Resource Nationalism in International Investment Law

Foreign direct investment in the natural resource industries is fostered through the signing of concession agreements between the host state and the investor. However, such concessions are susceptible to alteration by the host state, meaning that many investors now require the insertion of stabilization clauses. These are provisions that require the host state to agree that it will not take any administrative or legislative action that would adversely affect the rights of the investor.

Arguing that it is necessary to have some form of flexibility in concession agreements, whilst still offering protection of the legitimate expectations of the investor, *Resource Nationalism in International Investment Law* proposes the insertion of renegotiation clauses in order to foster flexible relationships between the investor and the host state. Such clauses bind the parties to renegotiate the terms of the contract, in good faith, when prevailing circumstances change. However, these clauses can also prove problematic for both state and investor, owing to their rigidity. Using Zambia as a case study, it highlights the limitations of the efficient breach theory to emphasize the need for contractual flexibility.

Sangwani Patrick Ng'ambi is a lecturer in International Investment Law and Assistant Dean at the University of Zambia.

Resource Nationalism in International Investment Law

Sangwani Patrick Ng'ambi

LONDON AND NEW YORK

First published 2016
by Routledge

2 Park Square, Milton Park, Abingdon, Oxfordshire OX14 4RN
711 Third Avenue, New York, NY 10017

Routledge is an imprint of the Taylor & Francis Group, an informa business

First issued in paperback 2018

Copyright © 2016 Sangwani Patrick Ng'ambi

The right of Sangwani Patrick Ng'ambi to be identified as author of this work has been asserted by him in accordance with sections 77 and 78 of the Copyright, Designs and Patents Act 1988.

All rights reserved. No part of this book may be reprinted or reproduced or utilised in any form or by any electronic, mechanical, or other means, now known or hereafter invented, including photocopying and recording, or in any information storage or retrieval system, without permission in writing from the publishers.

Notice:
Product or corporate names may be trademarks or registered trademarks, and are used only for identification and explanation without intent to infringe.

British Library Cataloguing in Publication Data
A catalogue record for this book is available from the British Library

Library of Congress Cataloging-in-Publication Data
Ng'ambi, Sangwani Patrick, author.
  Resource nationalism in international investment law / Sangwani
  Patrick Ng'ambi.
    pages cm
  Includes bibliographical references and index.
  ISBN 978-1-138-95158-7 (hbk)—ISBN 978-1-315-66811-6 (ebk)
  1. Investments, Foreign—Law and legislation. 2. Mineral
  investment. 3. Mineral investment—Zambia. I. Title.
  K3830.N496 2016
  346'.092—dc23   2015019525

ISBN: 978-1-138-95158-7 (hbk)
ISBN: 978-1-138-61455-0 (pbk)

Typeset in Baskerville by
Keystroke, Station Road, Codsall, Wolverhampton

To my mother, Daisy Nkhata Ng'ambi

Contents

Table of cases	xi

1 Introduction   **1**
   1.1 Background 1
   1.2 An overview of resource nationalism 3
        1.2.1 The resource nationalism cycle 3
        1.2.2 The obsolescing bargain model 5
        1.2.3 The rigidity of stabilization clauses 5
   1.3 Outline of the chapters 8

2 Foreign direct investment and resource nationalism   **13**
   2.1 Introduction 13
   2.2 Foreign direct investment defined 14
        2.2.1 Conflicting approaches to the interpretation
            of investment 15
        2.2.2 'Foreign' 23
   2.3 'Foreign direct investment' and the resource nationalism cycle 25
        2.3.1 The need for foreign capital 26
        2.3.2 The obsolescing bargaining model 28
        2.3.3 The resource nationalism cycle 30
   2.4 Mitigating political risk 39
        2.4.1 Political risk insurance 39
        2.4.2 Contractual clauses 40
   2.5 Conclusion 42

3 The effect of stabilization clauses   **44**
   3.1 Introduction 44
   3.2 The doctrine of permanent sovereignty over natural resources 45
        3.2.1 Evolution of the doctrine 47

viii Contents

      3.2.2 Legal status of the principle of permanent sovereignty over natural resources 49

3.3 *The definition and purpose behind stabilization clauses 52*
      3.3.1 Types of stabilization clauses 53
      3.3.2 The effect of stabilization clauses 55

3.4 *Case law on stabilization clauses 58*
      3.4.1 Earlier decisions 58
      3.4.2 The Libyan nationalization cases 62
      3.4.3 Subsequent decisions 68

3.5 *Conclusion 74*

4 Compensation under international investment law   76

4.1 *Introduction 76*

4.2 *Standards of compensation in international investment law 77*
      4.2.1 The Hull principle 78
      4.2.2 Appropriate compensation 80
      4.2.3 Lost future profits 83

4.3 *The efficient breach theory under international investment law 91*

4.4 *Conclusion 97*

5 The resource nationalism cycle in Zambia   99

5.1 *Introduction 99*

5.2 *The evolution of mining in Zambia 101*
      5.2.1 Commercial mining in Northern Rhodesia 101
      5.2.2 Independence and nationalization of the mines 104
      5.2.3 Privatization of the mines 109

5.3 *The resource nationalism cycle in Zambia: from privatization to the windfall tax 114*
      5.3.1 Entering into agreements 115
      5.3.2 The shortcomings of privatization 117
      5.3.3 Lessons for Zambia 125

5.4 *Conclusion 128*

6 Flexibility through renegotiation clauses   130

6.1 *Introduction 130*

6.2 *Renegotiation clauses defined 131*

6.3 *Contracts without a renegotiation clause 135*
      6.3.1 *Rebus sic stantibus* under international law 137
      6.3.2 Common law systems 140
      6.3.3 Civil law systems 141
      6.3.4 Hardship clauses 142

Contents ix

6.4 *Contracts with a renegotiation clause 144*
  6.4.1 Triggering event 145
  6.4.2 The effect of the change on the contract 146
  6.4.3 The objectives of the renegotiation 147
  6.4.4 The procedure 148
  6.4.5 Course of action should the renegotiation fail 149
  6.4.6 A proposed renegotiation clause in the event of windfall profits 156
6.5 *Conclusion 158*

7 Conclusion 160

Bibliography 166
Index 181

Table of cases

AGIP v Popular Republic of Congo (1982) 21 ILM 726 .... 69, 78, 86

Aluminum Co. of America v Essex Group Inc. 449 F. Supp. 53 (W.D. Pa. 1980) 141

Amco v Indonesia (1984) 23 ILM 351 .... 26, 136

AMINOIL (American Independent Oil Company) v Kuwait (1982) 21 ILM
976 .... 46, 70–2, 76, 85–6, 128, 133, 148, 149, 151–2

Amoco International Finance Corp. v Government of the Islamic Republic of Iran (1987)
15 Iran–US CT Rep 189 .... 71, 73

Asian Agricultural Ltd v Republic of Sri Lanka (Award) (1990) 4 ICSID
Rep 245 80

Banco Nacional de Cuba v Chase Manhattan Bank 658 F.2d 875
(2d Cir. 1981) 82

Barcelona Traction [1971] ICJ Reports 1 23

Bayindir v Pakistan ICSID Case No. ARB/03/29 (IIC 27 (2005)) 18

Benvenuti et Bonfant v People's Republic of Congo (1982) 21 ILM 740 .... 5, 86–7

Bergesen v Joseph Muller Corp. 710 F .2d 928 (2d Cir. 1983) 154

*Biloune and Marine Drive Complex Ltd v Ghana Investments Centre and
the Government of Ghana* (1990) 95 ILR 183 88

Biwater v Tanzania ICSID Case No. ARB/05/2 20

BP v Libya (1979) 53 ILR 297 .... 6, 58, 62–3, 65–6, 68

Canal de Craponne (1876) (Cour de Cassation) 142

Chinn, Oscar (1934) PCIJ Series A/B No. 63 57

Chorzow Factory PCIJ Series A. No. 17 .... 77, 84

CME v Czech Republic (http://italaw.com/sites/default/files/
case-documents/ita0180) 9

CMS Gas Transmission Co v Argentina (2003) 42 ILM 788 24

*Compañia de Aguas del Aconquija SA and Vivendi Universal v Argentine
Republic* (2002) 41 ILM 1135 24

*Company Z (Republic of Xanadu) v State Organization ABC
(Republic of Utopia)* (1983) 8 YB Comm Arb 94 72–3

Congo v Uganda 2005 ICJ Reports 168 51

CSOB v Slovakia (1999) 14 ICSID REV-FILJ 251 20

Davis Contractors Ltd v Fareham Urban District Council [1956] AC 696 (HL) 140

xii Table of cases

Delagoa Bay and East African Railway (US and Great Britain v Portugal)
(1900), quoted in M.M. Whiteman, *Damages in International Law:*
Volume 3 87–8
East Timor (Port v Austrl.) 1995 ICJ 90 .... 51, 154
Ebrahimi v Iran (1994) 30 Iran–US CTR 80
EnCana v Republic of Ecuador (2006) LCIA Case UN3481, 49 72
Enron Corporation and Ponderosa Assets LP v Argentine Republic ICSID
Case No. ARB/01/3, Decision on Jurisdiction (Ancillary Claim)
(2 August 2004) 24
Establishment of Middle East Country X v South Asian Construction Co.
(1987) 12 YCA 97 136
Fedax NV v Venezuela (1998) 37 ILM 1378 .... 15–16, 17, 20
Foresti, Laura de Carli and Others, Piero v South Africa ICSID Case No.
ARB(AF)/07/01 (2010) 38
Gabčíkovo-Nagymaros Project, Case Concerning the (Hungary v Slovakia)
[1997] ICJ Rep 92 .... 128, 137
Helman v Egypt ICSID Case No. ARB/05/19 18
Himpurna California Energy Ltd v PT (Persero) Perusahaan Listruik Negara
(2000) 25 YB Comm Arb 13 88–9
Hungarian State Enterprise v Yugoslav Crude Oil Pipeline (1984)
9 YCA 69 136
Indian Cement Co v Pakistani Bank ICC Case No. 1512 136–7
Joy Mining Machinery Ltd v Egypt (2004) 19 ICSID Rev-FILJ 486 .... 17, 18
Karaha Bodas Co. v Perusahaan Pertambangan Minyak Das Gas
Buni Negara 364 F.3d 274 (5th Cir. 2004); 190 F. Supp. 2d 936
(S.D. Tex. 2001) 89–90
Lanco v Argentina ICSID Case No. Arb/97/6, Decision on Jurisdiction
(8 December 1998) 40 ILM 457 (2001) 24
Lemire v Ukraine (2002) YBCA 133 143
Lena Goldfields Ltd v USSR (1950–51) 36 Cornell Law Quarterly
31 .... 59–60, 84
LESI SpA and ASTALDI v Algeria ICSID Case No. ARB/05/3
(IIC 150 (2006)) 18, 17, 21
LESI-Dipenta v Algeria (2004) 19 ICSID Review-FILJ 246 .... 17–18, 21
LETCO v Liberia (1989) 2 ICSID Reports 343 69
Libyan American Oil Company (LIAMCO) v Libya (1977)
62 ILR 141 .... 50, 58, 62–3, 65–6, 67–8, 74
Libyan American Oil Company (LIAMCO) v Libya (1981) 20 ILM 1 .... 41, 84–5, 94
Lithgow v United Kingdom (1986) 8 EHRR 329 81–2
Maffezini v Spain (2001) 16 ICSID Rev—FILJ 212 154
Malaysian Historical Salvors Sdn Bhd (MHS) v Malaysia ICSID
Case No. ARB/05/10 IIC 289 (2007) 16
Marbury v Madison 5 U.S. 137 (1803) 36
Maritime National Fish v Ocean Trawlers [1935] AC 524 140

Table of cases xiii

Mavrommatis Palestine Concessions (Greece v Great Britain), Judgment of
30 August 1924, PCIJ (Series A) No. 2 154
MCI v Ecuador ICSID Case No. ARB/01/8 (25 September 2007)
IIC 303 (2007) 20
Methanex Corp v United States of America, Award of 5 August 2005 73
MHS v Malaysia ICSID Case No. ARB/05/10, IIC 289
(2007) 18–19, 21
Mitchell v Democratic Republic of Congo ICSID Case No. ARB/99/9 (2006)
IIC 172 17
Mulundika and Others v The People [1995–1997] ZR 20 36
Mwiinda v Gwaba (1974) ZR 188 102
National Carriers Ltd v Panalpina (Northern) Ltd [1981] AC 675 140
North Sea Shelf Case (1969) ICJ Rep 4 149
Parkerings-Compagniet v Lithuania, Award of 11 September 2007,
ICSID Case No. ARB/05/8 73–4
Patuha Power Ltd v PT (Persero) Perusahaan Listruik Negara in M. Kantor
'The Limits of Arbitration' (2004) 2 *Transnational Dispute Management* 89
Pey Casado v Chile ICSID Case No. ARB/98/2, (2008) IIC 324 18
Phillips Petroleum Co. Iran v Islamic Republic of Iran (1987) 21 Iran–US
CTR 79 83
Phoenix v Czech Republic ICSID Case No. ARB/06/5, Award of
15 April 2009 16
Portugal v Germany (1930) Ann Dig. Int'l L. Cases 150 78
Railway Traffic between Lithuania and Poland, PCIJ Series A/B No. 42 149
Revere Copper & Brass Inc. v Overseas Private Investment Corporation
(1978) 17 ILM 1321 68–9
Romak v Uzbekistan UNCITRAL, PCA Case No. AA280 21
Salini Construttori SpA v Morocco (2003) 42 ILM 609
(ICSID) 16–17, 19, 20, 21
Sapphire International Petroleum Ltd v National Iranian Oil Co (NIOC)
(1967) 35 ILR 136 .... 6, 60–1, 83–4, 87, 88, 126
Saudi Arabia v Arabian American Oil Co (Aramco) (1963) 27
ILR 117 .... 6, 56, 61–2
Scafom International BV v Lorraine Tubes (Belgian Supreme Court) 139
Sobhuza II v Miller and Others [1926] AC 518 102
Société Ouest Africaine des Bétons Industriels (SOABI) v State of Senegal
(1988) 2 ICSID Rep 164 .... 87, 88
Starret Housing Corp v Islamic Republic of Iran (1987) 16 Iran–US
CTR 112 84
Sumitomo v Avagliano, 457 U.S. 176 (1982) 23
Tecnicas Medioambientales Tecmed SA v United Mexican States (2004)
43 ILM 133 88
Tennants (Lancashire) Ltd v C S Wilson & Co Ltd [1917] AC 495
(HL) 140

xiv Table of cases

Texaco Overseas Oil Petroleum Co / California Asiatic Oil Co v Libya (1978)
17 ILM 1 .... 6, 49, 50–1, 58, 62–3, 65–7, 68, 94, 152
Tippets, Abbett, McCarthy, Stratton v TAMS AFFA (1984) 6 Iran–US
CTR 219 76
Tsakiroglou & Co Ltd v Noblee Thorl GmbH [1962] AC 93 (HL) 140
Upton (1903) Ven Arb 173 77
Walton Harvey Ltd v Walker & Homfrays Ltd [1931] 1 Ch 274 140
Wena Hotels Ltd v Arab Republic of Egypt (2000) 6 ICSID Rep 67 88
Williams & Humbert v W & T Trademarks [1986] AC 368 82
Wintershall AG v Qatar (1989) 28 ILM 795 149–51

Chapter 1

Introduction

1.1 Background

Foreign direct investment involves 'the transfer of tangible or intangible assets from one country to another for the purpose of their use in that country to generate wealth under the total or partial control of the owner of the assets'.[1] Acquiring such an interest in another economy will invariably create a contractual relationship between the investor and the host state, which could span for a period of up to 30 years or more.[2] During the said period, the investor will pour substantial resources into the host state in order to foster viable operations. The investor expects to recoup this initial investment and also to make a profit from it over the period that the contract subsists. In the long term, however, the contract may become susceptible to various political risks.

As a result of these risks, historically, there was a general reluctance to invest in developing countries owing to the non-commercial risks which threatened the investments. These non-commercial risks manifested themselves inter alia through political risks, which led to war and any other civil disturbance or an outright regime change, typically through extra-democratic means such as military coups. Such events would often be succeeded by seizure of foreign owned property through nationalization or indirect seizure by making it more onerous for concessionaires to run their operations. This led to efforts by the international community, led by the International Monetary Fund and the World Bank to encourage investment in developing countries.[3]

Many of these non-commercial and political risks are addressed by insurance schemes through the Multilateral Investment Guarantee Agency (MIGA), which

---

1 M. Sornarajah, *The International Law on Foreign Investment* (3rd edn, Cambridge University Press 2010) 8. See also *International Monetary Fund, Balance of Payments Manual* (International Monetary Fund 1993) 86.
2 Rudolph Dolzer and Christoph Schreuer, *Principles of International Investment Law* (2nd edn, OUP 2012) 21.
3 ibid. See also *World Bank, Legal Framework for the Treatment of Foreign Investment* (World Bank 1992).

2 Resource nationalism in international investment law

operates under the auspices of the World Bank.[4] In addition, the World Bank encouraged potential host states to create an environment that attracted foreign direct investment. For many resource rich nations, this involved liberalizing their economies and revising their investment codes. The purpose of this was to enable developing countries to attract new capital, the transfer of technology and know-how, the creation of jobs, increased access to other markets and the strengthening of the local private sector.[5]

Host states thus began introducing investment friendly legislation. Such legislation included various incentives, including preferential tax breaks for a given period. In addition, they addressed issues such as compensation for expropriated property, provisions for externalization of profits and dispute settlement. For example, the Zambian Development Agency Act 2006 provides tax incentives for investments that exceed US$500,000 and these are to last for a period of five years.[6] Furthermore, if the investor is operating in a priority sector or rural area, then they are exempt from paying customs duties on any machinery acquired.[7] The Act also provides that any disputes arising out of the privatization process are to be settled by arbitration. This legislation is a means through which Zambia, as a host state, consents to have such disputes settled by arbitration.[8]

Furthermore, should the government expropriate the investor's property, the latter is entitled to compensation, which 'shall be made promptly at the market value and shall be fully transferable at the applicable exchange rate in the currency in which the investment was originally made, without deduction for taxes, levies and other duties, except where those are due'.[9] Moreover, investors are allowed to transfer profits made from their operations.[10] Neighbouring Namibia has similar provisions in its Foreign Investment Act.[11]

Certainly, since the 1980s, the flow of foreign direct investment to developing countries has increased dramatically.[12] A plethora of resource rich nations have been recipients of this foreign capital. The relationship between resource rich host states and foreign investors is governed inter alia through concession agreements between the aforementioned parties. The purpose of the concessions is to enable

---

4 See Ibrahim F.I. Shihata, 'The Multilateral Investment Guarantee Agency' (1986) 20 *International Lawyer* 485–97. See also Article 2(a) of the Convention Establishing the Multilateral Investment Guarantee Agency 1985.

5 *Invesment Law Reform: A Handbook for Development Practitioners* (World Bank 2010) 6.

6 See sections 55 and 56 of the Zambian Development Agency Act.

7 Section 57 of the Zambian Development Agency Act.

8 Andrea Marco Steingruber, *Consent in International Arbitration* (OUP 2012) 119–201.

9 Section 19 of the Zambian Development Agency Act.

10 Section 20 of the Zambian Development Agency Act.

11 Act No. 27, 1990.

12 Zakia Afrin, 'Foreign Direct Investments and Sustainable Development in the Least Developed Countries' (2004) 10 *Annual Survey of International & Comparative Law* 215, 217 and Tim Büthe and Helen Milner, 'The Politics of Foreign Direct Investment into Developing Countries: Increasing FDI through International Trade Agreements?' (2008) 52 *American Journal of Political Science* 741, 742.

the investor to explore and exploit their natural resources for a period of time. During the course of operations, investors are to pay the host state taxes and royalties, often at a preferential rate.

Within these concessions, investors will often seek additional contractual undertakings from the host state, designed to protect their investment even further. These invariably come in the form of stabilization clauses which are express undertakings on the part of the host state that they will not unilaterally jeopardize the investor's interests through legislative or administrative means. Given the length of concession agreements, a change of prevailing circumstances may episodically necessitate the renegotiation of certain terms of the contract. Stabilization clauses lead to rigidity, when what the parties need is flexibility.[13] In this book, I therefore argue that in addition to stabilization clauses, renegotiation clauses should also be included. These, in turn, will foster a flexible relationship between the two parties to the concession.

1.2 An overview of resource nationalism

1.2.1 The resource nationalism cycle

The investor is exposed to various risks when commencing operations in the host state. These risks are particularly evident in the advanced stages of the resource nationalism cycle.[14] This cycle begins when the host state grants a concession to the investor, who is invariably a foreign company. The cycle ends with the host government wishing to exert greater control over its natural resources, once the operations have commenced and have become more profitable.

Resource rich nations, typically, do not possess sufficient capital or know-how needed to explore and exploit their vast endowments of natural resources. Invariably, resource rich nations rely heavily on foreign direct investment, which brings in the much needed capital and other peripheral benefits.[15] Government policy is usually structured towards attracting foreign direct investment. They will do this through liberalizing the economy and also including tax incentives in the concession agreements. The agreement is usually structured in a way that the investor will run the operations and generate and retain its profits. However, out of these profits, the investor is expected to pay the host state taxes and a royalty. These terms are negotiated at a time when prices of the particular

---

13 Anne van Aaken, 'International Investment Law Between Commitment and Flexibility: A Contract Theory Analysis' (2009) 12 *Journal of International Economic Law* 507, 509.

14 See generally Thomas W. Wälde, 'Renegotiating Acquired Rights in the Oil and Gas Industries: Industry and Political Cycles Meet the Rule of Law' (2008) 1 *Journal of World Energy Law and Business* 55.

15 James C. Baker, *Foreign Direct Investment in Less Developed Countries: The Role of ICSID and MIGA* (Quorum Books 1999) 5.

4 Resource nationalism in international investment law

natural resource are experiencing a low.[16] The government, to encourage investment, may adopt a very liberal stance and grant the investors various legal and fiscal incentives.[17]

When the prices begin to experience a sustained upward trend, the perception is that the foreign investor is making a larger profit. In such an instance, the host state may wish to exert greater control over its natural resources. This may be influenced by a national anti-investment sentiment. Stoking the fires of this nationalistic mood, might be the fact that, owing to low tax and royalty rates, the state is not fully maximizing the benefits of this windfall in the price of the nation's natural resource.

Whether or not the government takes a resource nationalist stance also depends largely on the type of political regime in the host state. Resource nationalism will typically occur where the political pressure exists and there are few checks and balances on the executive. An authoritarian regime is less likely to adopt a resource nationalistic stance, because even though there are fewer checks and balances, there are no elections and therefore the political pressure is not quite present. They may only act if their political hegemony is threatened. A democratic regime is also less likely to adopt a resource nationalist stance. This is owing to the fact that, whilst the political pressure may exist by way of regular elections, ultimately the checks and balances that typically exist in a fully democratic state may preclude them from acting in a manner that has an adverse effect on the investor.

The host state is most likely to adopt a resource nationalistic stance in a hybrid system. This is a system where the executive is still accountable to the people through set elections but where once in power it is less susceptible to checks and balances. Under such a system, the host state is likely to adopt a resource nationalistic stance because it is influenced by their need to retain power in the next election and there are no institutional mechanisms in place to prevent it from taking actions that will increase its actions of doing so. An example of such a system is Russia.

Once the host state takes a resource nationalist stance and seeks ways and means to have a greater share in the profits being generated by the investor, it ultimately means taking a less liberal stance than that taken during the negotiation stage. In moderate cases, this may mean a revision of the tax incentives that the foreign investors are receiving. In extreme cases, this may even lead to the outright nationalization of the investor's assets.[18]

---

16 Wälde (n 14) 55.

17 Thomas W. Wälde and George Ndi, 'Stabilizing International Investment Commitments: International Law Versus Contract Interpretation' (1996) 31 *Texas International Law Journal* 215, 223.

18 G. Joffé, P. Stevens, T. George, J. Lux and C. Searle, 'Expropriation of Oil and Gas Investments: Historical, Legal and Economic Perspectives in a New Age of Resource Nationalism' (2009) 2 *Journal of World Energy and Business* 3, 22.

1.2.2 The obsolescing bargain model

The obsolescing bargain model states that concession agreements are susceptible to later alteration by the host government once operations have commenced.[19] During the negotiation stages, investors are very aware that most resource rich nations depend on their capital to explore and exploit their natural resources. They are also aware that all the incentives given by the host state could easily be taken away once operations commence. Because the state needs the investment, it is in a relatively weaker position because at this point the investors could easily take their capital to a jurisdiction where they have the best chances of maximizing their investment. In this sense, the investor has a wider selection than the host government, who really has to make do with a relatively small number of investors seeking to enter its jurisdiction.

Taking advantage of this fact, the investor will use its economic muscle to request conditions from the host state that will work to the former's benefit. However, there remains the possibility that once the operations have commenced, the host state could then intervene by utilizing the legislative and administrative prerogatives at its disposal. For example, the host state could, through its legislature, pass laws to reverse any tax incentives previously granted or simply to foster the process of nationalizing the investor's asset, as mentioned above. It could also use its national army to occupy the premises of the investor's operations.[20] In this sense, once operations have commenced, the host state becomes the stronger party and the investor is in a considerably weaker position than it was during the negotiating stage.[21]

1.2.3 The rigidity of stabilization clauses

Wary of the eventualities raised in section 1.2.2 above, foreign investors will often insist on the insertion of various clauses into the concession agreement. They may, for example, insert arbitration clauses into the contract as a means of ensuring that, should a dispute arise, it will be heard in a neutral forum outside the scope of national law. They may also insist on the insertion of stabilization clauses into the concession agreement.[22] These are provisions that generally state that, for a given period of time, the government is precluded from making any legislative changes or taking administrative action that will have an adverse effect on the rights contained within the concession agreement.

---

19 See generally Raymond Vernon, *Sovereignty at Bay: The Multinational Spread of US Enterprises* (Longman 1971).
20 See *Benvenuti et Bonfant v People's Republic of Congo* (1982) 21 ILM 740.
21 See Sornarajah (n 1) 281.
22 Piero Bernardini, 'Investment Protection under Bilateral Investment Treaties and Investment Contracts' (2001) 2 *Journal of World Investment* 235, 241.

6 Resource nationalism in international investment law

Therefore, in an instance where there is a conflict between the contractual rights contained within the concession containing a stabilization clause and subsequent municipal law, the former will always take precedence.[23] Although arbitral tribunals, for practical reasons, do not claim the right to compel specific performance, their respect for stabilization clauses and the sanctity of contracts is reflected in the compensation awards they render.[24]

The difficulty with such a position is that it leads to rigidity in the contracts. Such rigidity may not withstand the realities of the mines and minerals industry. The world prices of natural resources, such as copper and oil for example, are rather mercurial. A mineral that costs a certain amount one year may experience a dramatic increase in subsequent years. This was certainly evidenced in my case study on the Republic of Zambia as detailed in Chapter 5 of this book, which had seen a dramatic increase in the flow of foreign direct investment.[25] This increase was largely as a consequence of the liberalization of the Zambian economy, which was undertaken subsequently to the fall of socialism which took place in 1991.[26]

The Zambian economy has historically been linked to copper production. Prior to liberalization of the economy, the mines were in state hands, under the auspices of Zambia Consolidated Copper Mines (ZCCM). After 1991, however, the government embarked on a privatization programme. This eventually culminated in the mines being split into seven and being sold to foreign mining companies. To attract these companies, the Government of Zambia, amongst other things, offered a preferential tax regime. Mineral royalties were to stand at 0.2 per cent, which was lower than the 3 per cent stipulated in the Mines and Minerals Act. Furthermore, the corporate tax rate was reduced from 35 per cent to 25 per cent.[27]

In 2004, when most of the concessions were signed, the price of copper stood at US$2421.48 per ton on the London Metal Exchange (LME). In July 2006, this increased dramatically to US$7726.74 per ton. By October 2007, this had further increased to US$8020.59 per ton. These dramatic increases led to calls for the Government of Zambia to reconsider the preferential tax regime that the mining companies were enjoying. In 2008, the Government of Zambia acceded to these

---

23 See *Sapphire International Petroleum Ltd v National Iranian Oil Co (NIOC)* (1967) 35 ILR 136; *Saudi Arabia v Arabian American Oil Co (Aramco)* (1963) 27 ILR 117; *BP v Libya* (1979) 53 ILR 297; and *Texaco Overseas Oil Petroleum Co / California Asiatic Oil Co v Libya* (1978) 17 ILM 1.

24 See Jason W. Yackee, 'Pacta Sunt Servanda and State Promises to Foreign Investors Before Bilateral Investment Treaties: Myth and Reality' (2009) 32 *Fordham International Law Journal* 1550.

25 See generally Muweme Muweme, 'Foreign Direct Investment: What Difference for Zambia?' (2001) 50 *Jesuit Centre for Theological Research Bulletin* http://www.jctr.org.zm/publications/968-muwemecsr/file (last accessed 12 June 2015).

26 See generally John Lungu, 'Copper Mining Agreements in Zambia: Renegotiation or Law Reform?' (2008) 117 *Review of African Political Economy* 403.

27 John Lungu, *The Politics of Reforming Zambia's Mining Tax Regime* (Southern Africa Resource Watch 2009) 15.

calls.[28] First, it passed the Mines and Minerals Development Act of 2008, which cancelled all concessions entered into prior to the passage of the aforementioned act. Subsequently, the Government of Zambia proceeded to raise the corporate tax and royalty rates to 30 per cent and 3 per cent respectively.[29] This was done, ostensibly, to ensure that the people of Zambia benefited from the high copper prices.[30]

Contained within the cancelled concessions were stabilization clauses.[31] If the matter were to be decided by an arbitral tribunal, it is likely that the government's action may have pecuniary consequences.[32] Even though the stabilization clause purports to prevent host states from unilaterally abrogating the contract, in the event that commodity prices escalate it is clear that governments are unlikely to abide by the terms of contracts that are too rigid. As noted by Joffé and others: 'Despite the inclusion in original contracts of stabilization clauses designed to anticipate and counter the risk implicit in the obsolescing bargain, this outcome is inevitable. Stabilization clauses have rarely been effective since producer governments still enforced changes in contractual terms to reflect their perception of their right to capture additional rent'.[33]

It has thus been observed that long-term agreements must be seen as susceptible to continuous adjustment, rather than 'a body of fixed rights and obligations impervious to political, economic and social changes'.[34] It has further been observed that:

> Such an approach would, of course, constitute a radical departure from traditional doctrine, but, as has already been pointed out, the Anglo–American theory of contract has not always remained fossilized and inflexible. A departure from current traditional doctrine is therefore not necessarily inimical to the common interest of both investors and host governments.[35]

A change of circumstances is made inevitable, because of the mercurial nature of natural resource prices. Once prices experience a sustained upward trend, this will

---

28 Jan-Bart Gewald and Sebastiaan Soeters, 'African Miners and Shape-shifting Capital Flight: The Case of Luanshya/Baluba' in Alastair Fraser and Miles Larmer (eds), *Zambia, Mining, and Neoliberalism: Boom and Bust on the Globalized Copperbelt* (Palgrave 2010) 166.

29 Lungu, *The Politics of Reforming Zambia's Mining Tax Regime* (n 27) 19.

30 Sangwani Ng'ambi, 'Stabilization Clauses and the Zambian Windfall Tax' (2010) 1 *Zambia Social Science Journal* 107, 107.

31 Evaristus Oshionebo, 'Stabilization Clauses in Natural Resource Extraction Contracts: Legal, Economic and Social Implications for Developing Countries' (2010) 10 *Asper Review of International Business & Trade Law* 1, 4.

32 Wälde and Ndi (n 17).

33 Joffé, Stevens, George, Lux and Searle (n 18) 22.

34 Samuel K.B. Asante, 'The Concept of Stability of Contractual Relations in the Transnational Investment Process' in Kamal Hossain (ed), *Legal Aspects of the New International Economic Order* (Frances Pinter 1980) 259.

35 ibid.

8 Resource nationalism in international investment law

trigger a resource nationalist stance. Host states are more likely either to raise taxes or nationalize assets belonging to the investor. Although in practice stabilization clauses do not prevent host states from taking such action, there are pecuniary consequences. Not only will the host state have to compensate the investor for the market value of the nationalized asset, but it will also have to compensate the investor for lost future profits.

Such conduct is only efficient if the host state makes some money even after having fully compensated the investor. The difficulty with this position is that, whilst it protects the legitimate expectations of the investor, it does not give the state sufficient leeway to exercise its legitimate public functions. Typically, when the state nationalizes it is not just for the purposes of maximizing wealth, but also for the purposes of reorganizing its socio-economic structures.

This book therefore advances the view that some form of flexibility is needed in concession agreements. This enables both the host state and the investor to negotiate the terms of the contract in such a way that the former can benefit from its natural resource without jeopardizing the interests of the latter. This flexibility could be fostered through the insertion of renegotiation clauses in concession agreements.[36] Such clauses bind the parties to renegotiate the terms of the contract, in good faith, when prevailing circumstances change. In the event that the parties fail to reach an agreement, the matter can be settled by a third party. This will usually be an international arbitrator.[37]

Such clauses can be contrasted with stabilization clauses. Although such clauses are respected by international arbitral tribunals, on the basis of *pacta sunt servanda*, the mercurial nature of natural resources will inevitably lead to a fluidity in the prevailing circumstances. The rigidity of these clauses may prove to be problematic for both the state and the investor in the long run. It has been seen that governments seeking to maximize the benefits of a windfall in prices will still unilaterally cancel contracts, despite an express undertaking not to do so.[38]

1.3 Outline of the chapters

This book is divided into seven chapters, including this introduction and the conclusion. Chapter 2 of this book begins by defining foreign direct investment.[39] It will then proceed to discuss the resource nationalism cycle. This particular chapter will look at the factors contributing to resource nationalism. It will demonstrate that resource rich nations, lacking in know-how and financial capacity, will often acquiesce in very liberal contractual terms, which largely favour the

---

36 See Jeswald W. Salacuse, 'Renegotiating International Project Agreements' (2000) 24 *Fordham International Law Journal* 1319, 1362–63.
37 Piero Bernardini, 'The Renegotiation of the Investment Contract' (1998) 13 *Foreign Investment Law Journal* 411, 415.
38 Joffé, Stevens, George, Lux and Searle (n 18) 22.
39 See ch 2.

investor, in order to attract much needed foreign direct investment. In this sense the host state is the weaker party because it needs the investment. Once the investment is sunk, however, the host state has various prerogatives at its disposal, which could be used to alter the terms of the concession. At this point the investor is the weaker party. This process describes what is referred to as the 'obsolescing bargaining model'.

Various factors contribute to the host state taking a more resource nationalist stance. It will be seen that it is primarily influenced by a sustained upward trend in the price of the natural resource. This may lead to the host state seeking to maximize the benefits accruing from the windfall in prices. There may also be political pressure. Chapter 2 will show that resource nationalism is easier to adopt in a system where the executive is still accountable to the people through elections, but has very few checks and balances. Chapter 2 will also show that in a bid to counter the risks emanating from resource nationalism cycle, investors will often insist on various clauses. One of these is the stabilization clause. Such clauses constitute provisions under which the host state is precluded from undertaking any legislative or administrative actions that will change the legal regime that exists at the time the investor is entering into the agreement.

Chapter 3 discusses the effect of stabilization clauses.[40] The first part discusses the principle of permanent sovereignty over natural resources. The principle was developed in the aftermath of the Second World War, when previously colonized nations began to attain their independence. With political independence, they also sought to have a greater influence on the exploration and exploitation of their natural resources, with which they were well endowed. This principle, it will be seen, is often invoked by states that unilaterally abrogate concession agreements that contain stabilization clauses. It will be seen that this argument is generally not looked upon with a kindly eye. Tribunals instead take the view that when states freely enter into agreements containing stabilization clauses, they are bound by them. This is because tribunals respect the sanctity of contracts and often cite *pacta sunt servanda* as the basis of their decisions. Under the sanctity of contracts, the will of the parties must be respected and the insertion of stabilization clauses is a reflection of that will. Therefore, they must be upheld. Thus, it will be seen that where a state unilaterally terminates a concession containing a stabilization clause before the term of the contract has elapsed, then there are pecuniary consequences.

These consequences are highlighted in Chapter 4 of this book.[41] This chapter will show that where the state breaches a contract with the investor, the former must compensate the latter. There are two standards propounded under international investment law: appropriate compensation and the 'Hull formula'. Under the former, compensation is determined on a case-by-case basis, taking into

40 See ch 3.
41 See ch 4.

account all the relevant circumstances. Under the latter, compensation ought to be prompt, adequate and effective. Regardless of the standard adopted, arbitral tribunals invariably award lost future profits (*lucrum cessans*) as part of the compensation package. In this sense, the law relating to compensation under international investment law promotes efficiency. That is to say, the parties to a concession have an incentive to perform unless doing so would be inefficient. The government would have acted efficiently if it made some money even after having compensated the investor for its sunk costs and lost future profits.

This is the very essence of the efficient breach theory under contract law, which will be covered in Chapter 4. In this chapter I argue that one of the pillars of the efficient breach theory is wealth maximization. That is to say that the objectives of the parties are fully translated into monetary terms. However, the limitation with this is that wealth maximization is not always the goal of the state. Typically, when the state terminates a contract it is for public purposes. The state typically terminates concessions because it seeks to reorganize its socio-economic policies. Thus, whilst the compensation standard promotes efficiency, it does not give the state sufficient flexibility to pursue its legitimate public functions.

To further illustrate this point, Chapter 5 of this book is a case study on Zambia and the windfall tax the government of the aforementioned jurisdiction introduced in 2008.[42] Zambia is a mono-economy which relies primarily on its vast copper reserves. The first part of the chapter will examine the early stages of the Zambian mining industry. It will be seen that, in the initial stages, all mining rights were vested solely in the British South Africa Company. These rights were obtained through a series of treaties signed with various tribal chiefs operating in Northern Rhodesia, as Zambia was called prior to its independence in 1964. This included Chief Lewanika, the Paramount Chief of Barotseland. The British South Africa Company had the authority to issue concessions and to receive a royalty from the revenue made from mining operations in Northern Rhodesia. By the time of independence, the copper mining industry was dominated by two corporations: the Anglo American Corporation and the Roan Selection Trust.

This dominance was a cause for concern to Kenneth Kaunda and his United National Independence Party (UNIP). Of particular concern was the fact that the two companies were foreign, reinvested little and the current regime did little to benefit the people of Zambia. President Kaunda and UNIP adopted a policy of 'humanism'. This was a socialist ideology under which the government saw it as their responsibility to look after every Zambian, under the auspices of a one-party state. In line with this ideology, the government proceeded to nationalize the mining industry and eventually gave it to Zambia Consolidated Copper Mines Limited (ZCCM), which was a state owned corporation.

For years the Government of Zambia achieved its goal of looking after the people of Zambia by providing various amenities including education, healthcare

---

42 See ch 5.

and jobs. However, this was to be short-lived. When the copper prices plummeted and world oil prices escalated in the mid-1970s, the Government of Zambia was compelled to borrow money to make up for the shortfall in the national budget that this caused. This eventually led to a debt crisis. The subsequent economic crisis led to questions about the legitimacy of the UNIP Government and its ability to handle the country's affairs. President Kaunda was thus compelled to reintroduce multi-party democracy to Zambia in 1990. His UNIP Party was defeated by Frederick Chiluba's Movement for Multiparty Democracy (MMD), which swept into power in 1991.

The new government adopted a more liberal approach to the economy and proceeded to privatize the mining companies. Although privatization brought some benefits, it also brought some hardships to the people living in mining towns, including loss of jobs, loss of healthcare facilities and degradation of schools, roads and the environment. This was further compounded by the huge appreciation in copper prices and tax incentives that the mining companies were enjoying.

This led a perception that the mining companies were gaining more from operations than the people of Zambia. There were, therefore, calls to increase the tax rate so that the people of Zambia could maximize the potential benefits they could receive from the foreign mining companies. The public discontent was reflected in the results of the 2006 General Election. Although the MMD ultimately won this election, it did lose a great deal of ground in the urban areas and mining towns of the Copperbelt. The Patriotic Front made significant gains, attributable to the fact that it promised effectively to increase taxes on mining companies and reduce taxes of mine workers. The MMD Government could not ignore these gains. Thus, the Zambian Government introduced the windfall tax in 2008. It did this by cancelling all development agreements that had been entered into before 2008, through the Mines and Minerals Development Act 2008. These development agreements contained stabilization clauses. However, despite these clauses the Zambian Government proceeded to take the resource nationalist stance it did.

In Chapter 6, I argue that some form of flexibility is needed in the contract and this can best be achieved by the insertion of renegotiation clauses in concession agreements.[43] As seen in previous chapters, it is not in the interest of either the investor or the state to have contracts that are too rigid. With regard to contracts that do not contain renegotiation clauses, the parties could still rely on the principle of *rebus sic stantibus* (changed circumstances). This can be relied upon if adverse circumstances occur during the life of the contract, which could not have been anticipated at the time that it was signed. The application of this principle is very limited and applies only to situations that have adversely affected the parties. That is not actually the case where there has been a windfall in the price of natural resources, because clearly the parties actually benefit from this.

43 See ch 6.

Thus, I advocate that the most appropriate course of action is the insertion of renegotiation clauses into concession agreements. Such a clause would stipulate the event that would trigger the renegotiation, the effect of the trigger event on the parties, the objectives to be achieved during the course of renegotiation and, finally, the course of action that ought to be taken in the event that the renegotiation fails. Succeeding Chapter 6 will be my conclusion, which simply offers a summary of the main points raised in this book.[44]

44 See ch 7.

Chapter 2

Foreign direct investment and resource nationalism

2.1 Introduction

Foreign direct investment involves the transfer of tangible or intangible assets from one country to another. The purpose of this is to use those assets to generate wealth. These assets are either totally or partially controlled by the owner.[1] Among the myriad benefits this brings to resource rich nations is access to foreign capital. Typically, owing to a shortage of domestic capital, resource rich host states will have to rely on foreign capital as a means through which they can explore and exploit their natural resources. To attract foreign capital, the host state will thus offer various fiscal incentives to the investor.[2]

Investors on the other hand, are attracted to the host state by the prospect of making a profit once their initial investment has been sunk.[3] However, the long term nature of investment in resource rich nations renders the investor susceptible to a number of risks which jeopardize their chances of making a profit. One such risk is the resource nationalism cycle.[4] This is a cycle that typically manifests when the price of the natural resource experiences a boom. The windfall profits that this boom generates will often elicit opportunistic behaviour on the part of the state. The state will seek to gain greater control over its natural resources in order to maximize the benefits of the windfall profits. This may include increasing taxes or simply nationalizing assets belonging to the investor.[5]

These risks can be mitigated through various means. One of these means is political risk insurance. This could be done through private insurers or through government sponsored schemes such as the Overseas Private Insurance

---

1 M. Sornarajah, *The International Law on Foreign Investment* (3rd edn, Cambridge University Press 2010) 8.
2 Kenneth K. Mwenda, *Contemporary Issues in Corporate Finance and Investment Law* (Penn Press 2000) 9.
3 See Yair Aharoni, *The Foreign Investment Decision Process* (Library of Congress 1966) 168–71 and Jeswald Salacuse, *The Law of Investment Treaties* (OUP 2010) 231.
4 Paul Stevens, 'National Oil Companies and International Oil Companies in the Middle East: Under the Shadow of Government and the Resource Nationalism Cycle' (2008) 1 *Journal of World Energy Law & Business* 5.
5 Salacuse, *The Law of Investment Treaties* (n 3) 286.

14 Resource nationalism in international investment law

Corporation (OPIC) and the Multilateral Investment Guarantee Agency (MIGA).[6] Investors could also protect themselves through the insertion of various clauses into the concession agreement. For example, in order to ensure that disputes are heard in a neutral forum outside the fray of the host state's jurisdiction, the parties can insert an arbitration clause.[7] Moreover, to prevent the sort of opportunism induced by the resource nationalism cycle, stabilization and renegotiation clauses are often included in the concession agreement.[8]

The aim of this chapter is to discuss foreign direct investment, the risks associated with it and the means through which these risks are mitigated. Section 2.1 of this chapter explores the meaning of the term 'foreign direct investment' and section 2.3 examines the resource nationalism cycle and the risks emanating therefrom. Section 2.4 will serve as an overview of the mechanisms investors utilize in mitigating those risks and, finally, section 2.5 will consist of a conclusion.

2.2 Foreign direct investment defined

Definitions of foreign direct investment can be found in various national laws and investment protection treaties.[9] For example, the United Nations Conference on Trade and Development (UNCTAD) defines foreign direct investment as 'an investment involving a long-term relationship and reflecting a lasting interest and control by a resident entity in one economy . . . in an enterprise resident in an economy other than that of the foreign investor'.[10] From this definition we can see that there must be a transfer of assets from one jurisdiction to another. The investment must be made to acquire a lasting interest in an enterprise operating in an economy other than that of the investor. The investor's purpose is to have an effective choice in the management of the enterprise.

Portfolio investment falls outside the scope of this definition. This is owing to the fact that portfolio investment was seen as an ordinary commercial risk of which the investor is generally aware. This is because the investor takes upon himself the risks associated with such investments. If the investor suffers a loss of any kind he cannot sue the domestic stock exchange or the public utility running it. There is no basis upon which the investor can seek a remedy.[11]

---

6 A.F.M. Maniruzzaman, 'The Issue of Resource Nationalism: Risk Engineering and Dispute Management in the Oil and Gas Industry' (2009) 5 *Texas Journal of Oil Gas and Energy Law* 79, 99.

7 Rudolph Dolzer and Christoph Schreuer, *Principles of International Investment Law* (2nd edn, OUP 2012) 235–36.

8 Thomas W. Wälde, 'Renegotiating Acquired Rights in the Oil and Gas Industries: Industry and Political Cycles Meet the Rule of Law' (2008) 1 *Journal of World Energy Law and Business* 55, 67.

9 Engela C. Schlemmer, 'Investment, Investor, Nationality and Shareholders' in Peter Muchlinski, Federico Ortino and Christoph Schreuer (eds), *The Oxford Handbook of International Investment Law* (OUP 2008).

10 UNCTAD World Investment Report 2006, 293.

11 Sornarajah, *The International Law on Foreign Investment* (n 1) 8–9.

2.2.1 Conflicting approaches to the interpretation of investment

Myriad investment disputes are tabled before the International Centre for Settlement of Investment Disputes (ICSID).[12] In order for the tribunal to accept jurisdiction over a matter, it will have to concern an 'investment'. This is provided for in Article 25 of the Convention on the Settlement of Investment Disputes between States and Nationals of Other States (ICSID Convention), which states that:

> The jurisdiction of the Centre shall extend to any legal dispute arising directly out of or in relation to an investment between a Contracting State (or any constituent subdivision or agency of a Contracting State designated to the Centre by that State) and a national of another Contracting State, which the Parties to the dispute consent in writing to submit to the Centre.

The term investment is not defined under the ICSID Convention.[13] From the *travaux préparatoires*, it is clear that the draftsmen of the ICSID Convention had attempted to adopt a definition of investment. This potential definition is found in Article 30 of the draft convention, which defined investment as: 'any contribution of money or other assets of economic value for an indefinite period or, if the period be defined, for not less than five years'.[14] However, this definition was ultimately discarded.[15] The framers thought it was perhaps better to leave the term 'investment' to be defined by states in their own agreements.[16] The importance of some sort of definition or at least guidelines regarding what constitutes an investment cannot be overemphasized. This is because, whether or not the ICSID tribunal accepts jurisdiction depends largely upon whether the subject matter tabled before it involves an investment.[17]

Attempts have been made by ICSID tribunals to interpret the term investment. Arbitral tribunals are generally agreed on the fact that the term investment depends on the four factors identified in the early case of *Fedax NV v Venezuela*.[18] These are: (i) that the investment should exist for a certain duration; (ii) the multinational corporation should gain regular profits and returns; (iii) there must be

---

12 Andrea Marco Steingruber, *Consent in International Arbitration* (OUP 2012) 28–29.
13 Georges R. Delaume, 'ICSID Arbitration and the Courts' (1983) 77 *American Journal of International Law* 784, 795.
14 Julian D. Mortenson, 'The Meaning of "Investment": ICSID's *Travaux* and the Domain of International Investment Law' (2010) 51 *Harvard International Law Journal* 257, 286.
15 ibid 281.
16 See Christopher Schreuer, *The ICSID Convention: A Commentary* (Cambridge University Press 2001) 121–25.
17 William Rand, Norbert N. Hornick and Paul Friedland, 'ICSID's Emerging Jurisprudence: The Scope of ICSID's Jurisdiction' (1986) 19 *New York University Journal of International Law and Politics* 33, 35.
18 (1998) 37 ILM 1378, para 43.

16 Resource nationalism in international investment law

an assumption of risk; and (iv) there must be a contribution to the economic development of the host state. Where there appears to be disagreement amongst the tribunals is on whether or not all four elements ought to be contemporaneously present.

The tribunal in *Malaysian Historical Salvors Sdn Bhd (MHS) v Malaysia*[19] (MHS) identified the two main categories adopted by arbitral tribunals in determining what activity amounts to an investment. These are the 'jurisdictional approach' on one hand and the 'typical characteristics' approach on the other. Under the jurisdictional approach the tribunal will invariably deny jurisdiction if not all of the elements identified in the *Fedax* case are present. On the other hand, the typical characteristics approach is more flexible and states that all four elements need not be present at the same time. Both approaches will be discussed in turn.

2.2.1.1 The jurisdictional approach

The jurisdictional approach was first adopted in *Salini Construttori SpA v Morocco*.[20] The question before the arbitral tribunal in this case was whether a civil construction contract constituted an investment. The arbitral tribunal first looked at the bilateral investment treaty (BIT) between Italy and Morocco under which this dispute was brought. It held that the contract did indeed fall within the definition of investment under the aforementioned BIT.[21] However, the tribunal then went on to discuss whether it was an investment under Article 25 of the ICSID Convention. The tribunal noted that the Convention itself was silent on what constituted an investment.[22] It thus opined that: 'investment infers: contributions, a certain duration of performance of the contract and a participation in the risks of the transactions . . . In reading the Convention's preamble, one may add the contribution to the economic development of the host State of the investment as an additional condition'.[23]

The tribunal further added that the elements identified may be interdependent. For example, the level of the risk undertaken may be contingent on the amount of money contributed and the duration of the contract. For this reason the tribunal opined that the criteria should be assessed conjunctively rather than disjunctively.[24]

---

19 ICSID Case No. ARB/05/10 IIC 289 (2007).
20 (2003) 42 ILM 609 (ICSID).
21 ibid, para 49.
22 ibid, para 51.
23 ibid, para 52. It must be noted that further criteria have since been added by the award rendered in *Phoenix v Czech Republic*, ICSID Case No. ARB/06/5, Award of 15 April 2009. In this case the tribunal refused to rely exclusively on the *Salini* test. It held that, for an activity to qualify as an investment, the following criteria ought to be considered: '1 – a contribution in money or other assets; 2 – a certain duration; 3 – an element of risk; 4 – an operation made in order to develop an economic activity in the host State; 5 – assets invested in accordance with the laws of the host State; 6 – assets invested *bona fide*': ibid 45, para 114.
24 ibid.

In other words, all elements should be present concurrently or the subject matter cannot amount to an investment. The tribunal also noted that the risk undertaken by the investor should not merely be an economic risk but a qualified risk.[25] The difficulty with this is that the tribunal does not define what constitutes a qualified risk. Consequently, it is difficult to be persuaded of the arbitral tribunal's reasoning.[26]

The jurisdictional approach was also adopted in *Joy Mining Machinery Ltd v Egypt*.[27] That is to say that all the elements identified in *Fedax* should be present at the same time. The tribunal preferred the jurisdictional approach because in its view any other approach would have turned Article 25 of the ICSID Convention into 'a meaningless provision'.[28] In this particular case the arbitral tribunal considered the activity in question as merely commercial, since 'the production and supply of the kind of equipment involved in this case is a normal activity of the Company, not having required a particular development of production that could be assimilated to an investment'.[29]

Furthermore, the arbitral tribunal noted that the contract made no mention of foreign investment nor was there an express intention on the part of the investor to activate Egypt's authorization procedures for foreign investment.[30] The tribunal also held that since the total price of the supply had actually been paid at the beginning of the contract, this negated any possibility of gaining regular profits and returns. In addition, it found that the company's actions did not involve a qualified risk but were merely a commercial risk. Once again, the tribunal did not mention what amounted to a qualified risk. The tribunal ultimately denied jurisdiction, notwithstanding its concession that the operation did contribute to the economic development of the host state.[31]

The importance of economic contribution was highlighted in the subsequent case of *Patrick Mitchell v Democratic Republic of Congo*,[32] another case which adopted the jurisdictional approach. The arbitral tribunal held that because economic contribution to the host state was an 'obvious and unquestioned' effect of an investment it was therefore an objective requirement.[33] This position was brought into doubt by the two *LESI* cases in which the arbitral tribunals did not think economic contribution was particularly important. In *LESI-Dipenta v Algeria*,[34] for

---

25 ibid.
26 Paolo Vargiu, 'Beyond Hallmarks and Formal Requirements: a "*Jurisprudence Constante*" on the Notion of Investment in the ICSID Convention' (2009) 10 *Journal of World Investment and Trade* 753, 758.
27 (2004) 19 ICSID Rev-FILJ 486.
28 ibid, para 50.
29 ibid, para 56.
30 ibid.
31 ibid, para 57.
32 ICSID Case No. ARB/99/9 (2006) IIC 172.
33 ibid, para 30.
34 (2004) 19 ICSID Review-FILJ 246.

example, the arbitral tribunal said that for an activity to constitute an investment it should fulfil three conditions: 'a) the contracting party has made contributions in the host country; b) those contributions had a certain duration; and c) they involved some risks for the contributor'.[35] In the tribunal's view, contribution to the economic development of a country was not an essential requirement because it is 'something that is difficult to ascertain and that is implicitly covered by the other three criteria'.[36] The arbitral tribunal in *LESI SpA and ASTALDI v Algeria*[37] adopted a similar if not identical position.[38] Both tribunals accepted jurisdiction.

However, in the subsequent case of *Bayindir v Pakistan*,[39] the tribunal accepted jurisdiction but based on the *Salini* test.[40] The tribunal held that 'to qualify as an investment, the project must represent a significant contribution to the host state's development'.[41] In *Pey Casado v Chile*[42] the tribunal also adopted a jurisdictional approach but, as in the *LESI* cases, it disregarded the importance of the investor's contribution to the development of the host state. As far as the tribunal was concerned, 'economic development' is encompassed in the other three requirements anyway. Furthermore, in its view the criteria should be viewed as requirements rather than hallmarks.[43] To do otherwise, as was stated in *Joy Mining*, would render Article 25 of the ICSID Convention meaningless. In *Helman v Egypt*[44] the tribunal adopted an even more restrictive definition of investment when it said that: 'to be characterized as an investment a project must show a certain duration, a regularity of profit and return, an element of risk, a substantial commitment, and a significant contribution to the host State's development'.[45]

The subsequent case of *MHS v Malaysia*[46] is interesting because although the sole arbitrator ostensibly took a jurisdictional approach here he seems to be suggesting that a certain activity could constitute an investment despite the absence of certain requirements. This results in what has been described as a confused decision.[47] The arbitrator in this case first noted that there was an absence of regularity of profits and returns. In his opinion, however, this element was immaterial because the criterion is not always decisive and because it had 'not been

---

35 ibid, section 2.2, para 13(iv).
36 ibid.
37 ICSID Case No. ARB/05/3 (IIC 150 (2006)).
38 *LESI and ASTALDI*, para 72(iv).
39 ICSID Case No. ARB/03/29 (IIC 27 (2005)).
40 ibid, para 130.
41 ibid, para 137. See also the cases of *Jan de Nul v Egypt*, ICSID Case No. ARB/04/13 (IIC 114 (2006)); *Saipem v Bangladesh*, ICSID Case No. ARB/05/07 (IIC 280 (2007)), para 99; *Kardasspoulos v Georgia*, ICSID Case No. ARB/05/18 (IIC 294 (2007), para 116.
42 ICSID Case No. ARB/98/2, (2008) IIC 324.
43 ibid, para 232.
44 ICSID Case No. ARB/05/19.
45 ibid, para 77.
46 ICSID Case No. ARB/05/10, IIC 289 (2007).
47 Vargiu, 'Beyond Hallmarks and Formal Requirements' (n 26) 761.

Foreign direct investment and resource nationalism 19

held to be an essential characteristic or criterion in any other case cited in this Award'.[48] The arbitrator also noted that, although the investor had made a commitment by expending his own funds, 'the size of the contributions were in no way comparable to those found in *Salini*, *Bayindir*, and *Joy Mining*'.[49]

The arbitrator held further that the operation was not for the requisite time-frame of two to five years as stipulated in *Salini*. Although the project itself ran for a period of two years the contract itself was meant to be completed within 18 months.[50] Thus, the actual duration was merely incidental. In other words, the arbitrator was relying more on the timeframe that was contractually foreseen by the two parties, because: '[t]he nature of the project meant that the Claimant could have completed it within a shorter period than two years and was in fact contractually required to do so within 18 months'.[51] The arbitrator went on to say that

> although the Claimant satisfies the duration characteristic or criterion in the quantitative sense, it fails to do so in the qualitative sense. However, such failure does not, by itself, mean that the project was not an investment within the meaning of Article 25(1) since a holistic assessment of all the hallmarks still needs to be made.[52]

The arbitrator further noted that the risk involved was a typical business risk and not a qualified risk. Once again, the tribunal did not define what amounted to a qualified risk.[53] The arbitrator ultimately denied jurisdiction on the basis that the activity did not contribute to the economic development of the host state. In the arbitrator's view, this particular hallmark was the most important because: 'the other typical hallmarks of "investment" are either not decisive or appear only to be superficially satisfied'.[54] This decision was eventually annulled, which shows the inadequacy of the jurisdictional approach. The annulment committee noted that the constrictive approach adopted by the arbitrator ignored 'the bilateral and multilateral treaties which today are the engine of ICSID's effective jurisdiction'.[55] The *ad hoc* Committee favoured the typical characteristics approach because it was more in line with the intentions of the draftsmen of the ICSID Convention.

2.2.1.2 The typical characteristics approach

The typical characteristics approach is less restrictive than the jurisdictional approach in that a tribunal may still accept jurisdiction notwithstanding the fact

---

48 *MHS v Malaysia* (n 46) para 108.
49 ibid, para 109.
50 ibid para 110.
51 ibid, para 110.
52 ibid, para 111.
53 ibid, para 112.
54 ibid, para 131.
55 ibid, para 73.

that all the four elements are not present at the same time. The initial purpose behind excluding a definition of investment under the ICSID Convention was to ensure that Article 25 remained adaptable to the transient nature of international investment.[56] The typical characteristics approach is more consistent with this intention than the jurisdictional approach.[57]

The first tribunal to adopt a typical characteristics approach was that in *CSOB v Slovakia*.[58] Here the tribunal opined that, although the activity involved in this case did not satisfy the other criteria identified in the *Fedax* case, it did nonetheless involve a significant contribution to the economic development of the host state. For this reason it was an investment under the ICSID Convention.[59] The tribunal justified this overdependence on economic development by stating that: 'these elements of the suggested definition, while they tend as a rule to be present in most investments, are not a formal prerequisite for the finding that a transaction constitutes an investment as that concept is understood under the Convention'.[60] The tribunal essentially took the view that it is not necessary to have all the *Fedax* criteria present. By extension therefore, a project could be classified as an investment under Article 25 of the ICSID Convention despite some of those elements not being present. In *MCI v Ecuador*[61] the tribunal stated that the hallmarks identified by previous arbitral tribunals were to be regarded as mere examples as to elements that determine the existence of an investment.[62]

The tribunal in *Biwater v Tanzania*[63] also chose not to adopt the rigid *Salini* test, and instead called for 'a more flexible and pragmatic approach . . . which takes into account the factors identified in *Salini*, but along with all the circumstances of the case'.[64] They were of the opinion that there was no justification for the constrictive approach adopted in *Salini* because the criteria adopted did not appear in the ICSID Convention nor were they fixed and mandatory according to the law. The arbitral tribunal ultimately said that: 'it is doubtful that arbitral tribunals sitting in individual cases should impose one such definition which would be applicable in all cases and for all purposes'.[65]

2.2.1.3 Jurisprudence constante *on the term investment*

Clearly there are problems with this dichotomy in approaches towards defining the term investment. This is owing to the fact that it leads to uncertainty. This

---

56 Vargiu, 'Beyond Hallmarks and Formal Requirements' (n 26) 763.
57 ibid.
58 (1999) 14 ICSID REV-FILJ 251.
59 ibid, para 88.
60 ibid, para 90.
61 ICSID Case No. ARB/01/8 (25 September 2007) IIC 303 (2007).
62 ibid, para 71.
63 ICSID Case No. ARB/05/2.
64 ibid, para 316.
65 ibid, para 313.

Foreign direct investment and resource nationalism   21

is especially more so with the very problematic jurisdictional approach. The jurisdictional approach is objectionable for three reasons.[66] First, it is objectionable because it is inconsistent with the rationale behind not having a definition of investment in the first place. Secondly, arbitral tribunals adopting the jurisdictional approach tend to have a propensity to ignore the definitions of investments contained in bilateral investment treaties. An example of this was in the *MHS* proceedings. This was also the case in *Romak v Uzbekistan*.[67]

Although this was not an ICSID case, it accentuates this point. Romak, a Swiss-based firm, had entered into a contract for the supply of wheat to Uzbekistan. When Romak ran into difficulties receiving payment, it initiated arbitral proceedings against the aforementioned state. One of the issues raised here is whether this constituted an investment. Article 1(2) of the BIT between Switzerland and Uzbekistan rendered a very broad definition of investment to include 'every kind of asset' that had some economic value.[68] Romak asserted that this is the definition that ought to be followed. The arbitral tribunal rejected this subjective definition and refused to interpret the BIT in a way that would 'render meaningless the distinction between investments, on the one hand, and purely commercial transactions on the other'.[69]

The tribunal further disagreed with the contention that 'the definition of "investment" in UNCITRAL proceedings (i.e. under the BIT alone) is wider than in ICSID Arbitration'.[70] Such a suggestion, in the tribunal's view, would widen or narrow the substantive protections offered under the BIT and thus lead to unreasonable results.[71] The tribunal saw no basis for adopting a definition of 'investment' that was different to that adopted by ICSID tribunals. It thus adopted the objective criteria adopted in *Salini*, instead of utilizing the definition adopted in the BIT. In the tribunal's view, the contract for the supply of wheat was a one-off commercial transaction and therefore did not fall under the definition of 'investment' in accordance with the *Salini* test.[72] This illustrates arbitral tribunals' propensity to ignore the definitions contained in BITs in favour of the jurisdictional approach highlighted above.

Finally, the jurisdictional approach has its inner contradictions.[73] On the one hand it attempts to espouse a formal definition of investment by identifying certain elements. However, on the other hand, there is no consistency in the case law with regard to which requirements are applicable and which ones are not. The tribunal in *Salini* required four criteria to be present, whereas that in the *LESI* cases only required three.

---

66 Vargiu, 'Beyond Hallmarks and Formal Requirements' (n 26) 765–66.
67 UNCITRAL, PCA Case No. AA280.
68 ibid 23, para 101.
69 ibid 46, para 185.
70 ibid 48, para 193.
71 ibid, para 194.
72 ibid 57, para 222. See also ibid 62, paras 242–43.
73 Vargiu, 'Beyond Hallmarks and Formal Requirements (n 26) 766.

A more adequate approach is the typical characteristics approach. This is because it gives the arbitral tribunals the flexibility needed in determining whether they have jurisdiction, on a case-by-case basis.[74] Although this does not make the law more certain, it at least ensures it makes it more likely that an activity will amount to an investment. Moreover, arbitral tribunals are able to take into account BITs that invariably include their own definitions of investment.[75] The only difficulty with this, of course, is that it is so open ended that it still renders it difficult for the parties to determine what does in fact amount to an investment.[76] The advantage, however, is that because it is so open ended, it gives the ICSID tribunal the opportunity to capture as many disputes as possible. This in turn allows the tribunal to decide a matter on its merits, rather than dismissing it because of a mere technicality.

To address the problem of having two divergent approaches to the definition of investment, it is suggested that tribunals ought progressively to establish a *jurisprudence constante*; that is to say, they must have a range of decisions that constantly reaffirm the same interpretation of the term investment. This will progressively make a general rule out of that interpretation.[77] It does not become precedent per se, but rather it will become one that will have a persuasive effect on subsequent arbitral tribunals. As Vargiu notes:

> For the establishment of a *jurisprudence constante* on the notion of investment however, a step back would be needed from the advocates of both approaches. Supporters of the 'jurisdictional' approach should recognise that there is nothing in the ICSID Convention that requires a project to satisfy formal requirements in order to be qualified as an investment. On the other hand, some more formalism should be adopted by the advocates of the 'typical characteristics' approach, in order to define with more certainty what those 'typical characteristics' are in practice.[78]

Certainly a *jurisprudence constante* would ensure some form of predictability in the law, in the same way that the common law does. Furthermore, with the flexibility that it entails, having a *jurisprudence constante* perhaps makes it more likely that a certain activity will indeed qualify as an investment. This is especially so if the *jurisprudence constante* established leans more in favour of a typical characteristics approach, which is wide and leaves open the possibility of examining definitions promulgated in the BITs from which the arbitrators draw their jurisdiction. Furthermore, as noted above, it is also in agreement with the wishes of those that drafted the ICSID Convention.

74 ibid.
75 ibid.
76 ibid 766–67.
77 Vargiu, 'Beyond Hallmarks and Formal Requirements' (n 26) 15.
78 ibid 767–68.

2.2.2 'Foreign'

The term 'foreign' is also somewhat problematic. This is owing to the fact that investors tend to operate through their subsidiaries, which are typically incorporated in the host state. For example, if a given company wanted to operate in a country such as South Africa, it would need to incorporate its subsidiary in the aforementioned jurisdiction. Because this subsidiary is incorporated in South Africa it technically ceases to be a foreign corporation, despite the fact that the constitution of its shareholders remains largely foreign. This may present a potential problem if the host state does something to injure the interests of the multinational corporation.

Such a problem is illustrated in the *Barcelona Traction*[79] case. In this case the firm was incorporated in Canada; however, an alleged 88 per cent of its shareholders were Belgian. The company was operating in Spain where, in 1938, the Spanish Government declared the company bankrupt and took some other detrimental actions against Barcelona Traction. The corporation itself did not have *locus standi* in the International Court of Justice and therefore needed a state to bring an action against Spain on its behalf.

The Canadian Government would not take the case to the International Court of Justice on behalf of Barcelona Traction. However, because a majority of the company's shareholders were Belgian, the Government of Belgium took the action to the International Court of Justice, stating that this company was its national. The International Court of Justice held that Belgium had no right to sue. The International Court of Justice held that the determining factor in the nationality of a corporation is where it is actually incorporated, as opposed to the composition of its shareholders.[80]

Clearly, because investors operate through their subsidiaries which are incorporated locally, the *Barcelona Traction* position if applied rigidly may potentially cause problems vis-à-vis the protection of the investment. This is owing to the fact that under international law only the state of which the corporation is a citizen may bring action in the International Court of Justice. However, if the corporation is a citizen of the host state then it is unlikely that the latter will bring an action against itself in the International Court of Justice. To overcome this challenge, states will explicitly include 'shares' within the definition of investment in their treaties.[81]

Rigidly applying the *Barcelona Traction* case may also create an obstacle to an injured corporation seeking redress before the ICSID Tribunal. According to Article 25(2)(a) of the ICSID Convention, a person must be a national of a contracting state other than 'the State party to the dispute'. Thus, technically

---

79 [1971] ICJ Reports 1.
80 Paragraph 70 of the judgment. See also *Sumitomo v Avagliano*, 457 U.S. 176 (1982).
81 Sornarajah, *The International Law on Foreign Investment* (n 1) 12.

24   Resource nationalism in international investment law

a subsidiary incorporated in the host state would not qualify under this part. However, this dilemma is resolved under Article 25(2)(b) of the ICSID Convention, which states:

> [a]ny juridical person which had the nationality of the contracting State party to the dispute in that date and which, because of foreign control, the parties have agreed should be treated as a national of another contracting State for the purposes of this Convention.

This is important because under ICSID the corporation has to be a national of a state other than the host state. If the subsidiary is incorporated in the host state then technically it is a national of that state. Article 25(2)(b) addresses that by enabling corporations that are controlled by foreigners still to bring an action before the ICSID tribunal, despite them being incorporated in the host state.

Shareholders may also bring an action under ICSID.[82] The actual size of the investment is of no consequence. Thus there is no requirement that the investor be a majority shareholder; all that matters is that an investment was made.[83] The Annulment Committee in *Vivendi* stated that: 'whatever the extent of its [the shareholder's] investment . . . it was entitled to invoke the BIT in respect of conduct alleged to constitute a breach of substantive protection under the BIT'.[84]

The tribunal in the *Lanco* case had a similar opinion. In this case Lanco had 18 per cent of the issued shares in a corporation that had obtained a concession from the Government of Argentina. During the dispute, Argentina contended that because Lanco only had 18 per cent of the shares and was therefore a minority shareholder, it was not a party to the contract and did not have *locus standi*. The tribunal disagreed. This was owing to the fact that the BIT did not require the investor to have a majority share in the corporation. For this reason, Lanco was a party to the contract and the ICSID tribunal did indeed have jurisdiction.[85] The *Lanco* decision was confirmed by the cases of *CMS Gas Transmission Co v Argentina*[86] and *Enron v Argentina*.[87]

The aim of this section was to discuss the meaning of investment. This is owing to the fact that a tribunal will only accept jurisdiction over a matter if it involves an investment. The importance of this cannot be overemphasized. As the next

---

82 Schlemmer (n 9) 83.

83 *CMS Gas Transmission Co v Argentina* (2003) 42 ILM 788.

84 *Compañia de Aguas del Aconquija SA and Vivendi Universal v Argentine Republic* (2002) 41 ILM 1135, para 50.

85 *Lanco v Argentina*, ICSID Case No. Arb/97/6, Decision on Jurisdiction (8 December 1998) 40 ILM 457 (2001) para 10.

86 *CMS Gas Transmission Co v Argentina* (n 83) 788.

87 *Enron Corporation and Ponderosa Assets LP v Argentine Republic*, ICSID Case No. ARB/01/3, Decision on Jurisdiction (Ancillary Claim) (2 August 2004) http://ita.law.uvic.ca/documents/Enron-DecisionJurisdiction-FINAL-English.pdf (last accessed 31 May 2015).

section shows, the advanced stages of the resource nationalism cycle will often lead to the host state wishing to maximize the benefits that the investor derives from the former's natural resource. Host states do this either by reversing any tax breaks that the investor was given upon signing the concession or by outright nationalization. As a general rule, in either situation the host state may be liable to compensate the investor, should the latter choose to initiate arbitral proceedings. In order for the tribunal to accept jurisdiction and thus compensate the investor, the subject matter of the dispute must involve an investment, as highlighted above.

2.3 'Foreign direct investment' and the resource nationalism cycle

Resource rich host states typically seek foreign direct investment because they lack the financial, technological capacity to explore and exploit their natural resources.[88] Therefore, they have to rely on foreign direct investment to provide this. Investors are attracted to the host state by the prospect of making a profit. However, there are also political risks associated with making long-term investments. In particular, the host state may revoke any incentives granted to the investor in order to attract the initial investment. In addition, the state could nationalize the investors' assets.

This section begins by discussing the need for exogenous capital, in order for the host state to explore and exploit its natural resources. This is invariably necessitated by a paucity in domestic capital.[89] It will then go on to discuss the obsolescing bargaining model, which describes the asymmetrical relationship between the investor and the host state, and the paradigmatic shift in bargaining power that occurs once the investment has been sunk.[90] It will then discuss the resource nationalism cycle.[91] This is a cyclical pattern, which begins with the host state seeking foreign investment when the price of the natural resource is relatively low and ends when the price of the natural resource appreciates. In such a case, the host state would wish to exercise greater control over its natural resource, which may lead to higher taxes or outright nationalization.

---

88 Hasan S. Zakariya, 'Sovereignty Over Natural Resources and the Search for a New International Order' in Kamal Hossain (ed), *Legal Aspects of the New International Economic Order* (Frances Pinter 1980) 212.

89 A.A. Fatouros, *Government Guarantees to Foreign Investors* (Columbia University Press 1962) 16 and E.I. Nwogugu, *The Legal Problems of Foreign Investment in Developing Countries* (Manchester University Press 1965) 2.

90 See generally Raymond Vernon, *Sovereignty at Bay: The Multinational Spread of US Enterprises* (Longman 1971) and Brandon Marsh, 'Preventing the Inevitable: The Benefits of Contractual Risk Engineering in the Light of Venezuela's Recent Oil Field Nationalization' (2008) 13 *Stanford Journal of Law Business & Finance* 453, 457.

91 Maniruzzaman, 'The Issue of Resource Nationalism: Risk Engineering and Dispute Management in the Oil and Gas Industry' (n 6) 81.

2.3.1 The need for foreign capital

Foreign direct investment brings a plethora of advantages to the host state.[92] For this reason it is argued that the host state must afford absolute protection to the investor.[93] The wide array of benefits fostered through foreign direct investment are highlighted by Baker, who observes that 'foreign direct investment' provides:

> additional equity capital, transfer of patented technologies, access to scarce managerial skills, creation of new jobs, access to overseas market networks and marketing expertise, reduced flight of domestic capital abroad, more rigorous appraisal of investment proposals, diffusion of improved technologies, long-term commitment to successful FDI projects, and catalytic effects leading to associated lending for specific projects.[94]

The substantial benefits that foreign direct investment brings to the host state have been also highlighted by the World Bank.[95] In its Guidelines on the Treatment of Foreign Direct Investment it recognized that, inter alia, foreign direct investment facilitates the transfer of capital.[96] Typically, resource rich nations lack the domestic capital in order to explore and exploit their natural resources. The scarcity of this capital thus necessitates the importation of foreign capital.[97] Attracting foreign direct investment could be achieved by granting incentives to the investor. Even more importantly, however, host states need to grant concession agreements to the investor, which reduce the impact of risk and uncertainty.[98] They could also foster the creation of a good investment climate through their investment codes.[99]

On the other hand, dependency theorists argue that foreign direct investment ought to be rejected, because it does more to exacerbate poverty in developing countries than it actually does to ameliorate it.[100] According to this view, investments are typically made by multinational corporations, which are invariably headquartered in developed countries. They carry out their operations through subsidiaries in developing countries.

The subsidiaries will always make decisions and policies which benefit their parent companies and shareholders, who are often from developed countries. Given this fact, multinational corporations serve the interests of their developed countries rather than the interests of the developing country in which they are

---

92 Nathan M. Jensen, *Nation-States and the Multinational Corporation* (Princeton 2006) 23–39.
93 *Amco v Indonesia* (1984) 23 ILM 351 at 369 (para 23).
94 James C. Baker, *Foreign Direct Investment in Less Developed Countries: The Role of ICSID and MIGA* (Quorum Books 1999) 5.
95 Seymour J. Rubin, 'World Bank: Report to the Development Committee and Guidelines on the Treatment of Foreign Direct Investment' (1992) 31 ILM 1363, 1379.
96 ibid.
97 Fatouros (n 89) 16; Nwogugu (n 89) 2.
98 Aharoni (n 3) 168–71.
99 Muna Ndulo, 'Foreign Investment and Economic Development' (1984) 11 *Cornell Law Forum* 6, 7.
100 Richard Peet, *Global Capitalism: Theories of Societal Development* (Routledge 1991) 43–8.

operating. As a consequence, developing countries become satellite economies which serve the interests of the developed states. Dependency theorists thus argue that development is virtually impossible until developing states break away from the economic subjugation that is facilitated by foreign direct investment. Thus, foreign direct investment ought to be rejected.

Certainly, there is some support for this view. Indeed, although investment does bring in foreign capital, much of this is externalized once operations have commenced. There is evidence that the outflows of capital are far greater than the inflows.[101] In fact, what goes out may even be twice as much as that which goes in.[102] This is undoubtedly problematic because if capital is not staying within the country then economic development is significantly stifled.

Moreover, by accepting foreign direct investment, the host government fosters the creation of a rentier state, under which the state receives 'substantial amounts of external economic rent'.[103] Amongst the many vices the rentier state leads to is the 'Dutch Disease'.[104] This name derives from the demise of the manufacturing industry in the Netherlands, after the discovery of a large natural gas field.[105] Essentially, the massive revenues being received by rentier states as a result of the economic boom spurred by natural resources means that the national currency becomes stronger in relation to the US dollar. This in turn makes imports cheaper and domestic products more expensive. As a result, all national industries, except the booming natural resource sector, decline, which in turn leads to the de-industrialization of the host state. Consequently, diversification of the economy is rendered more difficult.

Moreover, a decline in the local manufacturing industry leads to job losses for skilled labour.[106] This is evidenced by what occurred in Gabon. When oil was booming it meant that revenues increased. Those benefiting from the increased revenues were thus in a position to purchase foreign produced food, which in turn had a detrimental effect on the rural agricultural sector in Gabon.[107]

It would appear, therefore, that foreign direct investment does have its potentially negative impacts. However, it does have some positive ones as well. For this reason, to reject it outright would be extreme.[108] Because of the scarcity of domestic capital, the host state will ultimately need to source foreign capital, technology

---

101 See John R. O'Neal and Frances H. O'Neal, 'Hegemony, Imperialism and the Profitability of Foreign Investment' (1988) 42 *International Organization* 347.

102 S.M. Cunningham, 'Multinationals and Restructuring in Latin America' in C.J. Dixon, D. Drakakis-Smith and H. Watts (eds), *Multinational Corporations and the Third World* (Routledge 1986) 39, 46.

103 Douglas A. Yates, *The Rentier State in Africa: Oil Rent Dependency & Neocolonialism in the Republic of Gabon* (Africa World Press 1996) 12.

104 Oskan Bayulgen, *Foreign Investment and Political Regimes: The Oil Sector in Azerbaijan, Russia and Norway* (Cambridge University Press 2010) 77.

105 Yates (n 103) 27–28.

106 Bayulgen (n 104) 77.

107 Yates (n 103) 158–59.

108 Ndulo, 'Foreign Investment and Economic Development' (n 99) 8.

28 Resource nationalism in international investment law

and managerial know-how in order to explore and exploit its natural resources. Rejecting foreign direct investment will lead to the exact situation that dependency theorists are seeking to avoid; the impoverishment of the host state. What host states need to do instead is closely identify the problems that may arise as a result of foreign direct investment. From that point onwards, they are placed in a position to formulate means of minimizing the negative effects of foreign direct investment, whilst also formulating means of maximizing its positive ones.

The state could for example strengthen its labour laws in order to prevent exploitation of or discrimination against the local labour force. In addition to this, it could negotiate for better technology to be brought to the host state, thus protecting itself from becoming a dumping ground for poor quality products.[109] Moreover, it could train competent financial personnel and lawyers who in turn will be better placed to negotiate agreements between the investor and the host state they are representing. In addition, host states could formulate their policies so that more emphasis is placed on the quality of investment coming in, rather than simply the quantity. This is certainly the position China has taken in recent years.[110]

As seen in this sub-section 'foreign direct investment' has some positive impacts. However, 'foreign direct investment' has also come under some intense scrutiny and some of these misgivings are justified. Clearly, shutting out 'foreign direct investment' is not the answer. This is owing to the fact that, in order to develop national industries, developing countries need capital. One means by which they can obtain this capital is through 'foreign direct investment'. Host states should therefore focus on attracting investment in a way that benefits them as well as the investor. Some means through which this can be accomplished have been highlighted above. However, states must also be cognizant of the fact that the foreign investor may encounter many risks when transferring capital from the home state to the host state. The purpose of the next section is to discuss these potential risks.

2.3.2 The obsolescing bargaining model

Under the obsolescing bargaining model, it is hypothesized that concession agreements containing significant undertakings on the part of the host state are susceptible to later changes once the investment has been sunk.[111] When deciding whether to invest in a particular country, the foreign investor's primary consideration is whether it will recoup its initial investment and make a profit on top of that. In order to achieve this goal, investors will need certain guarantees from the host state. This would include the guarantee that a favourable legal situation that exists

---

109 ibid.
110 Wenshua Shan, Norah Gallagher and Sheng Zhang, 'National Treatment for Foreign Investment in China: A Changing Landscape' (2012) 27 *ICSID Review* 120, 125.
111 See generally Vernon (n 90) and Marsh (n 90) 457.

at the time of negotiation will not then be rescinded at a later date.[112] For this reason, foreign investors need assurances on the part of the host state, that 'they will receive, both today and in the future, a definite legal treatment, specified in the relevant legal instruments, and that consequently they need not fear any major changes in local legal or political conditions that would be unfavourable to their interests'.[113]

On the other hand, it is the state's expectation that the foreign capital and the technical know-how that the investor will bring, shall in turn lead to the state benefiting from the exploration and exploitation of natural resources. In the latter case, this is fostered through the payment of royalties and other taxes to the host state once operations have commenced. The idea here is that the state receives some sort of tax from the investor on the basis of the fact that it owns the minerals but has permitted some other entity to use them.[114]

Three factors appear to affect the balance of power at the negotiating stage. The first is low prices of the natural resource, the second is lack of technological and managerial capacity and the third is the existence of alternative investment options for the investor.[115] Thus, at the negotiation stage, the host state needs to present itself as a sufficiently attractive investment destination. This is especially so if the investor is considering a plethora of investment destinations. Because it is the state that needs the investor's capital at this stage, it is in a considerably weaker bargaining position than the investor. This may further be exacerbated by a lacklustre response to initial attempts by the host state to attract foreign direct investment. Knowing this, the investor is in a position to demand various incentives and the insertion of various contractual clauses aimed at protecting the investment, and the state often has to acquiesce to those demands.[116]

Once the investment has been sunk, it is the state that becomes the stronger party. This is because, once operations have commenced, the investor is not exactly in a position to dismantle its equipment and extricate itself from the host state.[117] The investor is thus in a considerably weaker position than the host state at this stage, which has at its disposal various legislative and administrative prerogatives. The state could opportunistically increase taxes, impose heavy regulatory burdens or, in an extreme case, expropriate the investor's asset. This is particularly likely to occur in the advanced stages of the resource nationalism cycle.[118]

---

112 Fatouros (n 89) 63.
113 ibid.
114 Muna Ndulo, 'Mineral Taxation in Zambia' (1975–1977) 7–9 *Zambia Law Journal* 33, 35–36.
115 Vlado Vivoda, 'Resource Nationalism, Bargaining and International Oil Companies: Challenges and Change in the New Millennium' (2009) 14 *New Political Economy* 517, 520.
116 Bayulgen (n 104) 18.
117 Eric A. Posner and Alan O. Sykes, *Economic Foundations of International Law* (Harvard University Press 2013) 288.
118 Joseph Nwaokoro, 'Enforcing Stabilization of International Energy Contracts' (2013) 3 *Journal of World Energy Law & Business* 103, 105.

30 Resource nationalism in international investment law

2.3.3 The resource nationalism cycle

The advanced stages of the resource nationalism cycle occur when the state seeks to exert greater control over natural resource development and to limit the operations of the foreign investor.[119] This will often be sparked when the price of the natural resource escalates. The state will wish to gain a greater share of the profits being generated by the investor. This will be done by increasing taxes or simply by nationalizing the investor's asset. Resource nationalization often occurs in cyclical patterns, hence the term 'resource nationalism cycle'.[120] An example of a country that has undergone various resource nationalism cycles is Venezuela, where oil plays a 'central role as the engine of the economy'.[121] Exploration and exploitation of Venezuela's oil reserves remained largely in the hands of private investors until the industry was nationalized in the 1970s. It was then privatized in the 1990s. The oil industry was eventually renationalized in the 2000s.[122]

By 1928, Venezuela had become one of the world's leading oil exporters.[123] Under the dictatorship of General Juan Vicente Gómez, concession agreements were granted to the Standard Oil Company and the Royal Dutch Oil Company, who operated in Venezuela for a period of 23 years. In 1943, the Government of Venezuela enacted the Petroleum Law, which increased taxes and also extended existing concessions for almost 40 years. This was later amended by the government of Rómulo Betancourt and his Democratic Action Party, which amended the 1943 Petroleum Law and increased government taxes on the oil industry's profits to 50 per cent. The government was overthrown by a military coup in 1948.[124] The Government of Venezuela thus once again became a dictatorship, under Marcos Pérez Jimenéz.[125] Although he supported foreign oil companies, Marcos Pérez Jimenéz was ousted in 1958.[126]

When Betancourt was elected to power in 1958, he increased the government's share of oil profits from 50 to 60 per cent. His government also founded the Organization of Petroleum Exporting Countries (OPEC) along with Saudi Arabia,

---

119 Paul Stevens, 'National Oil Companies and International Oil Companies in the Middle East: Under the Shadow of Government and the Resource Nationalism Cycle' (2008) 1 *Journal of World Energy Law & Business* 5.

120 Maniruzzaman, 'The Issue of Resource Nationalism: Risk Engineering and Dispute Management in the Oil and Gas Industry' (n 6) 81.

121 Terry Lynn Karl, *The Paradox of Plenty: Oil Booms and Petro-States* (University of California 1997) 101.

122 See Elisabeth Eljuri and Clovis Treviño, 'Venezuela: On the Path to Complete "Oil Sovereignty", or the Beginning of a New Era of Investment?' (2009) 2 *Journal of World Energy Law & Business* 259, 260–61.

123 Marsh (n 90) 458–59.

124 Karl (n 121) 95.

125 Miguel Tinker Salas, 'Staying the Course: United States Oil Companies in Venezuela, 1945–1958' (2005) 32 *Latin American Perspectives* 147, 156.

126 ibid 161–62.

Kuwait, Iraq and Iran. The goal of this organization was to create a cartel which ensured the welfare of its member countries by fixing oil prices.[127]

When Rafael Caldera was elected president in 1969, Venezuela was experiencing a period of robust economic growth, which was influenced by political stability and rising oil prices. In 1971, Caldera raised the oil profit tax to 70 per cent. In addition, he passed the Hydrocarbons Reversion Law, which provided that all oil company assets would go to the state once the concessions had elapsed. In 1973, Caldera was succeeded by Carlos Andrés Pérez, who centred his presidential campaign on the notion that Venezuelans should control its extraordinary petroleum reserves.[128] During that year OPEC increased oil prices from US$3.50 per barrel to US$10 per barrel. This windfall in the price of oil emboldened the Government of Venezuela to effect an ambitious plan to nationalize the oil industry.[129]

In 1976, the Government of Venezuela nationalized its entire petroleum industry and placed all foreign companies under the administrative supervision of the Petróleous de Venezuela SA (PDVSA). The PDVSA was a state owned oil and natural gas company. When oil prices subsequently fell, Venezuela's economy experienced a recession. Not only did Venezuela's GDP decline; it also experienced heavy job losses. In order to keep the economy afloat, the Government of Venezuela resorted to foreign borrowing.[130] In response to falling oil prices, OPEC resolved to halve oil production in 1981. Attempts were made to resuscitate Venezuela's economy through the successive governments of Jaime Lusinchi, who took over in 1983 and Carlos Andrés Pérez, who returned to power in 1988. Foreign direct investment remained relatively low.

It was when Rafael Caldera succeeded Pérez in 1994 that a new business plan was introduced for the PDVSA, which eventually culminated in the privatization of Venezuela's oil industry. This occurred under the programme known as Apertura Petrolera (literally, 'petroleum opening') under which Venezuela promoted foreign direct investment in oil projects.[131] Although this programme certainly did attract a great deal of foreign investment, it also provoked criticism from within Venezuela. One notable critic was Hugo Chavez, who was elected President of Venezuela in December 1998. His policies progressively culminated in the renationalization of the Venezuelan petroleum industry.[132]

---

127 Francisco Parra, *Oil Politics: A Modern History of Petroleum* (IB Tauris 2004) 89.
128 Thomas J. Pate, 'Evaluating Stabilization Clauses in Venezuela's Strategic Association Agreements for Heavy-crude Extraction in the Orinoco Belt: The Return of a Forgotten Contractual Risk Reduction Mechanism for the Petroleum Industry' (2009) 40 *University of Miami Inter-American Law Review* 347, 368.
129 ibid.
130 Karl (n 121) 154.
131 Jason Pierce, 'A South American Energy Treaty: How the Region Might Attract Foreign Investment in the Wake of Resource Nationalism' (2011) 44 *Cornell International Law Journal* 417, 425.
132 ibid. See also Pate (n 128) 376.

It can thus be seen that the oil companies went from private hands and thence to the state in the 1970s. It was then privatized in the 1990s before being renationalized again in the 2000s by the government of Hugo Chavez. Since renationalization, however, Venezuela's oil production has decreased. Moreover, owing to a lack of technical expertise, the nationalized entities have been unable to explore and exploit resources from 'mature and geologically complex' fields.[133] An example of this is the reserves under Lake Maracaibo.

Moreover, because of these technical shortages, the PDVSA has been forced to shut down various oil wells. This is further compounded by the fact that the Chávez administration had effectively used the PDVSA as a cash-cow through which it could implement its social policies. This meant that the PDVSA was severely constrained financially, which in turn had an impact on its capacity to reinvest in new projects and its deteriorating infrastructure.[134] As a consequence of its lack of technological, managerial and financial capacity, and the need for expansion, it is likely that Venezuela will once again need to rely heavily on foreign direct investment.[135] By 2009, the government was already beginning to tone down its nationalistic rhetoric in a bid to attract foreign direct investment.[136]

2.3.3.1 Attracting foreign direct investment

The resource nationalism cycle often begins when the state grants a concession to the investor and ends with the state seeking to gain greater control over the natural resource once operations have commenced. Typically, when an investor enters the host state he is granted a concession, which will stipulate that the former is to explore and exploit the natural resources and the latter is to receive taxes and royalties from the profits generated. As mentioned earlier, the state does not have sufficient capital or know-how in the first place in order to invest in any new operations.

As a means of exploring and exploiting its vast natural resources, the host state will therefore rely on foreign direct investment. To foster the flow of foreign direct investment, the state will grant various incentives through the concession agreement. This is done in order to attract much needed investment to its jurisdiction. At the time that the investment is being attracted, the price of the natural resource is relatively low.[137]

During this period the prospect of privatizing previously nationalized oil or mining companies also becomes attractive. There may be various motives for this. One reason may be to replace any outdated infrastructure, as was the case with

---

133 Javier Corrales and Michael Penfold, *Dragon in the Tropics: Hugo Chávez and the Political Economy of Revolution in Venezuela* (Brookings 2011) 85.
134 ibid 87–88.
135 ibid 89.
136 ibid 90.
137 Wälde (n 8) 55.

Russia in the 1990s.[138] In addition, privatized entities are perceived to operate more efficiently.[139] This view may particularly gain credence and be augmented in situations where production in these state owned corporations has indeed decreased. This can be seen in countries such as Venezuela. In 1970, prior to the first nationalization, Venezuela was producing up to 3.5 million barrels of oil a day. Subsequent to nationalization, the production of oil slumped to as low as 1.5 million barrels a day in 1985. Following reprivatization in the 1990s, production was 3.06 million barrels a day in 1997.[140] This reduced again after Hugo Chavez renationalized the oil industry.[141]

Moreover, privatization cuts the losses of a host state if it has had to obtain loans, in order to keep these entities and the economy afloat. It is much more convenient for the state to have a foreign investor managing, exploring and exploiting the oil or mining industry at a profit, whilst the former simply receives taxes and royalties from the latter. This is especially attractive if the general consensus is that the price of the host state's natural resource will remain low for the foreseeable future.[142]

2.3.3.2 An appreciation in natural resource prices

The difficulty arises when the price of the natural resource experiences a sustained upward trend.[143] Once resource prices boom, it leads to opportunistic behaviour by host governments who wish to capture the benefits of the windfall profits that are being generated by the investor.[144] It is argued that 'nationalization of natural resource industries tends to occur when the price of the corresponding commodity is high'.[145] There is therefore a correlation between a rise in the price of the host state's natural resource and the rise of resource nationalism. Evidence of this is certainly seen by the nationalizations that took place in Latin America, which were influenced largely by a spike in oil prices between 2003 and 2008.[146]

---

138 Daniel R. Sieck, 'Confronting the Obsolescing Bargain: Transacting Around Political Risk in Developing and Transitioning Economies Through Renewable Energy Foreign Direct Investment' (2010) 33 *Suffolk Transnational Law Review* 319, 328.

139 See Narjess Boubakri, Jean-Claude Cosset and Omrane Guedhami, 'Liberalization, Corporate Governance and the Performance of Privatized Firms in Developing Countries' (2005) 11 *Journal of Corporate Finance* 767.

140 United States Energy Information Administration (2012) http://www.eia.gov/countries/analysisbriefs/Venezuela/venezuela.pdf (last accessed 31 May 2015).

141 ibid.

142 Rohit Negi, 'The Micropolitics of Mining and Development in Zambia: Insights from the Northwestern Province' (2011) 12 *African Studies Quarterly* 27, 37.

143 See Roderick Duncan, 'Price or politics? An Investigation of the Causes of Expropriation' (2006) 50 *Australian Journal of Agricultural and Resource Economics* 85.

144 ibid 88–89.

145 Roberto Chang, Constantino Hevia and Norman Loayza, 'Privatization and Nationalization Cycles' (2010) National Bureau of Economic Research Working Paper Series, Working Paper 16126 at 6 http://www.nber.org/papers/w16126 (last accessed 31 May 2015).

146 Ian Bremmer, *The End of the Free Market* (Portfolio 2010) 56–59.

The perception that occurs here is that the foreign investor is making a large profit, whilst the host state is making only a fraction of that through very low taxes and royalties.[147] For this reason, the state will wish to exert a greater level of control over its natural resources, in order to obtain a greater share of the rent. Because the investor has sunk significant amounts of money and is making a large gain, nationalization seems to be an attractive prospect in the short to medium term.

This may be compounded by the perception that since the resource is rooted in the soil, it may be a one-off extraction of wealth. Moreover, policy-makers may be dismayed by the amounts of profits that mining and oil companies are making in contrast to the taxes being received by the host state. Calls for nationalization may be intensified, especially where the concessions were granted shortly before a commodity boom takes place.[148] This may be further exacerbated by societal inequalities, eroding infrastructure and even environmental degradation caused by mining and oil companies. The host state will thus progress either to increase taxes or nationalize the investor's assets.[149]

2.3.3.3 The role of national systems and institutions

As a general rule, states are more likely to nationalize not only when prices are high, but also when national institutions are weak.[150] Therefore, the likelihood of a state adopting resource nationalist policies depends largely on the type of political regime governing the host state in question. Resource nationalist policies are influenced not only by the desire to capture more revenue from a windfall in prices but also a desire by states to retain their political hegemony.[151] Whether or not they are able to act upon their motives depends largely on whether institutional constraints in the form of checks and balances on the exercise of executive power actually exist. Under authoritarian systems, political hegemony depends less on the electorate than it does under democratic and hybrid systems.

It is argued, therefore, that states are less likely to adopt resource nationalist policies. This is despite the fact that checks and balances are virtually non-existent. Similarly, democratic governments are unlikely to adopt resource nationalist policies, because although they are more susceptible to electoral pressure, this is

---

147 Øystein Noreng, *Oil and Islam: Social and Economic Issues* (Wiley 1997) 111–115.

148 A. Butler, 'Resource Nationalism and the African National Congress' (2013) 113 *Journal of the Southern African Institute of Mining and Metallury* 11, 13.

149 G. Joffé, P. Stevens, T. George, J. Lux and C. Searle, 'Expropriation of Oil and Gas Investments: Historical, Legal and Economic Perspectives in a New Age of Resource Nationalism' (2009) 2 *Journal of World Energy and Business* 3, 22.

150 See Sergei Guriev, Anton Kolotilin and Konstantin Sonin, 'Determinants of Nationalization in the Oil Sector: A Theory and Evidence from Panel Data' (2009) 27 *The Journal of Law, Economics & Organization* 301.

151 Ekim Arbtali, 'Political Regimes, Investment Risk and Resource Nationalism: An Empirical Analysis' at 21 http://regconf.hse.ru/uploads/7da62134fab330f54f067e5cd2e603c40298cd7e. pdf (last accessed 31 May 2015).

counterbalanced by the strong institutions that exist in such systems. Hybrid systems are the most likely to adopt resource nationalist policies because they are not only answerable to the electorate, but such systems are also characterized by weak institutions.

Under authoritarian regimes, the government is less susceptible to the demands of the populace than would be the case in a democracy. For this reason, it is easier for the government to ignore the socio-economic demands of the people.[152] There are very few checks and balances and very little popular pressure when dealing with a non-democratic government.[153] On the one hand, this makes it easier for the host state to secure very favourable pro-investment terms for the multinational corporation, when it is entering into the country. In turn, this actually attracts higher levels of foreign direct investment.[154] Moreover, host states are in a position to deal ruthlessly with those opposing multinational corporations and use the state machinery to quash any demonstrations.[155] On the other hand, however, an autocratic regime is very likely to encroach upon these favourable terms in instances where they see a threat to their hold on power.[156]

The lack of institutional constraints in this instance will almost certainly be accompanied by lack of policy credibility and ultimate instability.[157] In such an instance, states may actually resort to resource nationalism in order to appease interest groups that in turn will support the non-democratic regime. Because there are no constraints in a non-democratic regime, it heightens the chances of expropriatory action on the part of the host state.[158]

Such an action is less likely under a democratic regime. This is owing to the fact that democratic regimes typically provide the mechanisms that will ameliorate political risk.[159] For this reason, democratic countries tend to have higher flows of 'foreign direct investment' than their autocratic counterparts.[160] Under a democratic system, the government is not only accountable to the people, but it is also characterized by strong institutions which perform checks and balances on the

---

152 Geoffrey Garrett and Peter Lange, 'Internationalization, Institutions and Political Change' in Robert O. Keohane and Helen V. Milner (eds), *Internationalization and Domestic Politics* (Cambridge University Press 1996) 48, 61 and Paul Brooker, *Non-Democratic Regimes: Theory, Government and Politics* (Macmillan 2000) 167–69.

153 Nathan M. Jensen, 'Democratic Governance and Multinational Corporations: Political Regimes and Inflows of Foreign Direct Investment' (2003) 57 *International Organization* 587, 593.

154 ibid.

155 Quan Li, 'Democracy, Autocracy and Expropriation of Foreign Direct Investment' (2009) 42 *Comparative Political Studies* 1098, 1106.

156 Arbtali (n 151) 24.

157 Bayulgen (n 104) 56.

158 ibid.

159 Jensen, *Nation-States and the Multinational Corporation* (n 92) 80.

160 ibid 85.

161 Larry Diamond, *Developing Democracy: Toward Consolidation* (Johns Hopkins University Press 1999) 11; Philippe C. Schmitter and Terry Lynn Karl, 'What Democracy Is . . . and Is Not' (1991) 2 *Journal of Democracy* 75, 76.

36 Resource nationalism in international investment law

executive.[161] One very key aspect that might protect the safety of foreign investments is stability of policy. Policy-makers in democratic institutions may also adopt a *status quo* approach, in favour of foreign investors.[162] This might render it more onerous for politicians to make sweeping economic changes that may detrimentally affect multinational corporations.

Furthermore, executives operating in a democratic country may also have the other arms of government to contend with. These are the legislature and the judiciary. Sweeping economic reforms will invariably require legislative changes. If the incumbent does not have a majority in the legislature, it may be harder to get certain measures through. A strong and independent judiciary will also be a consideration for the host state. Not only does the judiciary have the ability to render a judgment against the executive; it may also be in a position to strike down legislation that may be deemed unconstitutional.[163] On the other hand, in an event where it is seen as beneficial for its political future and there exist very few institutional restraints, the host country is likely to resort to resource nationalism.[164]

Under a hybrid system, the government still has an obligation to secure legitimacy through participation in elections during set terms in office. Three key features are typical in such systems: 'highly centralized state authority concentrated in the executive branch; formal institutions of democracy, including room for at least some candidates to oppose incumbent authorities on the ballot in elections to powerful posts; and the systematic gutting of these institutions and their frequent functional replacement by substitutions – often either outside the constitutional framework or in violation of the spirit of the constitution – that are created by and highly dependent on central authorities'.[165]

In sum, they are more susceptible to the demands of the electorate than their non-democratic counterparts. Moreover, they lack the types of institutional constraints that are typical in the type of democratic system highlighted in the preceding paragraph. There is a general dearth of strong institutions which are needed to hold the government accountable between elections. As a consequence, they are more likely to adopt short-term measures in order to please the masses.[166] They are thus more likely to impose a resource nationalist policy in instances where the electorate demands it. The probability of this occurring is increased further by the fact that there are virtually no checks and balances to hold the executive of the day accountable for its actions.

---

162 Nathan Jensen, 'Political Risk, Democratic Institutions and Foreign Direct Investment' (2008) 70 *The Journal of Politics* 1040, 1041.
163 See for example the famous case of *Marbury v Madison*, 5 U.S. 137 (1803). See also the Zambian Supreme Court case of *Mulundika and Others v The People* [1995–1997] ZR 20.
164 Li (n 155) 1109.
165 Nikolai Petrov, Masha Lipman and Henry H. Hale, *Overmanaged Democracy in Russia: Governance Implications of Hybrid Regimes* (Carnegie Endowment for International Peace 2010) 3.
166 ibid 11.

It has therefore been seen that whether or not a state resorts to resource nationalist policies also depends largely on the types of institutions operating within the host state. Host states with weak institutions and regular democratic elections, as we have seen under hybrid systems, are the most likely to resort to resource nationalism. On the other hand, democratic countries with strong institutions are the least likely to resort to resource nationalism. This is owing to the strong checks and balances that exist. Autocratic regimes are less likely to resort to resource nationalism than their hybrid counterparts, because although there exist fewer constraints upon executive power, they are not as susceptible to electoral pressure.

2.3.3.4 An expression of nationalism?

It is argued that when the state nationalizes, it is an expression of nationalism, rather than socialism.[167] In response to perceived foreign domination of the economy the state may then proceed to nationalize assets belonging to the investor. Nationalization certainly does eliminate the foreigner from the economic equation. However, in the process the host state is throwing out the baby with the bathwater, by eliminating foreign capital as well.[168] In the aftermath of an initial period of anti-foreigner euphoria, severe economic problems typically manifest. The consequence of this is that the resource rich nation moves from economic independence to economic downturn, which means that once again it has to resort to the use of foreign capital and expertise. The need to eliminate foreign domination from the economic paradigm is suddenly subjugated by the demand for development and modernization.[169]

Nationalism was the backdrop against which the Zambian Government nationalized the mining industry in the 1970s.[170] By 1968, during his famous Mulungushi reform speech, President Kaunda noted that economic activity in Zambia was still dominated by foreigners, mainly Asian and European.[171] The government had been urging the business community to 'Zambianize' their businesses by taking up Zambian citizenship and equipping Zambians with the skills to take up executive positions in these companies.[172] In a further attempt to 'Zambianize' corporations operating in Zambia the government thus proceeded to obtain

---

167 See Butler (n 148) 13 and Amy Chua, 'The Privatization-Nationalization Cycle: The Link Between Markets and Ethnicity in Developing Countries' (1995) 95 *Columbia Law Review* 223, 262.
168 ibid 266.
169 ibid.
170 Marcia Burdette, 'Nationalization in Zambia: A Critique of Bargaining Theory' (1977) 11 *Canadian Journal of African Studies* 471, 480.
171 Andrew Sardanis, *Africa : Another Side of the Coin: Northern Rhodesia's Final Years and Zambia's Nationhood* (I.B. Tauris 2011) 212.
172 ibid.

a 51 per cent equity stake in all companies, including those in the mining industry.[173] More recently, certainly when Zambia nationalized its oil industry, it did so in order for the state to have greater control over sectors of the economy that it deemed strategic.[174] This in turn would aid the government's policy of endogenous development.[175]

Very closely related to nationalism is the issue of ethnicity.[176] This is conceivable in instances where foreign investors may make alliances with ethnic minorities in developing countries. This may lead to resentment by the majority population and a potential backlash may consequentially follow. This may even be particularly prevalent in developing countries that are governed on democratic principles because, as with nationalism, they may end up voting in a government that works to the disfavour of the investor. Foreign investment may be at risk unless the host state has in place mechanisms to ensure that the majority populace are also enjoying the benefits of foreign investment. Failing this, it is very easy for the foreign investor and the economically dominant ethnic minority to become targets of nationalistic forces.

Countries such as South Africa and Malaysia have sought to deal with this issue through various means. South Africa has adopted black economic empowerment through their Black Economic Empowerment Act. This Act is calculated to ensure that previously disadvantaged groups including the black majority have access to the economic benefits that South Africa has to offer. However, this has been challenged as being in violation of investment treaties.[177] Without such mechanisms there will undoubtedly be hostility between the ethnic majority and the economically dominant minority. In turn, the foreign investor who has formed an alliance with the latter will also be in jeopardy. The alliance formed will become a potential target for nationalization in such instances.[178]

The aim of this section was to discuss the resource nationalism cycle. It has been seen that, at the beginning of the cycle, the host state will readily invite the foreign capital. It will also offer various incentives, to encourage the investor. However, once the investment is sunk, the host state will wish to exercise greater control over its natural resources. This will often occur when the price of the natural resource has appreciated, which in turn may lead to political pressure to raise taxes or to nationalize outright the investor's assets. This will adversely impact the investor. The next section therefore explores ways in which the investor will seek to protect itself from unilateral state actions that adversely affect it.

---

173 Burdette (n 170) 480.
174 Corrales and Penfold (n 133) 64.
175 ibid 63.
176 See Amy Chua, 'The Paradox of Free Market Democracy: Rethinking Development Policy' (2000) 41 *Harvard International Law Journal* 287; Amy Chua, 'Markets, Democracy and Ethnicity: Toward a New Paradigm for Law and Development' (1998) 108 *Yale Law Journal* 1.
177 See *Piero Foresti, Laura de Carli and Others v South Africa*, ICSID Case No. ARB(AF)/07/01 (2010).
178 Chua, 'The Privatization-Nationalization Cycle' (n 167) 223.

2.4 Mitigating political risk

There are various means of mitigating the risks highlighted in the preceding section.[179] This can be accomplished through the utilization of political risk insurance. It can also be done through the insertion of certain clauses in the concession agreements. The arbitration clause, which is invariably inserted into concession agreements, ensures that should a dispute between the host state and the investor arise, then this will be decided by a neutral forum operation outside of the mechanisms of the host state. They may also utilize stabilization clauses, which are intended to prevent the host state from utilizing its legislative and administrative functions to override previous undertakings.[180]

2.4.1 Political risk insurance

One of the means through which investors can protect themselves against the political risks highlighted in the preceding section is through political risk insurance. Amongst the government sponsored insurance schemes are the Overseas Private Insurance Corporation (OPIC) and the Multilateral Investment Guarantee Agency (MIGA). There are also a number of private insurers such as the American Insurance Group (AIG), Lloyd's of London, Sovereign Risk Insurance Limited, Chubb and Zurich Emerging Markets Solutions.[181]

OPIC operates with the backing of the Government of the United States.[182] It is required to operate on a self-sustaining basis.[183] As a result of this, the organization has recorded a profit for every year since its inception. OPIC 'helps U.S. businesses invest overseas, fosters economic development in new and emerging markets, complements the private sector in managing risks associated with foreign direct investment, and supports U.S. foreign policy'.[184] An advantage with OPIC is that it insures an investor's assets for up to 20 years, which is longer than its private counterparts.[185] It may also authorize loans.[186]

MIGA operates under the auspices of the World Bank. It was established in 1988 and has about 155 members. The main reason that it exists is to encourage the flow of investment to developing countries.[187] Article 11 of the MIGA

---

179 Maniruzzaman, 'The Issue of Resource Nationalism: Risk Engineering and Dispute Management in the Oil and Gas Industry' (n 6) 99.
180 Surya Subedi, *International Investment Law: Reconciling Policy and Principle* (2nd edn, Hart Publishing 2012) 101.
181 Maniruzzaman, 'The Issue of Resource Nationalism: Risk Engineering and Dispute Management in the Oil and Gas Industry' (n 6) 99.
182 Ashton B. Inniss, 'Rethinking Political Risk Insurance: Incentives for Investor Risk Mitigation' (2010) 16 *Southwestern Journal of International Law* 477, 488.
183 Overseas Private Investment Corporation, OPIC Handbook (2006) 4, http://www.opic.gov/sites/default/files/docs/OPIC_Handbook.pdf (last accessed 31 May 2015).
184 ibid.
185 Inniss (n 182) 489.
186 ibid.
187 See art 2 of the MIGA Convention.

Convention covers non-business risks such as nationalization, war or civil disturbance, breach of contract and any losses arising from any introduction of restrictions on the transfer of currency outside the host country by the government. Eligible types of investments are covered under Article 12 of the MIGA Convention. These include equity interests, non-equity direct investment and any medium or long-term forms of investment. Moreover, the investment must be made into a developing country in accordance with Article 14 of the MIGA Convention.

2.4.2 Contractual clauses

2.4.2.1 Dispute settlement clauses

One of the concerns of the investor is having its disputes heard by a non-neutral forum such as the national courts, if a dispute was to arise with the host state.[188] This is owing to the fact that the national courts, in developing countries at least, may not be fully independent of the executive. It is therefore within the realms of possibility that the national courts will render a decision against the investor even in the face of incontrovertible evidence. One way to avert this is through the insertion of a dispute resolution clause, which provides for arbitration or mediation. Mediation is a non-binding procedure that attempts to bring the parties together. This is fostered by a neutral third party, the mediator, who assists the parties in reaching their own decision.[189] The advantage with this approach is that it brings the parties together, which in the long run makes it easier to engage in long-term business transactions with one another. The difficulty with this approach, however, is that it is non-binding and therefore the parties can easily depart from any solutions propounded during the mediation proceedings.

Another means through which the parties can resolve their disputes is through arbitration. This is a process through which a dispute is heard by an individual or panel of individuals known as the arbitral tribunal. The tribunal obtains its jurisdiction from the arbitration clause itself. The advantage with a decision rendered by such a tribunal is that it is binding and enforceable. The process of seeking recognition and enforcement of non-domestic or foreign arbitral awards is fostered through the Convention on the Recognition and Enforcement of Foreign Arbitral Awards (the New York Convention).[190]

---

188 Sornarajah, *The International Law on Foreign Investment* (n 1) 286.
189 *World Intellectual Property Organization Guide to WIPO Mediation*, quoted in Tibor Várady, John J. Barceló and Arthur T. von Mehren, *International Commercial Arbitration: A Transnational Perspective* (3rd edn, Thomson & West 2006) 2–3.
190 http://www.uncitral.org/uncitral/en/uncitral_texts/arbitration/NYConvention.html (last accessed 31 May 2015).

Foreign direct investment and resource nationalism 41

Moreover, even if the state unilaterally terminates a contract containing an arbitration clause, the clause itself will continue to subsist.[191] This is owing to the principle of separability, which establishes the rule that the arbitration clause embedded in a contract is considered as separate from the main contract.[192] Therefore, even if the main contract lapses or becomes void, the general rule is that the arbitration clause itself continues to subsist. A state cannot therefore prevent being subjected to arbitration proceedings by simply terminating the contract. As observed by arbitrator Mahmassani in *LIAMCO v Libya*:[193]

> It is widely accepted in international law and practice that an arbitration clause survives the unilateral termination by that State of the contract in which it is inserted and continues in force even after that termination. This is a logical consequence of the interpretation of the intention of the contracting parties, and appears to be one of the basic conditions for creating a favourable climate of foreign investment.[194]

Supplementing the arbitration clause could be a choice of law clause. This is a particularly sensitive legal issue because it would involve two conflicting interests.[195] On the one hand the state is interested in preserving and protecting its national sovereignty. On the other hand the investor wishes to choose a legal order that is stable and predictable.[196] Depending on the bargaining power of the parties there are a few possible outcomes. The choice of law clause could refer exclusively to the law of the host state. Alternatively, the parties could choose a law which operates outside the fray of the national law of the host state. They could, for example, choose international law or the law of some other jurisdiction. Another potential alternative is the selection of a combination of both national and international law.[197]

2.4.2.2 Stabilization clauses

Investors will typically also insist on the insertion of stabilization clauses into concession agreements. As noted under the obsolescing bargaining model, the state may offer various incentives to the investor. However, these are subject to subsequent alteration by the host state, which possesses legislative and administrative prerogatives within its arsenal. It could therefore utilize these to override previous

---

191 Janet A. Rosen, 'Arbitration Under Private International Law: The Doctrines of Separability and Compétence de la Compétence' (1993) 17 *Fordham International Law Journal* 599.
192 ibid 606.
193 *Libyan American Oil Company (LIAMCO) v Libya* (1981) 20 ILM 1.
194 ibid 40.
195 Dolzer and Schreuer (n 7) 81.
196 ibid.
197 ibid.

42 Resource nationalism in international investment law

contractual undertakings, which in turn may jeopardize the investor's prospects of making a profit in the host state.[198]

As a buffer against this, stabilization clauses are inserted into concession agreements. These are clauses under which the state undertakes not to utilize its legislative and administrative prerogatives in a way that will have a detrimental effect on the investor. The concession agreement may even go on to specify those actions that are prohibited. This may include, for example, undertaking not to raise taxes for a period of time. These are what are referred to as tax stability clauses. The inclusion of these clauses is not only a major concern for investors but also for other stakeholders, such as lending financial institutions.[199] The lending institutions are typically the ones that will finance the projects. They too will need assurances that they will get their money back from the investor, once they make a borrowing.

Stabilization clauses could also be supplemented by the insertion of renegotiation clauses. The distinction between renegotiation clauses and stabilization clauses is that the latter focus more on the sanctity of contracts, whereas the former focus more on maintaining the economic equilibrium.[200] Stabilization clauses are discussed further in the next chapter, whereas renegotiation clauses will be discussed in Chapter 6 of this book.

2.5 Conclusion

It could thus be concluded that the discourse of foreign direct investment invariably involves long-term agreements. In the field of natural resources, this will typically be fostered inter alia through the granting of a concession agreement by the host state to the foreign investor. The investor can utilize its capital to explore and exploit the host state's natural resource. The former then pays royalties and taxes to the latter. It has been seen, however, that the long-term nature of these concession agreements renders the investor susceptible to various non-business risks.

One of these risks is the resource nationalism cycle. It has been seen from this chapter that this cycle begins when the host state, lacking in capital and expertise, will often solicit the aid of foreign investors. The latter in turn bring in the necessary capital, new technology and know-how to commence operations. It is the expectation of the investor to make a profit from the sunk investment. However, it has been seen that once operations commence and the natural resource experiences a sustained upward trend, the host state will seek to exercise greater control over the natural resource. It does so because it wishes to maximize the benefits

---

198 Sornarajah, *The International Law on Foreign Investment* (n 1) 281.
199 Maniruzzaman, 'The Issue of Resource Nationalism: Risk Engineering and Dispute Management in the Oil and Gas Industry' (n 6) 95.
200 Dolzer and Schreuer (n 7) 85.

accruing from high prices, which in turn lead to increased revenue for the investor. These revenues pale in comparison to the taxes and royalties accruing to the host state. Any incentives granted to the investor may be rescinded. This may mean either raising taxes or outrightly nationalizing the assets belonging to the investor.

This chapter has identified some of the mechanisms that exist in order to mitigate the risks involved in investing in resource rich nations. It has highlighted the availability of political risk insurance through publicly funded organizations such as MIGA and OPIC. In addition, it has highlighted that there are also private options available, such as Lloyd's of London or AIG. Moreover, investors could protect themselves through the insertion of certain clauses. The insertion of an arbitration clause, for example, ensures that all disputes between the host state and the investor are heard by a neutral forum that exists outside of the framework of the former's jurisdiction.

Moreover, to protect against the opportunism that manifests in the advanced stages of the resource nationalism cycle, investors will insist on the insertion of stabilization clauses. These are clauses stipulating that for the period within which the concession subsists, the host state will not take any administrative or legislative action that will have a material adverse effect on the profitability of the investment. The precise effect of these clauses will be discussed in the next chapter.

Chapter 3

The effect of stabilization clauses

3.1 Introduction

Under the obsolescing bargain model, it is clear that when a host state is entering into a concession with the investor, the former is prepared to accept whatever terms are dictated by the latter.[1] This is largely influenced by the fact that the host state often needs the investor's capital to exploit its natural resources. Thus, if it does not put itself in an adequately competitive position, it runs the risk of the investor seeking alternative jurisdictions in which to utilize its capital.[2] The investor is clearly in a stronger position during the negotiation stages of the contract because it is relying on a bargaining power derived from the state's need for foreign capital.[3] Once the concession is signed, and operations commence, it is the state that becomes the stronger party and the investor becomes the weaker party. This is because the state has various prerogatives at its disposal.

Thus, of concern to an investor when entering into a concession is whether the host government will abide by the terms of that agreement for the entirety of its term. It is clear that an ordinary contract, without stabilization clauses, will generally be governed by the municipal law of the host state.[4] From the investor's perspective, this means that the law can be altered at any time by the legislature of the host state and these laws can be amended in a way that disadvantages the concessionaire. Such a state of affairs puts the investor in a somewhat precarious position, especially in instances where a nationalistic mood sweeps the host state.[5] The advanced stages of the resource nationalism cycle typically occur in times when the investor is making windfall profits from the investment.[6] In times such as

---

1 See ch 2, 41–43.
2 ibid.
3 Erik J. Woodhouse, 'The Obsolescing Bargain Redux? Foreign Investment in the Electric Power Sector in Developing Countries' (2006) 38 *New York University Journal of International Law and Politics* 121, 130.
4 Sangwani Ng'ambi, 'Stabilization Clauses and the Zambian Windfall Tax' (2010) 1 *Zambia Social Science Journal* 107, 108.
5 See generally A.F.M. Maniruzzaman, 'The Issue of Resource Nationalism: Risk Engineering and Dispute Management in the Oil and Gas Industry' (2009) 5 *Journal of Oil and Gas Law* 79.
6 Vlado Vivoda, 'Resource Nationalism, Bargaining and International Oil Companies: Challenges and Change in the New Millennium' (2009) 14 *New Political Economy* 517, 520.

these the host state will reconsider the concessions and will seek to maximize the benefits attained from its natural resources.[7] It may consider altering tax legislation, so that it can gain a proportion of the windfall profits or simply nationalize the foreign company's assets.[8]

In order to address this issue, foreign investors thus insist on the insertion of stabilization clauses into the concession agreement.[9] These provisions are aimed at precluding host states from taking legislative or administrative measures that impede on the commercial interests of the investor.[10] These provisions are created for the protection of the investors, because the host government has various mechanisms at its disposal, which could potentially jeopardize the foreign investor's legitimate expectations of making a profit out of its investments. They protect the investment by rendering the concession immune from national law.[11]

Although the precise effect of stabilization clauses is still contentious, it is clear from the case law that arbitral tribunals respect the sanctity of contracts. As a consequence, there is an overwhelming amount of international jurisprudence which supports the contention that stabilization clauses are binding upon the state. Furthermore, the unilateral abrogation of these clauses has pecuniary consequences. Conceivably, this position has not been without its detractors, who argue that giving absolute legal effect to stabilization clauses impinges upon the state's sovereign prerogatives and the principle of permanent sovereignty over natural resources. This position has typically been dismissed by arbitral tribunals, who contend that states are exercising sovereignty when they bind themselves to concessions. Therefore, binding a state does not militate against permanent sovereignty over natural resources; it merely accentuates it.

In section 3.2 of this chapter, I will be looking at the principle of permanent sovereignty over natural resources, its evolution and status under international law. In section 3.3, I will be defining stabilization clauses and their intended purpose. In section 3.4, I shall explore the decisions of arbitral tribunals regarding stabilization clauses. Finally, section 3.5 will consist of a conclusion.

3.2 The doctrine of permanent sovereignty over natural resources

The end of the Second World War saw the dissolution of many colonial empires, when previously subjugated nations thus became independent and sovereign

---

7 See Thomas W. Wälde and George Ndi, 'Stabilizing International Investment Commitments: International Law Versus Contract Interpretation' (1996) 31 *Texas International Law Journal* 215, 220.

8 ibid.

9 J. Nna Emeka, 'Anchoring Stabilization Clauses in International Petroleum Contracts' (2008) 42 *International Lawyer* 1317, 1319.

10 Piero Bernardini, 'Stabilization and Adaptation in Oil and Gas Investments' (2008) 1 *Journal of World Energy Law and Business* 98, 100.

11 Frederick A. Mann, *Studies in International Law* (OUP 1972) 222–23.

states.[12] Many of these nations were well endowed in natural resources. As a facet of sovereignty and self-determination, these resource rich nations demanded the right to exploit their natural resources for the purposes of economic development and to better their prospects of economic growth.[13] To attain this goal resource rich nations saw the need to assert themselves on issues such as the control of their natural resources, which were in the hands of foreign companies.[14] It was felt that this state of affairs made nonsense of their newly acquired sovereignty and undermined their desire to develop and exploit their natural resources.[15]

Within the parameters of this goal was the need to reconsider the concession agreements formalized prior to their independence, a plethora of which were perceived as 'inequitable and onerous'.[16] This was certainly the case in *The American Independent Oil Company (AMINOIL) v Kuwait*,[17] where the concession was granted to AMINOIL before Kuwait had obtained her independence from Great Britain. This, of course, was by no means an isolated case. The need for developing countries to assert authority over natural resources led to the birth of the international law principle of permanent sovereignty over natural resources.[18]

The principle of permanent sovereignty over natural resources evolved through various United Nations General Assembly resolutions.[19] However, arguably the 'landmark resolution' was the United Nations General Assembly Resolution 1803 (XVII).[20] The evolution of the principle eventually culminated in the Charter of Economic Rights and Duties of States (CERDS), which as the name suggests highlights the rights and duties of states. The first part of this section will discuss the general evolution of the principle of permanent sovereignty over natural

---

12 A. Akinsanya, 'Permanent Sovereignty Over Natural Resources and the Future of Foreign Investment' (1978) 7 *Journal of International Studies* 124, 126.
13 Lilian A. Miranda, 'The Role of International Law in Intrastate Natural Resource Allocation: Sovereignty, Human Rights, and People-Based Development' (2012) 45 *Vanderbilt Journal of Transnational Law* 785, 794; Andreas R. Ziegler and Louis-Philippe Gratton, 'Investment Insurance' in Peter Muchlinski, Federico Ortino and Christoph Schreuer (eds), *The Oxford Handbook of International Investment Law* (OUP 2008) 526.
14 Samuel K.B. Asante, 'Restructuring Transnational Mineral Agreements' (1979) 73 *American Journal of International Law* 335, 340.
15 ibid.
16 Subrata Roy Chowdhury, 'Permanent Sovereignty Over Natural Resources: Substratum of the Seoul Declaration' in Paul de Wart, Paul Peters and Erik Denters (eds), *International Law and Development* (Martinus Nijhoff 1988) 61.
17 (1982) 21 ILM 976.
18 Lila Barrera-Hernándes, 'Sovereignty over Natural Resources under Examination: The Inter-American System for Human Rights and Natural Resource Allocation' (2006) 12 *Annual Survey of International and Comparative Law* 43, 45.
19 See General Assembly Resolution 523 (VI) of 12 January 1952, on Integrated Economic Development and Commercial Agreements.
20 Subrata Roy Chowdhury, 'Permanent Sovereignty Over Natural Resources' in Kamal Hossain and Subrata Roy Chowdhury (eds), *Permanent Sovereignty Over Natural Resources in International Law* (Frances Pinter 1984) 2. See also Emeka Duruigbo, 'Permanent Sovereignty and Peoples' Ownership of Natural Resources in International Law' (2006) 38 *George Washington International Law Review* 33, 38.

resources. The second part will discuss the legal status of the General Assembly resolutions.

3.2.1 Evolution of the doctrine

The principle of permanent sovereignty over natural resources essentially dictates that resource rich nations should have control over their natural resources. However, that control is contingent upon the state utilizing the resources for national development. In addition, in exercising the rights attached to this principle the state must act within the parameters of international law. The principle of permanent sovereignty over natural resources was developed over four phases.[21] The first phase took place from 1952 until the adoption of Resolution 1803 (XVII) in 1962. The second phase took place from 1962 until 1973, where 'the landmark resolution 1803 (XVII) was adopted, reiterated and reaffirmed in a number of other resolutions'.[22] The third phase occurred during the Sixth Special Session in May 1974, which eventually led to the adoption of the Charter on 12 December 1974. The fourth phase essentially occurs in the aftermath of 1974 – subsequent to the adoption of the Charter. Implicitly, the fourth phase is still in a state of evolution.

During the first phase, which occurred from 1952 until 1962, various resolutions had been passed relating to the principle of permanent sovereignty over natural resources. The focus was on the right of mineral rich countries to utilize their natural resources as part of their sovereignty, which in turn was a facet of self-determination.[23] The first of these was General Assembly Resolution 523 (VI), which recognized the right of under-developed countries 'to determine freely the use of their natural resources' with the added proviso that they do this in order to advance the economic development of their nations.[24] The sentiments expressed herein were echoed in the subsequent General Assembly Resolution 626 (VII),[25] which is seen as the genesis of the doctrine of permanent sovereignty over natural resources.[26]

Under General Assembly Resolution 1314 (XIII),[27] it was recognized that, in view of the fact that the right to self-determination as affirmed by the two

---

21 ibid 3–6.
22 ibid 3.
23 ibid.
24 General Assembly Resolution 523 (VI) of 12 January 1952.
25 General Assembly Resolution 626 (VII) of 21 December 1952. See also James N. Hyde, 'Permanent Sovereignty Over Natural Wealth and Resources' (1956) 50 *American Society of International Law* 854, 854.
26 See Miranda (n 13) 796; Duruigbo (n 20) 38. See also General Assembly Resolution 837 (IX) of 14 December 1954 and Jason W. Yackee, '*Pacta Sunt Servanda* and State Promises to Foreign Investors Before Bilateral Investment Treaties: Myth and Reality' (2009) 32 *Fordham International Law Journal* 1550, 1560.
27 General Assembly Resolution 1314 (XIII) of 12 December 1958.

Covenants drafted by the Human Rights Commission included 'permanent sovereignty over their wealth and natural resources', the Assembly needed to be fully informed on the doctrine. To facilitate this it established a Commission on Permanent Sovereignty comprised of both developed and developing countries, which was charged with conducting a 'full survey of the status of the permanent sovereignty of people and nations over their natural wealth'. It was to pay particular regard to 'the rights and duties of States under international law and to the importance of encouraging international co-operation in the economic development of under-developed countries'.[28] Surveys conducted by this Commission culminated in the landmark General Assembly Resolution 1803 (XVII),[29] which recognized: 'The right of peoples and nations to permanent sovereignty over their wealth and resources must be exercised in the interest of their national development and the well-being of the people of the State concerned'.

The second phase, which occurred from 1962 until 1973 has generally been described as one characterized by nationalism and states exerting greater control over the exploitation of their natural resources.[30] It comes as no surprise, therefore, that this period also consisted of a number of resolutions adopting, reaffirming and reiterating Resolution 1803 (XVII).[31] In addition, a Working Group on the Charter of the Economic Rights and Duties of States was established under Resolution 45 (III)[32] and enlarged under General Assembly Resolution 3037 (XXVII).[33]

The third phase occurred during the Sixth Special Session of the General Assembly, which took place on 1 May 1974. This session eventually led to the adoption of the Charter of Economic Rights and Duties of States.[34] There are many rights emanating from this Charter.[35] Its Article 2(2)(c) quite explicitly postulates that states have the right to 'nationalize, expropriate or transfer ownership

---

28 See General Assembly Resolution 1515 (XV) of 15 December 1960, re-emphasizing that whilst permanent sovereignty over natural resources had rights attached to it, these did come with duties.
29 General Assembly Resolution 1803 (XVII) of 14 December 1962. See also Marilda Rosado de Sá Ribeiro, 'Sovereignty Over Natural Resources Investment Law and Expropriation: The Case of Bolivia and Brazil' (2009) 2 *Journal of World Energy Law & Business* 129, 130 and Nico Schrijver, 'Natural Resource Management and Sustainable Development' in Thomas G. Weiss and Sam Daws (eds), *The Oxford Handbook on the United Nations* (OUP 2007) 596.
30 Janeth Warden-Fernandez, 'The Permanent Sovereignty Over Natural Resources: How it Has Been Accommodated Within the Evolving Economy' (2000) *CEPMLP Annual Review Article 4* at 3 http://www.dundee.ac.uk/cepmlp/gateway/?news=27955 (last accessed 12 June 2015).
31 Chowdhury, 'Permanent Sovereignty Over Natural Resources' (n 20) 3. See for example General Assembly Resolution 2158 (XXI) of 25 November 1966, General Assembly Resolution 2386 (XXIII) of 19 December 1968, General Assembly Resolution 2692 (XXV) of 11 December 1970, United Nations Conference on Trade and Development (UNCTAD) Resolution 88 (XII) of 19 October 1972 and General Assembly Resolution 3171 (XXVIII) of December 1973.
32 Resolution 45 (III) of 18 May 1972.
33 General Assembly Resolution 3037 (XXVII) of 19 December 1972. See also General Assembly Resolution 3082 (XXVIII) of 6 December 1973.
34 Resolution 3281 (XXIX).
35 See Nico Schrijver, *Sovereignty Over Natural Resources: Balancing Rights and Duties* (Cambridge University Press 1997) 258–98.

The effect of stabilization clauses **49**

of foreign property'. The condition attached is that the state pays 'appropriate compensation', which is to be settled under the auspices of domestic law and domestic tribunals, unless otherwise agreed.

Article 2(1) of the Charter says that the state can freely dispose of its natural resources. It is as a result of this right that states possess the authority to enter into agreements with multinational corporations. It is imperative, however, that these agreements are freely entered into.[36] Whilst a state can enter into an agreement, a question that has been intensely debated is whether a state can unilaterally abrogate these agreements.[37] Under the doctrine of permanent sovereignty over natural resources the state also has the right to regulate and supervise foreign investment[38] and the right to nationalize foreign owned property.[39] However, with this right also comes the duty to observe the tenets of international law vis-à-vis the taking of foreign owned property. This includes the duty to compensate foreign owned corporations. Furthermore, there is duty to utilize the natural resources in a way that advances economic development.[40]

The fourth phase occurred in the aftermath of the adoption of the Charter. The evolution and acceptance of this doctrine is determined by examining treaties that have been concluded since 1974. It has been noted that myriad treaties do reflect the rights and duties espoused in the Charter. However, given the adoption of bilateral investment treaties, which advocate full rather than appropriate compensation, the universal acceptance of the Charter may be questioned.[41]

3.2.2 Legal status of the principle of permanent sovereignty over natural resources

Because the Charter stems from a General Assembly resolution, there are questions as to whether the rights and duties contained therein are binding. On the one hand, it is argued that General Assembly resolutions are not binding.[42] It is recognized that the General Assembly does possess 'quasi-legislative' functions.[43] However, it is difficult to argue that the General Assembly is a legislative organ.[44]

---

36 *Texaco v Libya* (1978) 17 ILM, p. 1, paras 66–67.
37 For an overview see Esa Paasivirta, 'Internationalization and Stabilization of Contracts versus State Sovereignty' (1989) 60 *British Yearbook of International Law* 315, 316–23.
38 Article 2(2)(a).
39 Schrijver, *Sovereignty Over Natural Resources: Balancing Rights and Duties* (n 35) 271–74.
40 ibid 306–44.
41 Chowdhury, 'Permanent Sovereignty Over Natural Resources' (n 20) 5–6 and Schrijver, *Sovereignty Over Natural Resources: Balancing Rights and Duties* (n 35) 258–98.
42 See generally James Crawford, *The Creation of States in International Law* (2nd edn, OUP 2006) 113. See also Alan Boyle and Christine Chinkin, *The Making of International Law* (OUP 2007) 116 and Gregory J. Kerwin, 'The Role of United Nations General Assembly Resolutions in Determining Principles of International Law in United States Courts' (1983) 4 *Duke Law Journal* 876.
43 Philippe Sands and Pierre Klein, *Bowett's Law of International Institutions* (6th edn, Sweet & Maxwell 2009) 28.
44 ibid.

50 Resource nationalism in international investment law

First, this is owing to the fact that there is an objection to a two-thirds majority binding the minority. Secondly, to bind states under General Assembly resolutions may circumvent the traditional treaty-making process which, under some national constitutions, requires ratification in order for the state to be bound.[45]

On the other hand, to disregard completely the principles espoused in these General Assembly resolutions would be erroneous. Because of the general procedures that lead to the eventual vote and adoption of a resolution, it could be argued that they constitute evidence of customary international law.[46] A customary rule 'comes into existence only where there are acts of State in conformity with it, coupled with the belief that those acts are required by international law'.[47] General Assembly resolutions become customary norms on the basis that the General Assembly is itself a vehicle through which the states form and express the practice of international law are manifested.[48]

The resolution is drafted in such a way that it can win the support of the majority of the Assembly. Typically, more than a bare majority must be ensured before a vote will be called.[49] The resolution will often represent a harmonization of the conflicting views that might have been expressed, prior to the vote being called.[50] Therefore, by the time it is being adopted, it is an expression of the general consensus, which in turn can be construed as the formulation of a customary norm.[51]

This book supports the latter view. Arguably, the General Assembly resolutions pertaining to permanent sovereignty over natural resources do form a part of customary law. This view has been supported by various arbitral tribunals. For example, in the case of *Libyan American Oil Co. (LIAMCO) v Libya*,[52] the arbitrator held that: 'the said Resolutions, if not a unanimous source of law, are evidence of the recent dominant trend of international opinion concerning the sovereign right of States over natural resources'.[53] This clearly shows that even arbitral tribunals recognize the general resolutions on permanent sovereignty over natural resources as evidence of customary law.

This position was also reflected in *Texaco v Libya*.[54] Here, the arbitral tribunal took the view that Resolution 1803 reflected the tenets of customary international law.[55] It arrived at this conclusion on the basis that the said resolution

---

45 ibid.
46 ibid 27–28.
47 Samuel A. Bleicher, 'The Legal Significance of Re-citation of General Assembly Resolutions' (1969) 63 *American Journal of International Law* 444, 449.
48 M. Sornarajah, *The International Law on Foreign Investment* (3rd edn, Cambridge University Press 2010) 446.
49 Bleicher (n 47) 451.
50 ibid.
51 ibid.
52 (1977) 62 ILR 141.
53 ibid, para 100.
54 *Texaco v Libya* (n 36).
55 ibid 30.

The effect of stabilization clauses 51

referred to international law when it spoke of nationalization.[56] Moreover, the aforementioned resolution had received the universal assent of both developed and developing countries.[57] The tribunal further opined that General Assembly Resolution 1803 ought to be contrasted with the Charter of the Economic Rights and Duties of States, which in the arbitrator's view 'must be analyzed as a political rather than as a legal declaration concerned with the ideological strategy of development and, as such, supported only by non-industrialized States'.[58]

Furthermore, it could be argued that the resolutions pertaining to permanent sovereignty over natural resources are a reflection of rights and duties that already existed under international law.[59] For example, it was already generally recognized that the state had the right to nationalize.[60] Once the state nationalized, it also had an obligation to pay compensation.[61] This is therefore another reason why it could be argued that the resolutions pertaining to permanent sovereignty over natural resources are generally binding.

In addition, the principle of permanent sovereignty over natural resources has been accepted by the International Court of Justice. This position was reflected in the *East Timor* case.[62] In more recent times the principle of permanent sovereignty over natural resources has gained more recognition. In *Congo v Uganda*[63] the International Court of Justice recognized permanent sovereignty over natural resources as 'a principle of customary international law'.[64] Given the fact that decisions of the International Court of Justice are a source of international law, it could thus be asserted that the principle of permanent sovereignty over

---

56 ibid 29. See also Stephen M. Schwebel, 'The Story of the U.N.'s Declaration on Permanent Sovereignty over Natural Resources' (1963) 49 *American Bar Association Journal* 463, 469.
57 ibid.
58 ibid 30. See also Andreas Lowenfeld, 'Investment Agreements and International Law' (2003) 42 *Columbia Journal of Transnational Law* 123, 124 and Eduardo Jimenez de Aréchaga, 'Application of the Rules of States' Responsibility to the Nationalization of Foreign-owned Property' in Kamal Hossain (ed), *Legal Aspects of the New International Economic Order* (Frances Pinter 1980) 225.
59 Karol N. Gess, 'Permanent Sovereignty over Natural Resources: An Analytical Review of the United Nations Declaration and Its Genesis' (1964) 13 *International and Comparative Law Quarterly*, 398, 411 and R.R. Baxter, 'International Law in "Her Infinite Variety"' (1980) 29 *International and Comparative Law Quarterly* 549, 564.
60 Schrijver, *Sovereignty Over Natural Resources: Balancing Rights and Duties* (n 35) 271–74.
61 ibid.
62 *East Timor (Port v Austrl.)* [1995] ICJ Reports 90. See the dissenting opinions of Weeramantry J at 204 and Skubiszeweski J at 264.
63 *Case concerning Armed Activities on the Territory of the Congo (Democratic Republic of the Congo v Uganda)* [2005] ICJ Reports 168.
64 ibid. para 244. Note, however, that it does not apply in situations of 'looting, pillage and exploitation of certain natural resources by members of the army of a State militarily intervening in another State'. Judge Koroma in his declaration contends that the ICJ's acknowledgement of the principle as a customary norm implies that the rights and duties emanating from it 'remain in effect at all times, including *during armed conflict and occupation*' (para 11). This can be contrasted with ad hoc Judge Kateka, who said that: 'The PSNR was adopted in the era of decolonization and the assertion of the rights of newly independent States. It thus would be inappropriate to invoke this concept in a case involving two African countries. This remark is made without prejudice to the right of States to own and or dispose of their natural resources as they wish' (para 56).

52 Resource nationalism in international investment law

natural resources is a legitimate one and so are the rights and duties emanating therefrom.

It could thus be argued that the principle of permanent sovereignty over natural resources is firmly accepted under international law.[65] It is under this principle that states are able to enter into concession agreements with investors. It is further argued that, under this principle, the word 'permanent' entails that the state has the right to exit these agreements at any given time, regardless of an agreement not to do so.[66] It might appear, therefore, that there is a clash between this principle and the insertion of stabilization clauses in concession agreements. The next part of this chapter will discuss stabilization clauses and the attitudes of courts and international tribunal to the permanent sovereignty argument.

3.3 The definition and purpose behind stabilization clauses

At the time of signing a concession, there exists an asymmetrical relationship between host state and the investor.[67] This asymmetrical relationship exists as a result of the myriad legislative and administrative prerogatives that the state has at its disposal. These prerogatives could be employed by the state, in a way that is calculated to jeopardize the investor's prospects of making a profit once it actually sends its capital. The state could for example prematurely terminate the contract and nationalize assets belonging to the investor by utilizing the legislative process.[68] Similarly, the state could raise taxes, which could either have the effect of significantly reducing the investor's profits or simply make it more onerous or expensive to run operations in a given jurisdiction.[69]

Premature termination or alteration of the mining agreements could have a huge impact on the mining operations. This is owing to the fact that, in the first instance, commencing with an exploration project in resource rich countries can be very expensive and laborious. Mining and oil companies alike almost invariably explore various areas before they eventually attain success. Once they

---

65 Robert Dufresne, 'The Opacity of Oil: Oil Corporations, Internal Violence, and International Law' (2004) 36 *New York University Journal of International Law and Politics* 331, 354; Chowdhury, 'Permanent Sovereignty Over Natural Resources' (n 20) 1; Kamal Hossain, 'Introduction' in Kamal Hossain and Subrata Roy Chowdhury (eds), *Permanent Sovereignty Over Natural Resources* (Frances Printer 1984) ix–xx, ix; A.F.M. Maniruzzaman, 'International Development Law as Applicable Law to Economic Development Agreements: A Prognostic View' (2001) 20 *Wisconsin International Law Journal* 1, 23; and Nico Schrijver, 'Natural Resources, Permanent Sovereignty Over' (2010) *Max Planck Encyclopedia of Public International Law* 8, http://ilmc.univie.ac.at/uploads/media/PSNR_empil.pdf (last accessed 3 June 2015).
66 Eduardo Jimenez de Aréchaga, 'State Responsibility for the Nationalization of Foreign Owned Property' (1978) 11 *New York University Journal of Law and Politics* 179, 179–80.
67 See ch 2, 41–43.
68 Abdullah Faruque, 'Validity and Efficacy of Stabilization Clauses: Legal Protection vs Functional Value' (2006) 23 *Journal of International Arbitration* 317, 317.
69 Joseph Nwaokoro, 'Enforcing Stabilization of International Energy Contracts' (2013) 3 *Journal of World Energy Law & Business* 103, 104.

The effect of stabilization clauses   53

do, they will need to make up for the shortfall created by the failed projects. In addition, mineral prices are somewhat mercurial in that they tend to fluctuate and depreciate owing to a plethora of factors that are beyond the scope of this book.[70]

With this much uncertainty in the venture it is understandable therefore that any additional uncertainties in this equation are unlikely to render the business venture unprofitable.[71] Predictability in the law, particularly the fiscal regime, is therefore an imperative factor in determining whether the investor will sign a concession.[72] The investor will therefore insist on some assurances that the sanctity of contract is respected and that it will be guaranteed against the arbitrary exercise of state power, which would alter or unilaterally abrogate the investor's contractual rights.[73]

3.3.1 Types of stabilization clauses

To address these concerns highlighted above, investors will invariably insist on the insertion of stabilization clauses in their concession agreements. These are clauses which 'specifically seek to secure the agreement against future government action or changes in law'.[74] The clause purports to do so by immunizing the contract from the municipal law by internationalizing it.[75] Thus, at least in the abstract, any alteration in the law should have no effect on the concession whatsoever if it contains a stabilization clause.[76]

There are various types of stabilization clauses. The first type is the 'stabilization clause *stricto sensu*'.[77] This clause seeks to ensure that the law existing at the time of the contract will continue throughout the life of the project.[78] Such a clause will, in theory, freeze the municipal law of the host state from the day that the contract is concluded until the contract itself expires. An example of such a clause is that contained in the Concession Agreement of 1933 between Iran and the Anglo Iranian Oil Company. It stated that the:

> Concession shall not be annulled by the Government and the terms therein contained shall not be altered either by general or special legislation in the

---

70 See generally Wälde and Ndi (n 7) 223–26.
71 ibid 227.
72 Faruque (n 68) 322.
73 M. Sornarajah, *The Settlement of Foreign Investment Disputes* (Kluwer 2000) 49.
74 Christopher T. Curtis, 'The Legal Security of Economic Development Agreements' (1988) 29 *Harvard International Law Journal* 317, 346.
75 A.F.M. Maniruzzaman, 'Some Reflections on Stabilisation Techniques in International Petroleum, Gas and Mineral Agreements' (2005) 4 *International Energy Law and Taxation Review* 96, 97 and generally A.A. Fatouros, 'International Law and the Internationalized Contract' (1980) 74 *American Journal of International Law* 134.
76 Bertrand Montembault, 'The Stabilisation of State Contracts Using the Example of Oil Contracts: A Return of the Gods of Olympia' (2003) 6 *International Business Law Journal* 593, 599–601.
77 Curtis (n 74) 346.
78 Faruque (n 68) 319.

future, or by administrative measures or any other acts whatever of the executive authorities.[79]

This implies, on a broader level, that if any legislative changes are made by the host state, this does not in any way alter the rights and obligations contained in the concession itself. It therefore follows that in the event where there is a conflict between the provisions of the contract and any subsequent legislation, the former will always take precedence.[80] Included within this category would be tax stability clauses. Again, these simply stipulate that, during the stability period, no new taxes will be introduced by the host state that override the incentives that may be contained in the concession agreement.

Another type is the 'intangibility clause'.[81] These are provisions within the contract which denote that the contract cannot be altered or abrogated without the mutual consent of the parties.[82] With these types of clauses the state does not actually surrender any legislative or administrative prerogatives per se. However, like the *stricto sensu* clauses, they do seek to prevent the state from unilaterally altering the terms of the contract. An example of such a clause is the one contained in the production sharing contract of Indonesia between Pertamina and Overseas Petroleum Investment Corporation and Treasure Bay Enterprise Ltd.[83] It stated that: 'This contract shall not be annulled, amended or modified in any respect, except by mutual consent in writing of the parties hereto'.[84]

The third type of stabilization clause one might encounter is the 'economic stabilization clause'.[85] An example of this is contained within the agreement between the Republic of Gabon and Vanco Gabon Ltd. It reads as follows:

> [T]he State guarantees to the Contractor, for the duration of the contract, the stability of the financial and economic conditions insofar as these conditions result from the Contract and from the regulations in force on the Effective Date.
>
> These obligations resulting from the Contract shall not be aggravated, and the general and overall equilibrium of the Contract shall not be affected in an important and lasting manner for the entire period of validity hereof. However, adjustments and modification of these provisions may be agreed upon by mutual consent.[86]

---

79 Esa Paasivirta, *Participation of States in International Contracts and Arbitral Settlement of Disputes* (Lakimiesluton Kustannus 1990) 162.

80 Faruque (n 68) 319.

81 Curtis (n 74) 346.

82 Faruque (n 68) 319; Rudolf Dolzer and Christoph Schreuer, *Principles of International Investment Law* (OUP 2008) 83.

83 Article 17.2 of the production sharing contract of Indonesia between Pertamina and Overseas Petroleum Investment Corp. and Treasure Bay Enterprise Ltd, quoted in Faruque (n 68) 319.

84 ibid.

85 ibid 320.

86 ibid.

The effect of stabilization clauses 55

This type of clause either prohibits the state from passing a law or taking administrative action that renders the contract more onerous or expensive to perform or ensures that in an instance where the government does pass such a law the government can examine these adverse economic consequences and restore to the investor economic equilibrium.[87]

3.3.2 The effect of stabilization clauses

There is much academic debate surrounding the precise effect of stabilization clauses.[88] There are two clearly identifiable categories in this respect. On the one hand, there are those who argue that stabilization clauses do offer absolute protection to the investor. On the other hand, there are those who are diametrically opposed to this. This views expressed in this book falls in the former category. In this section, I argue that stabilization clauses do offer absolute protection to the investor based on the fact that arbitral tribunals respect the sanctity of contracts, thus endorsing the maxim *pacta sunt servanda*. In order to ensure this absolute protection, however, investors must also ensure that there is an arbitration clause so that the case is determined in a neutral forum.

Stabilization clauses effectively do grant absolute protection to the investor. They purport to do this by circumventing the possibility of an agreement being prematurely terminated or modified by an Act of the legislative arm of the host state.[89] Thus, if a concession contains within it a stabilization clause and the host state proceeds to nationalize assets belonging to the investor, then the former would be committing an illegal act. Stabilization clauses immunize the concession agreement from municipal law by internationalizing it.[90] This effectively means that the concession agreement becomes subject to international law. Therefore, obligations and remedies available to both parties are also of an international character.[91] One of those international obligations is the international law principle of *pacta sunt servanda*.[92] This principle essentially espouses that agreements freely entered into shall be enforced according to their terms.[93] This is obviously not an

---

87 ibid.
88 See Paasivirta, 'Internationalization and Stabilization of Contracts Versus State Sovereignty' (n 37) 316–23.
89 David Suratgar, 'Considerations affecting Choice of Law Clauses in Contracts Between Governments and Foreign Nationals' (1962) 2 *Indian Journal of International Law* 273, 302.
90 See Henry De Vries, 'The Enforcement of Economic Development Agreements with Foreign States' (1984) 62 *University of Detroit Law Review* 1, 20–21; Margarita T.B. Coale, 'Stabilization Clauses in International Petroleum Transactions' (2002) 30 *Denver Journal of International Law and Policy* 217. See also Julien Cantegreil, 'The Audacity of the Texaco/Calasiatic Award: Rene-Jean Dupuy and the Internationalization of Foreign Investment Law' (2011) 22 *European Journal of International Law* 441.
91 F.V. Garcia Amador, 'Fourth Report on State Responsibility' (1959) 2 *Yearbook of the International Law Commission* 32, para 127.
92 *Black's Law Dictionary* (8th edn, 2004) 1140.
93 Andreas F. Lowenfeld, 'Lex Mercatoria: An Arbitrator's View' in Thomas E. Carbonneau (ed), *Lex Mercatoria and Arbitration* (Kluwer 1998) 89.

56 Resource nationalism in international investment law

absolute rule.[94] This principle is as applicable to agreements between the host state and private corporations as it is to agreements between the former and other states.[95] *Pacta sunt servanda* stems from respect for the sanctity of contracts. It is not an absolute rule. However, the default position is to lean against unilateral termination of existing agreements.[96] Thus, once a contract is entered into, its terms must be upheld and respected.

It has been argued that because the contract is 'immune from an encroachment by a system of municipal law', in the same manner as a treaty between two international persons, the contract is elevated to the status of a treaty. For this reason, it is only subject to international law.[97] This is partly the basis upon which the absolute protection theory has been opposed. On a conceptual level, it is indeed difficult to accept the contention that a contract with a private investor is equivalent to a treaty. This opposition is based on the premise that, by its very definition, a treaty is an agreement between two states. It can never be concluded between a state and an entity, such as a multinational corporation which is not a subject of international law. Furthermore, a treaty involves the mutual surrender of sovereign rights and these are rights which the investor does not have the capacity to surrender.[98] The clause may stipulate the proper law of the contract is international law or the general principles of law; however, this does not automatically transform the contract itself into an international agreement within the definition espoused in the Vienna Convention on the Law of Treaties.[99]

These sentiments were echoed in the case of *Saudi Arabia v ARAMCO*,[100] where the tribunal rejected the contention that the concession should be 'assimilated to an international treaty governed by the Law of Nations'. The law applicable in this case should be that of Saudi Arabia because 'this is the law of the country with which the contract has the closest natural and effective connection, unless another law is designated by the conclusive conduct of the parties'.[101] A state can limit its legislative powers on account of an international agreement with another state. Thus, generally speaking, if there is a treaty in place and the state violates it through legislative means, then this will have international consequences. It does

---

94 Patrick S. Atiyah and Stephen A. Smith, *Atiyah's Introduction to the Law of Contract* (6th edn, Clarendon Press 2006) 5–9 and Edwin Peel, *Treitel: The Law of Contract* (13th edn, Sweet & Maxwell 2011) 2–3.

95 Hans Wehberg, 'Pacta Sunt Servanda' (1959) 53 *American Journal of International Law* 775, 776.

96 R.Y. Jennings, 'State Contracts in International Law' (1961) 37 *British Yearbook of International Law* 156, 177.

97 Mann, *Studies in International Law* (n 11).

98 Sornarajah, *The Settlement of Foreign Investment Disputes* (n 73). See also S.K. Chatterjee, 'The Stabilization Clause Myth in Investment Agreements' (1988) 5 *Journal of International Arbitration* 97, 107.

99 Oliver Schachter, *International Law in Theory and Practice* (Brill 1991) 309 and C.F. Amerasinghe, 'State Breaches of Contracts with Aliens and International Law' (1964) 58 *American Journal of International Law* 881, 906. See also *Saudi Arabia v ARAMCO* (n 100)165–67.

100 (1963) 27 ILR 117, 165–67.

101 ibid 167.

not follow, however, that a contractual agreement with an individual or corporation can have the same effect.[102] It would thus appear that an agreement between a state and a corporation falls outside the scope of the Vienna Convention on Treaties. Therefore, it cannot be said to be a treaty or tantamount to one.

A further view espoused by opponents to the absolute protection theory is that private relations are not governed by international law as such. Thus, applying international law to private relations is misplaced and attempting to do so is akin to trying to apply 'the matrimonial laws of France or England to relations between cats and dogs'.[103] This is a relatively weak argument, considering the myriad sources of international law that private entities are able to rely upon in the modern era.[104]

Moreover, there are doubts as to whether stabilization clauses can limit a state's inalienable prerogatives.[105] One of these is the right to nationalize foreign owned property.[106] A state cannot surrender its sovereign prerogatives because these are often imperative if the state is to function. Thus, it is unclear whether a stabilization clause requiring the subjugation of mandatory rules of international law can produce its typical effect. However, there is a possibility that the reliance induced by the stabilization clause entitles the injured party to compensation for any damage caused by the said nationalization. This should be the case even where the breach of the stabilization commitment is not in itself rendered illegal by the arbitral tribunal.[107]

Opponents of the absolute protection theory have simply dismissed it as 'essentially self-serving . . . designed to support a very partisan, capitalist approach to contractual disputes'.[108] Indeed, it has been seen that there are conceptual problems with equating a contract to a treaty. For this reason it is difficult to accept this as a basis for binding a state to concession agreements which contain stabilization clauses. Given these views one might, therefore, hesitate in arriving at the conclusion that stabilization clauses are inherently valid and enforceable.[109] Although there is no consensus in the academic debate on this matter, it would

---

102 Martin Wolff, 'Some Observations on the Autonomy of Contracting Parties in the Conflict of Laws' (1950) 35 *Transactions of the Grotius Society* 143, 150–51.
103 Angelo P. Sereni, 'International Economic Institutions and the Municipal Law of States' (1959) 96 *Recueil des cours* 129, 210.
104 Sangwani Patrick Ng'ambi, 'The Effect of Stabilization Clauses in Concession Agreements' (2012) 43 *Zambia Law Journal* 57, 63.
105 Chatterjee (n 98) 110. See also *Oscar Chinn* (1934) PCIJ Series A/B No. 63, 23.
106 Bernardini (n 10) 101.
107 ibid. See also Lorenzo Cotula, 'Reconciling Regulatory Stability and Evolution of Environmental Standards in Investment Contracts: Towards a Rethink of Stabilization Clauses' (2008) 1 *Journal of World Energy Law & Business* 158, 165–67 and A.F.M. Maniruzzaman, 'The Pursuit of Stability in International Energy Investment Contracts' (2008) 1 *Journal of World Energy Law & Business* 121, 126 and 141; Felipe Mutis Te'llez, 'Conditions and Criteria For The Protection of Legitimate Expectations Under International Investment Law' (2012) 27 *ICSID Review* 432.
108 Derek W. Bowett, 'State Contracts With Aliens: Contemporary Developments on Compensation for Termination or Breach' (1988) 49 *British Yearbook of International Law* 49, 51–52.
109 Nwaokoro (n 69) 106 and John F. Crawford and Wesley R. Johnson, 'Arbitrating with Foreign States and Their Instrumentalities' (1986) 5 *International Financial Law Review* 11, 12.

appear that there are an overwhelming number of cases in support of holding states to undertakings made through stabilization clauses. The basis of this is the sanctity of contracts, as encapsulated by the maxim *pacta sunt servanda*. This means that all agreements must be upheld. After all, under the principle of the sanctity of contracts, it is the will of the parties that serves as the foundation of their agreement.[110] The insertion of stabilization clauses in concession agreements in the first place is an expression of that will.[111] For this reason, stabilization clauses should be upheld.[112]

3.4 Case law on stabilization clauses

The preceding section discussed the possible application of stabilization clauses in theory. The aim of this section is to explore the attitudes of arbitral tribunals towards the application of stabilization clauses. There is a plethora of arbitral awards dealing with this issue. In some awards the arbitrators contend that stabilization clauses do in fact afford absolute protection to the investor. An act breaching these would be an act of illegality.

In other awards, however, the arbitral tribunals have stated that to preclude a host government from nationalizing foreign owned assets by virtue of stabilization clauses would amount to an unwarranted encroachment upon state sovereignty. However, it would appear that the latter view is grossly under-represented. In fact, that argument is not looked upon with a kindly eye. Most arbitral awards explored in this section endorse the view that contracts undertaken are binding. It therefore follows that stabilization clauses are binding on the state.

This section is divided into three sub-sections. Section 3.4.1 will discuss the earlier decisions on the legal effect of stabilization clauses. There is a recognition even under these cases that stabilization clauses are binding on the state. Section 3.4.2 will discuss the three Libyan cases: *BP v Libya*,[113] *Texaco v Libya*[114] and *LIAMCO v Libya*.[115] These three cases are particularly significant because by and large they had a similar set of facts yet had different outcomes. Finally, section 3.4.3 will look at later cases. These also endorse the view that stabilization clauses are binding.

3.4.1 Earlier decisions

There are very few cases prior to the Second World War regarding disputes between states and investors.[116] This general paucity in early case law appears to

---

110 Peter Muchlinski, *Multinational Enterprises and the Law* (2nd edn, OUP 2007) 582.
111 ibid.
112 ibid.
113 (1979) 53 ILR 297.
114 (1978) 17 ILM 1.
115 (1977) ILR 141.
116 Yackee (n 26) 1572.

The effect of stabilization clauses **59**

have been influenced by the fact that there were doubts as to whether private parties had *locus standi* to bring cases before an international tribunal. In addition to this, international commercial arbitration and the infrastructure supporting it was still in its infancy.[117] Thus, in instances of injury to the investor by the host state, action would traditionally be brought by the home state of the investor under the umbrella of diplomatic protection.[118]

Any doubts as to whether an investor could pursue an action, in its own right, against the state were certainly dispelled by the case of *Lena Goldfields Ltd v USSR*.[119] This case involved Lena Goldfields, which was a company incorporated in 1908. The company had purchased 70 per cent of the shares in the Russian Lena Goldfields Company. In 1918, the new Soviet Government took power and proceeded to nationalize the property of mining companies without paying compensation. This, of course, included assets belonging to Lena Goldfields.

In 1925, after two years of difficult negotiations between the two parties, the Soviet Government finally granted Lena Goldfields a concession to mine gold and other metals in the Urals and Siberia. Part of the concession was to run for a period of 50 years and another part was to run for 37 years. Operations commenced later in 1925. However, these operations were interrupted by a shift in government policy on foreign capitalists in 1929.[120] The subsequent hostility and harassment that followed this rendered it incredibly difficult for Lena Goldfields to continue its operations. When negotiations between the Soviet Government and Lena Goldfields failed, the latter was compelled to initiate arbitral proceedings against the former.

Article 76 of the concession contained within it a stabilization clause. Under this clause, the Soviet Government had undertaken not to alter the agreement without Lena Goldfields' consent. In other words, it prohibited any unilateral action by the state that would adversely affect the rights of Lena Goldfields. The Court of Arbitration opined that the contract between the state and a private entity may be internationalized and that the 'general principles of law' may be applied in protecting the contractual interests of private entities such as Lena Goldfields.[121] The tribunal further held that, by repudiating the contract, the Soviet Government had unjustly enriched itself. Lena Goldfields was thus awarded a sum of US$65 million which included loss of future profits.[122] The arbitral tribunal did

---

117 ibid.
118 Edwin M. Borehand, 'Contractual Claims in International Law' (1913) 13 *Columbia Law Review* 457, 457.
119 Arthur Nussbaum, 'The Arbitration Between the Lena Goldfields Ltd. and the Soviet Government' (1950–51) 36 *Cornell Law Quarterly* 31, 42. This is a reproduction of the award, as the original was lost.
120 See V.V. Vedeer, 'The Lena Goldfields Arbitration: the Historical Roots of the Three Ideas' (1998) 47 *International and Comparative Law Quarterly* 747, 761.
121 ibid 30, para 22.
122 Yackee (n 26) 1575.

60 Resource nationalism in international investment law

not elaborate further the issue of stabilization clauses. However, the most notable facet of this case is that the arbitral tribunal held that something besides national law could govern a contract between the investor and the host government.[123]

The arbitral tribunal in the subsequent case of *Sapphire International Petroleum Ltd v National Iranian Oil Co.*[124] had a similar position. This case involved the National Iranian Oil Company (NIOC), which had entered into a joint venture with Sapphire International. Under terms stipulated by the agreement, the latter was to provide technical and financial assistance to NIOC with the goal of increasing production and exportation of Iranian oil. The stabilization clause under this agreement read as follows:

> No general or statutory enactment, no administrative measure or decree of any kind, made either by the government or by any governmental authority in Iran (central or local), including NIOC, can cancel the agreement or affect or change its provisions, or prevent or hinder its performance. No cancellation, amendment or modification can take place except with the agreement of the two parties.[125]

In order to carry out these operations, the two parties set up the Iranian Canadian Oil Company (ICRAN). The contract was effectively divided into two periods: the prospecting period and the extraction and sale period. During the prospecting period, all expenses were to be reimbursed to Sapphire through ICRAN. Once the extraction and sale period commenced, both the parties were jointly to cover all the expenses arising during the earlier period. Moreover, the contract stated that drilling was to commence within two years of the contract being finalized. Additionally, NIOC reserved the right to terminate the agreement with Sapphire if the latter failed to fulfil its obligations within the two-year period prescribed in the contract. In such an event, Sapphire would be compelled to pay a sum of US$350,000 to NIOC. A bank guarantee in NIOC's favour was provided to this effect.

When Sapphire commenced its operations, it claimed its expenses from NIOC. These expenses came to an amount of US$302,545.25. However, NIOC refused to reimburse these expenses. It based this refusal on the premise that it had not been consulted prior to the commencement of the works, which was a term of the contract. In July 1959 Sapphire thus wrote to the Shah of Iran requesting the government to reimburse its expenses. The Iranian prime minister responded on 5 September 1959. In his response he stated that NIOC was entitled to refuse

---

123 Coale (n 90) 227. See also *In the Matter of an Arbitration Between Petroleum Development (Trucial Coast) Ltd and the Sheikh of Abu Dhabi* (1952) 1 *International and Comparative Law Quarterly* 247, 260 and *Ruler of Qatar v International Marine Oil Company Ltd* (1953) 20 ILR 534.
124 (1967) 35 ILR 136.
125 ibid 140.

The effect of stabilization clauses 61

to make the refund because Sapphire had ostensibly not fulfilled its obligations. Sapphire was therefore referred back to NIOC to settle the dispute.

Given this background, and the ensuing dispute with NIOC, Sapphire decided that it would be too risky to sign a drilling contract with the former. On 24 July 1960, NIOC wrote to Sapphire informing the company that it had not yet commenced its drilling obligations. Six months later, in January 1961, NIOC cancelled the contract and proceeded to cash the US$350,000 indemnity provided by Sapphire. Sapphire thus initiated arbitral proceedings against NIOC. Because NIOC had failed to appoint an arbitrator, a sole arbitrator was appointed by the Swiss Federal Court, in accordance with Article 41 of the contract.

The arbitrator in this case found that the premature termination of the concession agreement imposed a duty on the state to compensate Sapphire International. He relied upon the principle of *pacta sunt servanda* to arrive at his decision. This principle dictates that contractual undertakings must be respected and he accordingly made an award in favour of Sapphire International. The tribunal found that NIOC had deliberately failed to fulfil its obligations and this amounted to a breach of contract.[126]

From the two earlier cases, it is quite clear that arbitral tribunals are more inclined to award in favour of the complainant investor if the defendant host state does not abide by its contractual obligations. As far as arbitral tribunals are concerned, once the state enters into a contract, it is bound by it and failure to honour it amounts to a breach of contract. This position has, however, been challenged in later cases. One of the arguments advanced is that interpreting a stabilization clause so as to preclude the host state from passing certain legislation in the public interest would be an encroachment on the doctrine of permanent sovereignty over natural resources. Arbitral tribunals have given due consideration to this argument but ultimately they have rejected it. This was certainly the position taken in *Saudi Arabia v Arabian American Oil Co. (ARAMCO)*.[127]

In the case of *ARAMCO* the Government of Saudi Arabia had entered into a contract with a company called Saudi Arabia Maritime Tankers Ltd, which belonged to the shipping tycoon Aristotle Onassis. His company was granted the exclusive right to transport Saudi oil; an agreement which was to subsist for a period of 30 years. The agreement, however, contravened an earlier one concluded with the Arabian Oil Company (ARAMCO) which had been granted, through a concession, the exclusive right to transport its own oil that it extracted from Saudi Arabia. A stabilization clause was contained within the concession agreement.

ARAMCO thus referred the matter to arbitration. During the proceedings, the government argued that that the stabilization clause was not binding upon the state. To hold otherwise in its view would militate against the sovereignty of

126 ibid 181.
127 (1963) 27 ILR 117.

62 Resource nationalism in international investment law

Saudi Arabia. The arbitral tribunal disagreed with this contention. The tribunal contended that:

> [b]y reason of its very sovereignty within its territorial domain, the State possess the legal powers to grant rights [by] which it forbids itself to withdraw before the end of the concession, with the reservation of the Clauses of the Concession Agreement relating to its revocation. Nothing can prevent a State, in the exercise of its sovereignty, from binding itself irrevocably by the provisions of a concession and from granting to the concessionaire irretractable rights. Such rights have the character of acquired rights.[128]

Effectively, the tribunal was stating that a state cannot go back on its decision once it has renounced the right to exercise some of its powers. Once the state has accepted a stabilization clause it gives the investor a 'legitimate expectation', which the government cannot then go back on.[129] The arbitral tribunal thus rejected the sovereignty argument. This demonstrates that, as a general rule, sovereignty cannot be an excuse for the state's failure to fulfil its contractual obligations.

The earlier cases therefore demonstrate that arbitral tribunals subscribed more to the view that stabilization clauses give absolute protection to foreign investors. Although concerns were raised that holding the state liable for breach of stabilization clauses may be incongruous with the sovereignty of the state, this argument is generally rejected by arbitral tribunals. The rationale behind this position is that entering into agreements is a facet of sovereignty, which the tribunals contend is in part surrendered once the states bind themselves to an agreement with a corporation. The next subsection will explore the position of the arbitral tribunals in the Libyan nationalization cases.

3.4.2 The Libyan nationalization cases

This subsection examines the cases that arose out of the Libyan Government's nationalization of foreign owned oil companies. The three cases I will be discussing in this subsection are *BP v Libya*,[130] *Texaco Overseas Oil Petroleum Co./California Asiatic Oil Co. v Libya*[131] and *LIAMCO v Libya*.[132] The juridical significance of these three cases stems from the fact that they had a similar if not identical set of facts.

---

128 ibid 168.
129 Prosper Weil, 'Les clauses de stabilization ou d'intangibilité insérées dans les accords de development économique' in *Mélangues offerts à Charles Rousseau* (A. Pedone 1974) 326. See also Martti Koskenniemi, 'What Use for Sovereignty Today' (2011) 1 *Asian Journal of International Law* 61, 62, who says: 'They had been able to bind themselves because they were sovereigns. If they were not able to bind themselves – and thus receive the benefits they were looking for – well, then they could not really be sovereigns, could they?'
130 Note 113.
131 Note 114.
132 Note 115.

The effect of stabilization clauses **63**

Despite this fact, they had rather divergent outcomes. Notwithstanding this fact, all three cases endorse the principle of *pacta sunt servanda*, which further accentuates my contention that arbitral tribunals respect the sanctity of contracts.

The genesis of these cases appears to be 1951 when Libya had attained her independence. She was an impoverished nation with very few known natural resources. As a consequence of this, Libya's population was sparse and uneducated. This was further compounded by the fact that 90 per cent of the country consisted of desert, which meant that Libya only possessed a small amount of arable land. Therefore, upon attaining her independence, Libya thus appeared to be a nation with very bleak economic prospects.[133]

This position was considerably altered between 1951 and 1979 with the discovery and exploitation of Libya's vast oil reserves. By 1979, Libya's income was estimated to have exceeded US$16 billion dollars from oil exports. This placed Libya among the world's top 15 richest nations. Moreover, at US$6,680 per capita income, Libya was the highest earner in Africa.[134]

The upturn in economic fortunes that Libya was enjoying were almost entirely based on her oil riches.[135] However, Libya lacked the capacity to extract its vast oil reserves. Therefore, in order to exploit these oil reserves the Government of Libya had to rely very heavily on the inflow of investment from foreign oil companies. To foster this process, the Government of Libya had to put in place a legal framework.[136] It therefore introduced the Libyan Petroleum Law of 1955. Under this Act was the framework through which oil concessions were granted. Of particular note was the standard deed of concession which, according to Article 9, was to be used when granting all concessions.

There were three key provisions within the standard concession agreements: the stabilization clause, the arbitration clause and the choice of law clause. The stabilization clause was contained in clause 16. After about three subsequent amendments, the final version of clause 16 read as follows:

(1) The Government of Libya, the Commission and the appropriate provincial authorities will take all steps necessary to ensure that the Company enjoys all the rights conferred by this Concession. The contractual rights expressly created by this Concession shall not be altered except by mutual consent of the parties.

(2) This Concession shall throughout the period of its validity be construed in accordance with the Petroleum Law and the Regulations in force on the date of execution of the Agreement of Amendment by which this

---

133 For a more elaborate socio-economic background see Robert B. von Mehren and P. Nicholas Kourides, 'International Arbitration Between States and Foreign Private Parties: The Libyan Nationalization Cases' (1981) 75 *American Journal of International Law* 476, 477–79.

134 The World Bank, *World Development Report* (1979).

135 Von Mehren and Kourides (n 133) 477.

136 ibid.

paragraph (2) was incorporated into this Concession Agreement. Any amendment to or repeal of such Regulations shall not affect the contractual rights of the Company without its consent.[137]

Clause 16, like most stabilization clauses, was inserted as a guarantee from the host government that it would not alter the contractual rights of the concession holders without the other party's consent. In other words, the Government of Libya would not deprive the oil companies of their enjoyment of the contractual rights bestowed upon them, unless the latter agreed to it.[138]

The arbitration clause was contained in clause 28(1). Under the aforementioned provision, the parties undertook to settle all disputes by arbitration rather than through the national forums. As a consequence, if a dispute arose it was to be referred to an arbitral tribunal consisting of two arbitrators and an umpire. The investor and the Government of Libya were to appoint one arbitrator each. The two appointed arbitrators were then to appoint a third arbitrator, the umpire. The party initiating the arbitral proceedings was required under this clause to make a written request to the other party informing it of the name of the arbitrator it had selected and specifying the nature of the dispute.[139] The other party then had to appoint its own arbitrator within 90 days. Failure to do so within the timeframe stipulated would lead to the appointment of a sole arbitrator by the vice-president of the International Court of Justice.[140]

Contained within clause 28(7) was the choice of law clause. The original choice of law provision read as follows: 'This Concession shall be governed by and interpreted in accordance with the Laws of Libya and such principles and rules of international law as may be relevant, and the umpire or sole arbitrator shall base his award upon those laws, principles and rules'. This was first altered in 1961 by royal decree, which effectively stated that where there was a conflict between Libyan law and international law then the former would take precedence. This was agreed to in 1963, according to clause 16.

Another change by royal decree took place in 1965 and was agreed to in 1966. On this occasion it was agreed that, rather than Libyan law superseding international law, only the principles of Libyan law that were common with those of international law should be applied in the governance and interpretation of the concession. In the absence of such principles in Libyan law, what should apply are the general principles of law including those applied by international tribunals. This change was affected because the concession holders were dissatisfied with the alteration in 1963. Altering the agreement ensured that if there were no principles

---

137 Note 113 at 322.
138 Ng'ambi, 'The Effect of Stabilization Clauses in Concession Agreements' (n 104) 72.
139 Clause 28(2).
140 Clause 28(3). See also Tibor Várady, John J. Barceló and Arthur T. von Mehren, *International Commercial Arbitration: A Transnational Perspective* (3rd edn, Thomson & West 2006) 114–115.

The effect of stabilization clauses   65

under Libyan law that overlapped with international law, then it would mean that the concession would be governed by the general principles of law instead. This, it was argued, would ensure that fairer treatment is afforded to the foreign oil companies.[141]

In 1969, the Government of Libya was overthrown by Colonel Muammar Gaddafi in a bloodless coup. Colonel Gaddafi thus became chairman of the Revolutionary Command Council of Libya. In November 1971, the Government of Iran invaded Abu Musa and the Greater and Lesser Tumb. These were located in the Persian Gulf. Although these islands were still nominally under British protection through a treaty, this treaty was due to expire the following day. Britain did virtually nothing to prevent Iran from occupying these islands. As a consequence, Britain received much condemnation from the Arab world. In December 1971, the Libyan Government, in retaliation, nationalized all assets belonging to British Petroleum in the Hunt/BP deed of concession through Decree No. 115.[142]

Early in 1973, the new Government of Libya attempted to gain direct equity participation in the oil concessions granted to foreign companies. The new government thus engaged in negotiations which did not go in its favour. Consequently, the Government of Libya elected to nationalize all of Bunker Hunt's interests in the Hunt/BP deed of concession. It cited America's support for Israel as the rationale for this particular nationalization. In the same year, the Government of Libya proceeded to nationalize 51 per cent of the assets belonging to TOPCO, CALASIATIC and LIAMCO through decree No. 66 of 1973.[143]

This occurred after direct equity participation negotiations between Libya and these companies had failed. Once again, American support for Israel in the Arab-Israeli conflict was cited as the reason for the nationalizations. In 1974, the Government of Libya proceeded to nationalize the remaining 49 per cent of LIAMCO's assets through Decree No. 10 of 1974.[144] It also did the same with the remaining 49 per cent of assets belonging to TOPCO and CALASIATIC through Decree No. 11 of 1974.[145]

The claimants BP, TOPCO/CALASIATIC and LIAMCO initiated arbitral proceedings against the Government of Libya. In all three cases, the oil companies had written to the Government of Libya indicating that they had appointed their

---

141   Amendments to the Petroleum Law, Libyan Rev. (January 1966) at 26, 27.
142   Libya: Law on the Nationalization of the British Petroleum Exploration Company (1972) 11 ILM 380.
143   See Libya: Law on Nationalization of Oil Companies Legislation and Regulations (1974) 13 ILM 60; other concession holders that were affected by this decree were: Esso Standard of Libya Inc., Grace Petroleum Corp., Esso Sirte Co., Inc., Shell Exploratie En Productie Maatschappij, Mobil Oil of Libya Inc., and Gelsenberg A.G. (Libya). There were some corporations that were not affected by this and these were Aquitaine Libye and Elf-Libye, which were French and Hispanica de Petrolos, which was a Spanish corporation.
144   Von Mehren and Kourides (n 133) 485.
145   Bernard Taverne, *Petroleum, Industry and Governments: A Global Study of the Involvement of Industry and Government in the Production and Use of Petroleum* (2nd edn, Kluwer 2008) 197.

arbitrator. The Government of Libya refused initially to participate in the arbitral proceedings. Thus, in all three instances, sole arbitrators were appointed by the vice-president of the International Court of Justice, as prescribed in clause 28(3).

The first case examined here is that of *BP v Libya*.[146] In this case, the arbitrator held that the Libyan Government's nationalization of BP's assets was illegal. In arriving at this decision, however, the arbitrator seems to have focused more on the fact that the taking was confiscatory. This was owing to the fact that two years had elapsed since the nationalizations had taken place and BP still had not received compensation.[147] The arbitrator said very little about the stabilization clause contained within the concession. In determining whether the Libyan Government was liable for breach of contract the arbitrator looked at the choice of law clause, which clearly stated that the law applicable here was the 'general principles of law'.[148] Under such a legal regime, this was clearly a breach of contract and BP was entitled to damages that were to be determined at a later date.[149] In the arbitrator's view, the rules dealing with repudiation of an agreement were 'too elementary and voluminous' to require any further elaboration.[150] This case represents an endorsement of the view that a state is bound to a contract with an investor. Failure to abide by such a contract does have pecuniary consequences.

The arbitrator in *Texaco Overseas Oil Petroleum Co./California Asiatic Oil Co. v Libya*[151] was far more elaborate in how he arrived at his decision. In this case the Government of Libya argued that stabilization clauses militated against the principle of permanent sovereignty over natural resources. In arriving at his decision, the arbitrator focused on the principle of *pacta sunt servanda*. He came to the conclusion that it was in fact possible for a sovereign state to bind itself to a contract with an investor.

In accordance with the choice of law clause in clause 28(7) of the concession, the arbitrator explored the principles of Islamic or Sharia law, which is a source of Libyan law. He observed that, in principle, all parties should abide by a contract under Sharia law. This rule is in fact applied more rigidly to the sovereign or government than it is to private parties. This is owing to the great discretionary powers available to the sovereign. Thus, to set an example to his or her subjects a sovereign is held to a greater standard than that applied to ordinary persons. This rule is applicable to agreements entered with non-Muslims.[152] The arbitrator further observed that even the General Assembly Resolution 1803 endorsed the view that foreign investment agreements are to be observed in good faith.[153]

146 Note 113.
147 ibid 329.
148 ibid 303.
149 ibid 357.
150 ibid 329.
151 Note 114.
152 ibid 23, para 65.
153 ibid 24, para 68.

The arbitrator noted that even the Charter on Economic Rights and Duties of states, whose binding force he rejected,[154] also explicitly states that 'international obligations' are to be fulfilled 'in good faith'.[155]

Moreover, the arbitrator held that the stabilization clause did not impinge upon the sovereign prerogatives of the State of Libya. This was essentially because all its sovereign powers still remained intact and could still be exercised on persons other than those to whom it owed contractual obligations. The arbitrator opined that: 'a State cannot invoke its sovereignty to disregard commitments freely undertaken through the exercise of this same sovereignty, and cannot through measures belonging to its internal order make null and void the rights of the contracting party which has performed its various obligations under the contract'.[156] In the arbitrator's view, contracts ought to be respected and to rule otherwise would undermine the credibility of states. This is by virtue of the fact that it would create an imbalance between the parties that connotes that the state is not bound but the investor is. This would directly unstitch the very fabric of the principle of good faith. For this reason such a position ought to be vehemently rejected.[157]

It is clear from the preceding case that the principle of permanent sovereignty over natural resources is not an excuse for the state's failure to uphold its contractual obligations. The decision in *Texaco* can be contrasted with that of *LIAMCO v Libya*.[158] In this case the arbitral tribunal held that stabilization clauses do not affect the state's sovereign right to expropriate a contract. To hold otherwise in its view would amount to an intolerable interference with a state's sovereignty. This case represents a recognition that arbitral tribunals can take into account the sovereignty argument.[159] Whether the *LIAMCO* award actually renders *pacta sunt servanda* futile is questionable.[160]

However, it must be noted that this position only pertained to the issue of damages. The arbitrator here was deciding upon whether to apply the 'Hull Principle', which prescribed adequate compensation and always required the inclusion of future profits. The arbitrator doubted the applicability of the Hull Principle under customary international law. The idea of including future profits in the compensation package was a controversial one in the arbitrator's view.[161] The arbitrator in this case found that the nationalization was lawful in the sense that it was non-discriminatory and for a public purpose. Thus, any determination of future profits ought to be considered in terms of 'equity' rather than 'adequacy'.

---

154 ibid 30, para 88.
155 ibid 31, para 90.
156 ibid 23–24, paras 65–68.
157 ibid 31, para 91.
158 Note 115 at 141.
159 Ng'ambi, 'Stabilization Clauses and the Zambian Windfall Tax' (n 4) 111.
160 Yackee (n 26) 1589, although cf. Andrew Guzman, 'Why LDCs Sign Treaties That Hurt Them: Explaining the Popularity of Bilateral Investment Treaties' (1998) 38 *Virginia Journal of International Law* 639.
161 *LIAMCO* (n 115) 131–32.

68 Resource nationalism in international investment law

Moreover, the arbitrator in *LIAMCO* acknowledged that the contract could not validly be terminated without the 'mutual consent of the contracting parties, in compliance with the said principle of the sanctity of contracts and particularly with the explicit terms of Clause 16 of the Agreements'.[162] Thus, to argue that this case represented a rejection of the sanctity of contracts would be a slight exaggeration.[163]

In sum, the Libyan decisions have similar outcomes; however, their arrival at these decisions were very different. *BP v Libya*[164] and *Texaco v Libya*,[165] on the one hand, espouse the belief that stabilization clauses do grant foreign investors absolute protection. Particularly from *Texaco* we can see that the contention that this affects the sovereignty of a nation is not entertained at all. On the other hand, *LIAMCO v Libya*[166] does entertain the sovereignty argument. However, given the context in which the decision was made, it can be argued that arbitral tribunals in all three cases respected the sanctity of contracts, albeit for different reasons.

3.4.3 Subsequent decisions

The subsequent cases are also generally homogenous in their support for the sanctity of contracts.[167] The first case explored here is that of *Revere Copper & Brass, Inc. v Overseas Private Investment Corporation*.[168] In 1967, Revere Jamaica Alumina Ltd, a subsidiary of Revere Copper & Brass, Inc., had entered into agreement with the Government of Jamaica. The former was to construct and operate a bauxite mining plant in Jamaica. This agreement provided for tax stability. Seven years later, however, a new government was elected in Jamaica, which stripped Revere of its incentives. Ignoring contractual provisions the newly elected government proceeded to raise taxes significantly. This had an adverse effect on Revere's operations and it was thus compelled to shut down its plant. The Overseas Private Investment Corporation (OPIC) rejected Revere Copper's expropriation claim. This was on the basis that the Government of Jamaica had not actually taken away Revere Copper's physical assets or its licence. Revere Copper thus initiated arbitral proceedings against OPIC.

The arbitral tribunal noted that the Government of Jamaica sought to obtain long-term commitments from foreign investors in order to exploit its natural resources.[169] It attracted this investment affording tax breaks and other assurances for limited periods of time to the investor. It was noted that it is in fact possible for governments to impose limits on their sovereign powers when they enter

---

162 ibid 62.
163 Yackee (n 26) 1590.
164 Note 113.
165 Note 114.
166 Note 115.
167 But cf. Dolzer and Schreuer, *Principles of International Investment Law* (n 82) 76.
168 (1978) 17 ILM 1321.
169 ibid.

into agreements with investors, in a similar fashion to when they issue long-term government bonds on foreign markets. The tribunal further stated:

> Under international law the commitments made in favour of foreign nationals are binding notwithstanding the power of Parliament and other governmental organs under the domestic Constitution to override or nullify such commitments Any other position would mean in this case that Jamaica could not in the exercise of its sovereign powers obtain foreign private capital to develop its resources or attract foreign industries. To suggest that for the purposes of obtaining foreign private capital the Government could only issue contracts that were non-binding would be meaningless. As the contracts were made in the sense that the commitments were set out in unqualified legal form, international law will give effect to them. For the purposes of this proceeding they must be regarded as binding.[170]

In the case of *AGIP v Popular Republic of Congo*,[171] for example, the arbitral tribunal rejected the sovereignty argument. As such, it was held that the agreement between the State of Congo and AGIP was binding. This case involved the Government of Congo, which had nationalized the nation's oil distribution sector in 1974. The only company that remained unaffected by these nationalizations was AGIP. The aforementioned company had entered into an agreement for the sale of 50 per cent of its shares to the Government of Congo. The agreement between the government and AGIP contained within it several stabilization clauses.

When Congo nationalized the company by decree, there were questions as to whether this action was compatible with the stabilization clause. The arbitral tribunal, in a similar fashion to earlier cases, held that the stabilization clauses contained within the concession concerned were freely entered into and accepted by the Government of Congo. The government still possesses its legislative and regulatory powers. However, those powers cannot be invoked against the investor with whom the host government has an agreement.[172] For this reason, the Government of Congo was under an international obligation to compensate AGIP for any damage suffered as a result of the nationalization.[173]

The subsequent case of *LETCO v Liberia*[174] takes a similar position. The ICSID Tribunal stated that the stabilization clause is there to protect against the arbitrary actions of the host state. The clause 'must be respected', otherwise the state will be allowed to avoid its contractual obligations too easily by utilizing its legislative prerogatives.[175]

---

170 ibid.
171 (1982) 21 ILM 726.
172 ibid 735, para 86.
173 ibid, paras 86–88.
174 (1989) 2 ICSID Reports 343.
175 ibid 368.

70 Resource nationalism in international investment law

The respect arbitral tribunals have for the sanctity of contracts is further observed in *AMINOIL v Kuwait*.[176] In this case the Ruler of Kuwait had granted the American Independent Oil Company (AMINOIL) a concession to explore and exploit oil and gas reserves in Kuwait's hold of the neutral zone between Kuwait and Saudi Arabia. This concession was to subsist for a period of 60 years. The agreement was signed in 1948 while Kuwait was still a British Protectorate. Within this agreement was a stabilization clause which read as follows:

> The Shaikh shall not by general or special legislation or by administrative measures or by any other act whatever annul this Agreement except as provided in Article 11. No alteration shall be made in terms of this Agreement by either the Shaikh or the Company except in the event of the Shaikh and the Company jointly agreeing that it is desirable in the interests of both parties to make certain alterations, deletions or additions to this Agreement.[177]

When Kuwait obtained her independence from Britain on 19 June 1961, the government then proceeded to amend the 1948 concession.[178] This was essentially to conform to the 50–50 profit-sharing pattern that had now become more commonplace in the Middle East.[179] When OPEC became more powerful throughout the Middle East, pressure mounted on AMINOIL to agree on greater participation by the government, as well as the imposition of higher taxes by the Kuwaiti Government. AMINOIL acquiesced in these changes.[180]

After the October War of 1973, oil prices quadrupled. This meant that AMINOIL's profits increased notwithstanding the fact that the government had increased tax and royalty rates. Negotiations continued and a new agreement was thus proposed by AMINOIL. This agreement stipulated that AMINOIL's profits would amount to 70 cents per barrel or US$18–20 million per year. The government, on the other hand, proposed a plan that would mean that AMINOIL would gain substantially lower profits of 25 cents per barrel, which translated to US$7.5 million per year.[181]

Although negotiations continued, in 1977 the Government of Kuwait finally issued Decree Law No. 124.[182] This decree effectively terminated the concession and provided that all property would revert to the state.[183] Under its Article 3, the decree established a Compensation Committee, whose task was 'to assess the fair compensation due to the Company as well as the Company's outstanding

---

176 (1982) 21 ILM 976.
177 ibid 990–91.
178 ibid 991.
179 See Andreas Lowenfeld, *International Economic Law* (2nd edn, OUP 2008) 503.
180 ibid.
181 ibid.
182 Note 176 at 998, para 29.
183 ibid.

The effect of stabilization clauses   71

obligations to the State or other parties'.[184] The state was then to 'pay what the Committee decides within one month of being notified of the Committee's decision'.[185] AMINOIL refused to appear before the committee and instead initiated arbitral proceedings in London pursuant to the 1948 agreement.

One of the fundamental questions raised during the arbitral proceedings was whether the stabilization clause rendered the nationalization decree unlawful. The tribunal observed that: 'a straightforward and direct reading of [the stabilization clause] can lead to the conclusion that they prohibit any nationalization'.[186] Nevertheless, the tribunal ultimately held that the stabilization clause did not preclude the Government of Kuwait from nationalizing assets belonging to AMINOIL.

The tribunal did reject the contention by the Government of Kuwait that the stabilization clauses added 'nothing to what would in any event be the legal position'[187] or, in other words, the stabilization clauses were merely affirming what the contract already said. The tribunal opined that, in interpreting the contracts, the object and purpose of the clause must be examined. Because one party to the contract was a state with various powers and prerogatives at its disposal, the purpose of this clause was to provide some sort of protection for the investor.[188] The Government of Kuwait also challenged the validity of the stabilization clauses because they were signed in 1948. This obviously occurred prior to the state having gained independence. The tribunal rejected this argument on the basis that the Government of Kuwait had expressly acquiesced to the stabilization clauses when it revised its agreements in 1961 and again in 1973.

Counsel for the Government of Kuwait further claimed that effecting the stabilization clause would militate against the principle of permanent sovereignty over natural resources.[189] The tribunal also rejected this argument. However, the tribunal did acknowledge that the stabilization clause in this agreement did not amount to an express undertaking on the part of the Kuwaiti Government that it would not nationalize. The tribunal did not dispute the fact that it is possible for the state to limit its right to nationalize assets belonging to foreign corporations. However, this would have to be expressly stipulated in the contract itself.[190] It cannot be implied from the wording that the state has fettered or surrendered its right to nationalize assets belonging to foreign investors. Furthermore, such a clause would have to cover only a relatively limited period.[191] In this particular case the stabilization was very general and did not expressly prohibit

---

184 ibid.
185 ibid.
186 ibid 1020, para 88.
187 ibid 1020, para 89.
188 ibid.
189 ibid 1021, para 90.
190 Cf. *Amoco International Finance Corp. v Government of the Islamic Republic of Iran* (1987) 15 Iran–US CT Rep 189.
191 Note 176 at 1022, para 91.

72 Resource nationalism in international investment law

nationalization.[192] Furthermore, the clause ran for a period of 60 years, which, in the arbitral tribunal's opinion, was 'especially long'.[193]

The tribunal further held that the purpose behind the stabilization clause was to protect against confiscatory termination and takeover. If the takeover is not confiscatory, it would not amount to a breach of the stabilization clauses. Since the government had made an offer of monetary compensation, the taking was not confiscatory.

This position of the majority was fiercely criticized by Arbitrator Fitzmaurice. Although he highlighted that his was not a dissenting opinion he did state that it was erroneous to imagine that monetary compensation makes the taking any less confiscatory. He gave an analogy of paying compensation to a person who has lost his leg. Paying compensation to one such injured person does not actually bring the leg back. When corporations such as AMINOIL insert stabilization clauses within their contracts the aim is not to obtain money; the aim is to ensure that the concession as a whole is not breached by the host state. Therefore, nationalization should always be rendered confiscatory, with or without compensation, 'because by virtue of their inherent character, they always are'.[194]

On the fundamental principle of *pacta sunt servanda* the tribunal noted the 'great changes' which the Concession had undergone since 1948. AMINOIL did accept these changes, albeit grudgingly. The tribunal also recognized that the changes that the contract had undergone were greatly influenced by the transformation in the way oil concessions were being dealt with across the Middle East and the world over. These were changes that had taken place progressively and ultimately gave a new character to the concession as a whole.[195]

Further evidence of support for *pacta sunt servanda* is found in the case *of Company Z (Republic of Xanadu) v State Organization ABC (Republic of Utopia)*.[196] The real names of the parties were not actually revealed in this case. However, it has been suggested that 'Utopia' was more than likely a francophone African state.[197] In this case the Republic of Utopia had repudiated a natural resources agreement. Citing the Charter on the Rights and Duties of States, the Government of Utopia contended that its repudiation was an act of sovereignty, that the arbitral tribunal had no jurisdiction and that it was not liable for the repudiation.

The arbitral tribunal rejected the contention that the Utopian Republic was not bound by the arbitration clause. In its view, it was a universally accepted position that governments are bound by arbitration clauses. Once it has signed an arbitration clause, the state cannot validly absolve itself of the obligations

---

192 Cf. *EnCana v Republic of Ecuador* (2006) LCIA Case UN3481, 49 para 173 and Maniruzzaman, 'The Pursuit of Stability in International Energy Investment Agreements' (n 107) 145.
193 Note 176 at 1023, para 95.
194 The Separate Opinion of Sir G. Fitzmaurice, ibid 1052, para 26.
195 ibid 1023, para 97.
196 *Company Z (Republic of Xanadu) v State Organization ABC (Republic of Utopia)* (1983) 8 YB Comm Arb 94.
197 Yackee (n 26) 1594.

The effect of stabilization clauses **73**

contained therein by a simple change in its national law or a unilateral abrogation of the contract.[198] An arbitral tribunal rendering an award in favour of the investor in no way encroaches upon the host state's sovereign right to alter its policies as it sees fit. This is owing to the fact that the tribunal did not claim the power to order specific performance; it only had the power to compel payment of an amount of compensation equivalent to performance.[199]

The tribunal also opined that the law on sovereign states entering into binding agreements was also very clear. It stated that: '[i]t cannot be maintained . . . that the Utopian State, by virtue of is national sovereignty, is unable to validly undertake its obligations . . . To deny . . . the faculty to validly bind itself would clearly entail an unacceptable limitation on its sovereignty'.[200]

The tribunal contended that, although the Utopian State had the right to change course and abandon its previously adopted policies, this did not mean that its non-performance of the contract with Company Z would be devoid of consequences. To rule otherwise would militate against the fundamental principle of *pacta sunt servanda*.[201]

A contrasting case is that of *Amoco International Finance Corp. v Government of the Islamic Republic of Iran*.[202] The arbitral tribunal took the view that internationalizing a contract is elevating the status of a contract to that of a treaty. Doing so elevates the status of a private corporation to that of a state. The arbitral tribunal contended that a private corporation should not be elevated to the status of a state. It further held that the right to expropriate is a fundamental attribute of sovereignty that cannot be considered as easily surrendered by the state.[203]

This rationale is flawed, however. This book has already acknowledged that a contract cannot be elevated to the status of a treaty because, by its very nature, a treaty is an agreement between two states. This is clearly not the case here. In addition, holding a state liable to a contract is simply acknowledging that where states enter into specific commitments with investors who might otherwise be reluctant to invest, they are bound by them.[204] The later case of *Parkerings v Lithuania*[205] also supports the sanctity of contracts. In this case the ICSID Tribunal held that:

> It is each State's undeniable right and privilege to exercise its sovereign legislative power. A State has the right to enact, modify or cancel a law at its

---

198 Note 196 at 109.
199 ibid 113.
200 ibid 113–114.
201 ibid.
202 Note 190. It must be noted, however, that it is now generally accepted that a contract can be elevated to an international level, where there is an umbrella clause in a bilateral investment treaty between the host state and the home state of the investor. See Stephan W. Schill, *The Multilateralization of International Investment Law* (Cambridge University Press 2014) 84–86.
203 ibid 243.
204 See *Methanex Corp v United States of America*, Award of 5 August 2005 (at Part IV, ch D, para 7).
205 *Parkerings-Compagniet v Lithuania*, Award of 11 September 2007, ICSID Case No. ARB/05/8, para 332.

74 Resource nationalism in international investment law

own discretion. Save for the existence of an agreement, in the form of a stabilization clause or otherwise, there is nothing objectionable about the amendment brought to the regulatory framework existing at the time an investor made its investment. As a matter of fact, any businessman or investor knows that law will evolve over time. What is prohibited however is for a State to act unfairly, unreasonably or inequitably in the exercise of its legislative power.[206]

From the foregoing, it could be argued that tribunals do support the sanctity of contracts. Even in cases where the breach of contract has been deemed legal, there has not been a direct challenge to the validity or legal effect of these clauses.[207] The earlier cases unanimously endorsed the view that where states had entered into specific commitments, they were bound by these and this was certainly a consideration in the compensation awards. Although arguments were raised that this position impedes on the principle of permanent sovereignty over natural resources, this argument has generally been rejected.

The trend of respecting the sanctity of contracts was generally continued in the Libyan nationalization cases. The possible exception to this rule is the award in *LIAMCO v Libya*.[208] However, even in this case the termination of the concession, although not illegal per se, was still a 'source of liability to compensate the concessionaire'.[209] The compensation award did include future profits.[210] Moreover, the arbitrator did not directly attack the validity of the stabilization clause. The subsequent cases also endorse the sanctity of contracts. Therefore, it has been demonstrated that stabilization clauses in concessions do bind the state to the concession for the period of time stipulated. If the state unilaterally terminates a concession, it will have to pay compensation.

3.5 Conclusion

The general consensus amongst the arbitral awards is that stabilization clauses are binding upon the state. Clearly, the contention that stabilization clauses grant the contract the same status as a treaty is extreme. However, it is clear that when a state enters into an express undertaking not to alter its laws for a stipulated period of time, then it is bound. It cannot alter its laws to supersede the express undertakings not to jeopardize the investor's assets for the period of time indicated in the stabilization clause.

Failure to abide by this will have consequences. In some instances the outright nationalization has been deemed illegal. Indeed, it has been seen that even where

---

206 ibid para 332.
207 Dolzer and Schreuer (n 82) 83.
208 Note 115.
209 ibid 60.
210 ibid 81.

the nationalization is deemed legal, the actual effect and validity of the stabilization clause has not actually been challenged. It is clear, therefore, that stabilization clauses are binding and arbitral tribunals respect the sanctity of contracts. It is also clear that permanent sovereignty over natural resources does not override *pacta sunt servanda*. Entering into a contract is an act of sovereignty. The state cannot then invoke this very principle to exit these contracts prematurely.

The difficulty with this, however, is that it leads to contractual rigidity, which is potentially insalubrious. Indeed, whilst the consequences of breaching a stabilization clause are a good deterrent to unscrupulous behaviour on the part of the state, one might argue that it is in the common interest of both parties to keep the investment going. The prices of natural resources are mercurial and industry patterns are likely to evolve. In either case, circumstances will change and the parties will inevitably have to change with them. It is for this reason that this book advocates that contractual mechanisms are inserted, which, in turn, will render the concession more flexible. These could come in the form of renegotiation clauses. These clauses, it is argued, have proved to be beneficial to both the host state and the investor because they enable both parties to seek 'an amiable settlement of their differences than to risk an open breach of the investment agreement'.[211]

---

211 Günther Jaenicke, 'Consequences of a Breach of an Investment Agreement Governed by International Law, by General Principles of Law or by Domestic Law of the Host State' in Detlev Dicke (ed), *Foreign Investment in the Present and New International Economic Order: Vol 2* (Warburg 1987) 193.

Chapter 4

Compensation under international investment law

4.1 Introduction

Under international investment law, a state is liable to pay compensation when it prematurely terminates its concession agreement with the investor.[1] The basis upon which compensation is to be assessed, however, is a controversial one.[2] This state of affairs is further compounded by the lack of clear guidance as to which standard of compensation is applicable under international investment law.[3] At present, there are two standards of compensation: appropriate compensation and the 'Hull principle'.

Under the appropriate compensation standard, it is advocated that compensation should be determined on a case-by-case basis, taking into account all the relevant circumstances.[4] The 'Hull formula' is more explicit. It espouses that compensation must be prompt, adequate and effective.[5] Adequate essentially means restoring the investor to a position that the latter would have been in had the breach not taken place. This would invariably involve including loss of future profits (*lucrum cessans*) in the concession agreement. This is typically measured by the discounted cash flow method, which entails looking at the gross receipts the enterprise expected to make in each future year of the concession, minus future expenditures. Issues such as inflation are also taken into account.[6]

This method is invariably applied by arbitral tribunals, including those that explicitly state that the standard of compensation applicable is 'appropriate compensation'.[7] Such a position is advantageous, because it places the investor in

---

1 Irmgard Marboe, *Calculation of Compensation and Damages in International Investment Law* (OUP 2009) 30, paras 2.81–2.91; Jeswald W. Salacuse, *The Three Laws of International Investment: National, Contractual, and International Frameworks for Foreign Capital* (OUP 2013) 314–15.
2 Ian Brownlie, *Principles of International Law* (6th edn, OUP 2003) 514.
3 Surya Subedi, *International Investment Law: Reconciling Policy and Principle* (2nd edn, Hart Publishing 2012) 151–53.
4 Eduardo Jiménez de Aréchaga, 'State Responsibility for the Nationalization of Foreign Owned Property' (1978) 11 *New York University Journal of International Law and Politics* 179, 188–8.
5 See *Tippets, Abbett, McCarthy, Stratton v TAMS AFFA* (1984) 6 Iran–US CTR 219, 225.
6 Guideline IV(6), 'World Bank 'Guidelines, on the Treatment of Foreign Direct Investment' (1992) 31 ILM 1379, 1383.
7 See *AMINOILl v Kuwait* (1982) 21 ILM 976, 1033, para 144.

a position he would have been had the termination not taken place.[8] Furthermore, the state only has an incentive to terminate a concession when it still manages to make a subsequent profit, even after indemnifying the investor, including lost future profits. This is efficient because, in a monetary sense, no party loses out and one party makes a gain.

It is argued that contract law in this way promotes efficiency, by giving the parties to the contract an incentive to perform, unless doing so would be inefficient.[9] This is the very essence of the efficient breach theory under contract law. One of the pillars of this theory is that the main goal of the parties to a contract is profit and wealth maximization. In other words the interests and objectives of the parties can fully be translated into monetary and pecuniary terms.

This is certainly a limitation to the applicability of the efficient breach theory to concession agreements because, in this context, one of the parties to the contract is the state whose goals cannot solely be quantified in monetary terms. When a state nationalizes or expropriates, it is often for a public purpose.[10] Wealth maximization is not the paramount concern of the state per se, but rather a reorganization of its socio-economic policies. In this sense, although the existing standards of compensation promote efficiency, they do not provide sufficient flexibility for governments whose objectives are often at variance with those of the foreign investor. Section 4.2 of this chapter will discuss the compensation standards under international investment law. Section 4.3 of this chapter will examine the efficient breach theory and its application under international investment law before concluding in section 4.4.

4.2 Standards of compensation in international investment law

In the event that the state nationalizes property belonging to a foreign investor, there is a duty to pay compensation.[11] As was stated by the arbitral tribunal in the *Upton* case,[12] states do have the right to 'appropriate private property for public purpose', however, and this right is unquestionable.[13] However, there is a duty to compensate the owner.[14] Classically, the purpose of compensation is to

---

8 See *Case Concerning German Interests in Upper Silesia (Chorzow Factory* case), PCIJ Series A. No. 17, at 47.

9 Barry E. Adler, 'Efficient Breach Theory Through the Looking Glass' (2008) 83 *New York University Law Review* 1679, 1680–81. See also Eric A. Posner and Alan O. Sykes, *Economic Foundations of International Law* (Belknap Press 2013) 25.

10 Andreas F. Lowenfeld, *International Economic Law* (2nd edn, OUP 2008) 564.

11 Muna Ndulo, 'The Nationalization of the Zambian Copper Industry' (1974) 6 *Zambia Law Journal* 55, 65; Paolo Vargiu, 'Environmental Expropriation in International Investment Law' in Tullio Treves Francesco Seatzu and Seline Trevisanut (eds), *Foreign Investment and Common Concerns: An International Law Perspective* (Routledge 2013) 206–221, 206.

12 (1903) Ven Arb 173.

13 ibid 194.

14 ibid.

78 Resource nationalism in international investment law

eliminate all the consequences of the state's action and restore the investor to a position he would have been in, had the state not breached its agreement.[15]

There are two standards of compensation under international law. One standard, encapsulated in the 'Hull principle', requires the state to pay 'prompt, adequate, and effective' compensation in the event of a nationalization. Of importance is the term 'adequate', which not only means compensating the investor for the full market value but also for lost future profits (*lucrum cessans*).[16] The other standard only requires the state to pay appropriate compensation, which is determined on a case-by-case basis. Section 4.2.1 will discuss the Hull principle, section 4.2.2 will discuss appropriate compensation and section 4.2.3 will discuss lost future profits.

4.2.1 The Hull principle

Under the Hull principle, the rule is that payment of compensation must be 'prompt, adequate, and effective'.[17] Adequate, according to this principle, means that the nationalizing state should put the investor in the same position that the latter would have been in had the nationalization not occurred. This may mean paying the market value of the enterprise. In addition, the state may also have to pay future profits or *lucrum cessans*.[18] Prompt means the payment must be made within a 'reasonable time'[19] and there should be no inordinate delays.[20] In addition to this, the interest rate payable should be such that it does not have an adverse effect on the adequacy of the compensation. Effective means that the currency should be freely convertible and there should be no restriction on its repatriation.[21]

In later years, the United States State Department further elaborated on the meaning of the term 'adequate'.[22] In its view, when American owned property is expropriated by the host state, the former must be paid full market value for its assets. Fair market value, it contended, was to be calculated as if the act of expropriation had not occurred. The United States State Department acknowledged that market value is not always ascertainable owing to the fact that there would have been no recent sales of comparable property. For this reason, the State Department utilizes three indirect valuation methods in determining market value.

---

15 Aréchaga, 'State Responsibility for the Nationalization of Foreign Owned Property' (n 4) 180.

16 See *AGIP v Congo* (1982) 21 ILM 726 and Richard J. Smith, 'The United States Government Perspective on Expropriation and Investment in Developing Countries' (1976) 9 *Vanderbilt Journal of Transnational Law* 517, 519.

17 Green Hackworth, *Digest of International Law: Volume 3* (US Government Printing Office 1942) 660–65.

18 Smith (n 16) 519.

19 *Portugal v Germany* (1930) Ann Dig. Int'l L. Cases 150, 151.

20 Pamela B. Gann, 'Compensation Standard for Expropriation' (1984) 23 *Columbia Journal of Transnational Law* 615, 620.

21 Restatement of the Foreign Relations Law of the United States (REVISED), §712, comment (Tent. Draft No. 3, 1982).

22 Smith (n 16) 519–20.

These are: the going concern approach, the replacement cost approach and the book value approach.

Under the 'going concern' approach, estimations of market value are based on the earning power of the company.[23] This includes considering loss of future profits, which are typically based on past earnings or estimates of future earnings. The United States State Department did recognise that it will not always be possible to apply this method where it is impracticable or unfair. This could, for example, manifest in an instance where the investment has not been operating long enough and therefore has a limited profit history. It was also recognized that this method is susceptible to government manipulations that may distort the profitability of the operations. This includes 'increased taxes, threat of cancellation of contractual or concessionary rights, or withdrawals of privileges'.[24]

It must be noted that tribunals have been rather cautious to award lost future profits because they can be speculative. This was illustrated in the separate opinion of Professor Brownlie in the case of *CME v Czech Republic*,[25] who opined that compensation must be both just and 'reflect the genuine value of the investments affected'.[26] The genuine value of the investment was to be compatible with a reasonable rate of return.[27] In his separate opinion, Professor Brownlie thus awarded a sum of US$160.9 million which, by his own admission, was significantly lower than that of the final award.[28] This shows that even in a tribunal there can be disagreement as to how to quantify loss to the investor.

Under the 'replacement cost' approach the party determining the amount of compensation payable should look at the cost of replacing the property at the time of the expropriation, 'less actual depreciation'.[29] Although this amount is greater than book value, it does not take into account earning power manifested through projected future profits. The State Department considered this approach 'generally less acceptable in most circumstances than the going-concern approach'.[30] It is also noted that this method is rarely applicable in instances of government takings and can only be utilized in instances where replacements that are identical to the ones taken can be purchased, which is rarely the case when assets are taken by the state. Moreover, because the investor's assets are usually so unique, estimating the value of replacement is impossible.[31]

---

23 See also James Crawford, *The International Law Commission's Articles on State Responsibility: Introduction, Text and Commentaries* (Cambridge University Press 2002) 226.
24 Smith (n 16) 520.
25 *CME v Czech Republic* 31, para 69 http://italaw.com/sites/default/files/case-documents/ita0180. pdf (last visited 5 June 2015).
26 ibid 43, para 106.
27 ibid 45, para 115.
28 ibid 47, para 121. The tribunal itself rendered an award of US$270 million.
29 Smith (n 16) 520.
30 ibid.
31 Campbell McLachlan, Laurence Shore and Matthew Weiniger, *International Investment Arbitration: Substantive Principles* (OUP 2010) 319.

80 Resource nationalism in international investment law

The 'book value' approach involves valuing assets at the 'acquisition cost less depreciation'.[32] In the State Department's view, this value 'bears little relationship for their actual value'.[33] This is illustrated in the case of *Asian Agricultural Ltd v Republic of Sri Lanka*.[34] The state in this case had a duty to provide full protection and security to the investment in question. Owing to the state's failure to do so, armed insurgents destroyed a shrimp farm in which the investor had a 48 per cent shareholding. The tribunal refused to order the state to pay for lost profits in this case. In the state's view, any potential purchaser would have been sceptical about the ability of the company to pull itself out of the red and whether future earnings could sufficiently offset past losses. Furthermore, the assets of the company paled in comparison to the loans it had taken out.[35]

In view of the fact that the investor could not be compensated for any future profits, the tribunal drew up a 'comprehensive balance sheet',[36] which was a reflection of the investor's assets and liabilities derived from a list of the company's 'tangible assets'.[37] This approach disregards various factors, such as the 'enterprises' contractual rights, know-how, goodwill, and management skills'.[38] It also merely measures what is on the company's balance sheet, which is usually determined by applying standard accounting principles.[39] It is no surprise, therefore, that this is the least acceptable method of valuation.[40]

In determining the method applicable, cognizance must be taken of all the circumstances of the case. Thus, the individual determining compensation may apply one or a combination of methods in arriving at a figure that will justly compensate the investor. The US State Department further recognized that compensation could also come in a non-monetary form of goods, kickbacks and other services.[41]

4.2.2 Appropriate compensation

The Hull formula can be contrasted with the 'appropriate compensation' standard. Under this banner, it is contended that the amount of compensation payable to the investor should be determined on a case-by-case basis.[42] In contrast

---

32 Smith (n 16) 520.
33 ibid.
34 *Asian Agricultural Ltd v Republic of Sri Lanka (Award)* (1990) 4 ICSID Rep 245.
35 ibid 292.
36 ibid 290.
37 ibid 291.
38 McLachlan, Shore and Weiniger (n 31) 319.
39 ibid 321. See also Paul D. Friedland and Eleanor Wong, 'Measuring Damages for the Deprivation of Income-Producing Assets: ICSID Case Studies' (1991) 6 ICSID *Review of Foreign Investment Law Journal* 400, 404.
40 Smith (n 16) 520.
41 ibid.
42 *Ebrahimi v Iran* (1994) 30 Iran–US CTR paras 88 and 95. See also Aréchaga, 'State Responsibility for the Nationalization of Foreign Owned Property' (n 4) 185.

Compensation under international investment law 81

to the Hull principle, there is no precise definition of what compensation is required under the 'appropriate compensation' standard.[43] The benefit of not having a precise definition is that it provides a flexible standard, which can accommodate all the prevailing circumstances when determining the issue of compensation.[44] This standard has been endorsed by the United Nations General Assembly, the European Court of Human Rights, the House of Lords and the United States Court of Appeals (Second Circuit).[45]

The appropriate compensation standard is endorsed in General Assembly Resolution 1803 (1962). An important facet of this General Assembly Resolution is that it was endorsed by both developed and developing nations. It must be noted, however, that even in this instance the United States took the term appropriate to mean prompt, adequate and effective, in accordance with the Hull formula.[46] General Assembly Resolution 1803 states that:

> 4. Nationalization, expropriation or requisitioning shall be based on grounds or reasons of public utility, security or the national interest which are recognized as overriding purely individual or private interests, both domestic and foreign. In such cases, the owner shall be paid appropriate compensation in accordance with the rules in force in the State taking such measures in the exercise of its sovereignty and in accordance with international law.[47]

Similar sentiments are expressed in the Charter on the Economic Rights and Duties of States (CERDS),[48] which recognizes the right of states to nationalize foreign property, provided that appropriate compensation is paid by the host state 'taking into account its relevant laws and regulations and all circumstances that the State considers pertinent'. It further states that in the event where the issue of compensation leads to controversy, the matter should be settled under the national laws and tribunals of the host state, unless it otherwise agreed.

The European Court of Human Rights, in *Lithgow v United Kingdom*[49] held that the right to nationalize and the right of a state to determine the amount of compensation payable to the individual were inextricably linked. The state is better placed to determine this because it has a wider knowledge of the 'society and its needs and resources'.[50] In view of this fact, the state is better placed to

43 Rudolf Dolzer, 'Expropriation for Nationalization' (1985) 8 *Encyclopedia of Public International Law* 214, 219; Andra Eisenberg, 'Different Constitutional Formulations of Compensation Clauses' (1993) 9 *South African Journal of Human Rights* 412, 418.
44 M. Sornarajah, 'Compensation for Expropriation. The Emergence of New Standards' (1979) 13 *Journal of World Trade Law* 108, 127–28.
45 See Eisenberg (n 43) 416–20.
46 Stephen M. Schwebel, 'The Story of the U.N.'s Declaration on Permanent Sovereignty over Natural Resources' (1963) 49 *American Bar Association Journal* 463, 465.
47 See also General Assembly Resolution 2158 (XXI) of 1966.
48 General Assembly Resolution 3281 (XXIX) of 1974.
49 (1986) 8 EHRR 329.
50 ibid 373.

82 Resource nationalism in international investment law

determine what measures it ought to take. The European Court of Human Rights could not divorce the United Kingdom's determination of compensation from its actual decision to nationalize 'since the factors influencing the latter will of necessity influence the former'.[51] Given these facts, the Court would not question the legislature's judgment in this respect, unless there were reasonable grounds to do so.[52] In the case of *Williams & Humbert v W & T Trademarks*,[53] the House of Lords considered the question of compensation when the Spanish Government nationalized the property of an English family. The House of Lords advocated appropriate compensation. As Lord Templeman noted, it was a firmly established principle that the state had the right to nationalize property and compensation had to be determined in this light.[54]

The American case of *Banco Nacional de Cuba v Chase Manhattan Bank*[55] arose out of the Cuban nationalizations. In this case, the US Court of Appeals (Second Circuit) held that failure to pay compensation would have been a violation of international law and that the standard applicable, would have been 'appropriate compensation'. However, the court also mentioned that 'appropriate' could also mean 'full compensation'. The Court of Appeal thus contended that:

> It may well be the consensus of nations that full compensation need not be paid 'in all circumstances' and that requiring an expropriating State to pay 'appropriate compensation' – even considering the lack of precise definition of that term – would come closest to reflecting what international law requires. But, the adoption of an 'appropriate compensation' requirement would not exclude the possibility that in some cases full compensation would be appropriate.[56]

The sentiments expressed in the preceding case are similar to those in the World Bank Guidelines on the Treatment of Foreign Direct Investment. Although the Guidelines begin by talking about 'appropriate compensation', they eventually state that it is only appropriate if it is 'adequate, effective and prompt'.[57] It is clear that no consensus exists on which standard of compensation applies in international investment law.[58] The Hull principle, it would appear, is not universally accepted.[59]

---

51 ibid.
52 ibid.
53 [1986] AC 368.
54 ibid 430–41.
55 658 F.2d 875 (2d Cir. 1981).
56 ibid 892–93.
57 See also Guideline IV(1) and Guideline IV(2) of 'World Bank Guidelines on the Treatment of Foreign Direct Investment' (1992) 31 ILM 1379, 1382.
58 Rudolph Dolzer, 'New Foundations of the Law of Expropriation of Alien Property' (1981) 75 *American Journal of International Law* 553, 553.
59 See Oscar Schachter, 'Compensation for Expropriation' (1984) 78 *American Journal of International Law* 121; Frank G. Dawson and Burns H. Weston, 'Prompt, Adequate and Effective: A Universal Standard of Compensation?' (1962) 32 *Fordham Law Review* 727.

However, it has been adopted in most, although not all, bilateral investment treaties.[60] In section 4.2.3 it will be seen that, although the tribunals do not explicitly endorse the Hull principle, it is still clear that the principles adopted under the aforementioned standard are recognized. This is reflected in the fact that arbitral tribunals invariably recognize that lost future profits should be included in the compensation award payable to the investor. In this sense, even though appropriate compensation might be the standard applied, the effect of these decisions reflects a standard of compensation that resembles the Hull principle.[61]

4.2.3 Lost future profits

Under the case law we shall discuss in this sub-section, it is clear that the state is under an obligation to pay lost future profits to the investor in the event that it prematurely terminates a concession. Loss of future profits have often been a factor in determining the fair market value of the property when it was taken.[62] It is argued by some writers that loss of future profits should only be included in the compensation package when the taking is deemed to be illegal.[63] However, in this sub-section it will be seen that loss of future profits are paid out even where the taking is deemed legal.[64] In this respect the arbitral tribunals make no distinction between legal and illegal takings. The rationale behind damages is to put the investor in the same pecuniary position that he would have been in had the contract been performed.[65] As observed by the tribunal in *Sapphire International Petroleum Ltd v National Iranian Oil Co.*:[66]

> This rule is simply a direct deduction from the principle *pacta sunt servanda*, since its only effect is to substitute a pecuniary obligation for the obligation which was promised but not performed. It is therefore natural that the creditor

---

60 Lowenfeld, *International Economic Law* (n 10) 564; McLachlan, Shore and Weiniger (n 31) 317; and Wenshua Shan, 'Is Calvo Dead?' (2007) 55 *American Journal of Comparative Law* 123. See also Wenshua Shan and Norah Gallagher, 'China' in Chester Brown (ed), *Commentaries on Selected Model Investment Treaties* (OUP 2013) 164–65, which discusses the Chinese Model BIT. Even though it avoids language such as 'adequate' as set out in the Hull formula, the actual calculation methods prescribed are not substantially different from the aforementioned standard of compensation.

61 Gann (n 20) 618; M.H. Mendelson, 'Compensation for Expropriation: The Case Law' (1985) 79 *American Journal of International Law* 414, 415.

62 *Phillips Petroleum Co. Iran v Islamic Republic of Iran* (1987) 21 Iran–US CTR 79, 123.

63 Derek W. Bowett, 'State Contracts With Aliens: Contemporary Developments on Compensation for Termination or Breach' (1988) 49 *British Yearbook of International Law* 49, 63. See also Ian Brownlie, *Principles of Public International Law* (7th edn, OUP 2008) 539 and Irmgard Marboe, 'Compensation and Damages in International Law: The Limits of "Fair Market Value"' (2006) 7 *Journal of World Investment and Trade* 723.

64 See also Crawford, *The International Law Commission's Articles on State Responsibility, Introduction, Text and Commentaries* (n 23) 226 and William C. Lieblich, 'Determinations by International Tribunals of the Economic Value of Expropriated Enterprises' (1990) 7 *Journal of International Arbitration* 37, 47–48.

65 *Sapphire International Petroleum Ltd v National Iranian Oil Co.* (1967) 36 ILR 136, 185–86.

66 ibid.

84 Resource nationalism in international investment law

should thereby be given full compensation. This compensation includes loss suffered (*damnum emergens*), for example expenses incurred in performing the contract, and the profit lost (*lucrum cessans*), for example the net profit which the contract would have produced. The award of compensation for lost profit or the loss of a possible benefit has been frequently allowed by international tribunals.[67]

The first decision examined here is that of the Permanent Court of International Justice in the *Case Concerning German Interests in Upper Silesia*.[68] This case represents an example of payment of future profits in a case where the state unilaterally abrogates a treaty. The Polish Government in this case had taken over a company in which German companies had rights. This was specifically prohibited by Article 6 of the Geneva Convention Concerning Upper Silesia. The aforementioned provision stated that, whilst the Polish Government had the general right to nationalize, it could not do so with property belonging to German nationals.[69] The German Government thus sued Poland for compensation. The Permanent Court of International Justice held that, in the event where a government breaches an undertaking, there is a general obligation to make reparations.[70] Such reparation in its view 'must, as far as possible, wipe out all the consequences of the illegal act and re-establish the situation which would have existed if that act had not been committed'.[71] This included the loss of future profits.[72]

The International Court of Arbitration in *Lena Goldfields* took a similar position.[73] In assessing damages, the tribunal found that, as a consequence of repudiating their agreement, the Soviet Union had unjustly enriched itself. Lena Goldfields was thus awarded a sum of £13 million. Included within this figure, implicitly, was loss of future profits, because Lena Goldfields had only invested an initial sum of US$20 million.[74]

Later arbitral tribunals have determined loss of future profits by examining past earnings of a company and then arriving at a figure. From this figure they then deduct any future payments that the nationalized entity would have had to make, such as taxes, royalties and operating costs. This was certainly the approach taken by the arbitral tribunal in the case of *Libyan American Oil Co. (LIAMCO) v Libya*.[75]

---

67 ibid 185–86.
68 Note 8.
69 ibid 21.
70 ibid 29.
71 ibid.
72 ibid 52, see also *Starret Housing Corp v Islamic Republic of Iran* (1987) 16 Iran–US CTR 112, 196–201.
73 Arthur Nussbaum, 'The Arbitration Between the Lena Goldfields Ltd. and the Soviet Government' (1950–51) 36 *Cornell Law Quarterly* 31, 42.
74 Jason W. Yackee, 'Pacta Sunt Servanda and State Promises to Foreign Investors Before Bilateral Investment Treaties: Myth and Reality' (2009) 32 *Fordham International Law Journal* 1550, 1575.
75 (1981) 20 ILM 1, 81.

Compensation under international investment law   85

The tribunal first acknowledged that, as a matter of sovereignty, the state did possess the right prematurely to terminate its concession agreement with Libya under international law. Although this premature termination was not illegal per se it did, however, constitute a 'source of liability to compensate the concessionaire'.[76] This would include loss of future profits.[77] The arbitrator stated:

> In such confused state of international law, . . . it appears clearly that there is no conclusive evidence of the existence of community or uniformity in principles between the domestic law of Libya and international law concerning the determination of compensation for nationalization in lieu of specific performance, and in particular concerning the problem whether or not all or part of the loss of profits (*lucrum cessans*) should be included in that compensation in addition to the damage incurred (*damnum emergens*).[78]

It was thus recognized that loss of future profits ought to be paid to LIAMCO. This was despite the fact that the nationalization was deemed legal. In determining the value of its compensation, LIAMCO hired an independent expert to make an evaluation, who estimated the amount of crude oil, liquids and gas that would have been produced for the remainder of the contract. LIAMCO utilized the official market price of July 1976 to estimate gross revenues it would have made until the contract elapsed in 1988. It did not upwardly adjust this amount to take into account any possible future increases in market prices. From this gross figure, it deducted operating costs and any taxes and royalties that it would have had to pay to the Libyan Government. The tax and royalty rates were based on those that existed prior to the nationalization measures taken in 1973. LIAMCO then applied a 12 per cent discount factor to the net figure, arriving at a valuation of US$186.27 million.[79] The tribunal reduced this figure to US$66 million as 'equitable compensation', owing to the fact that it did not take into account currency inflation that would almost certainly occur.[80]

Similarly, in the case of *The American Independent Oil Co. (AMINOIL) v Kuwait*,[81] the tribunal opined that the nationalization was legal. Notwithstanding this fact, the tribunal also included future profits when rendering its award on compensation. However, the tribunal examined all the circumstances of the case and opined that its award had to be consistent with the legitimate expectations of the parties concerned.[82] The tribunal further noted 'with reference to every long-term contract . . . there must necessarily be economic calculations, and the weighing-up

76 ibid 60.
77 ibid 81.
78 ibid 76.
79 Gann (n 20) 631.
80 Note 75 at 160.
81 (1982) 21 ILM 976.
82 ibid 1034, para 148.

86 Resource nationalism in international investment law

of rights and obligations, of chances and risks, constituting the contractual equilibrium'.[83]

In the tribunal's view, AMINOIL's expectations were reflected in the 1973 agreement between the parties, which had subsequently been modified by the Abu Dhabi formula, which led to the increase of tax and royalty rates payable to the Government of Kuwait.[84] Given the fact that AMINOIL had agreed to this formula, it meant that any calculation of future lost profits would have to give due consideration to it. Thus, the amount awarded to AMINOIL was based on a reasonable rate of return and not on the excessive one it presented, which was based on the lower taxes and royalty rates reflected in the earlier concession agreement.[85]

The International Centre for Settlement of Investment Disputes (ICSID) tribunals have also included lost future profits in their awards. The first case that illustrates this is *AGIP v Popular Republic of Congo*,[86] where the claimant's interest in a Congolese company was nationalized by the Government of Congo. In this case the arbitral tribunal applied the law of Congo, which incorporated elements of the French Civil Code, which provided that lost profits were recoverable.[87] Therefore, the tribunal awarded lost profits to AGIP.[88]

We can thus see that the ICSID tribunal also recognises that lost future profits ought to be included in the awards for compensation. However, it is reluctant to do so in instances where the lost future profits are indeterminable. This is usually in instances where the nationalized entity does not have a sufficient history of profit-making. In such an instance, any figure that would be arrived at would be purely conjectural as there would be no pre-existing figures to base it upon. It is for this reason that arbitral tribunals would be reluctant to award loss of profits in such an instance. This is illustrated in the case of *Benvenuti et Bonfant v People's Republic of Congo*.[89] This case concerned the Congolese Government, which had nationalized a company in which Benvenuti et Bonfant (B & B), an Italian corporation, had a 40 per cent equity interest.[90] B & B had entered into an agreement with the Congolese Government in which B & B was to build a bottle manufacturing plant in the host state.[91] Although plant production commenced in 1975, the owners of the corporation left Congo the following year, upon advice by the Italian embassy that its safety was in jeopardy.[92] Subsequently, the Congolese army occupied the plant. Although there was no formal act of

---

83 ibid.
84 ibid 1035, para 154.
85 ibid 1037–38, paras 160–63.
86 (1982) 21 ILM 726.
87 ibid 737, paras 98–100.
88 ibid 739, para 115, section (a)(ii)(D).
89 (1982) 21 ILM 740.
90 ibid 748, para 2.6.
91 ibid 749, para 2.9.
92 ibid 751, para 2.23.

expropriation, B & B contended that the actions of the Congolese Government had the effect of taking over its interest in the operation.

In determining the dispute the tribunal stated that it had the jurisdiction to decide the dispute *ex aequo et bono* (in justice and fairness) pursuant to Article 42(3) of the ICSID Convention.[93] B & B contended that the value of its 40 per cent ownership interest was CFA110,098,936. It arrived at this figure by taking into account lost projected profits that it was expected to make over the period that the agreement was to subsist.[94] The tribunal elected to appoint an independent expert to make the valuation. The expert advised that future profits could not be included in the award, owing to the fact that, during its one year of operation, no profits had actually been realized by the company. Therefore, given the fact that its profit history was virtually non-existent, the expert treated the expropriated company as a start-up rather than a fully operational entity. The expert then made an evaluation based on the most objective criteria at the time, which was the actual amount of the original investment and multiplied this by B & B's 40 per cent interest. In so doing, the expert came to a valuation of CFA122 million.[95] This actually exceeded the amount claimed by B & B.

The tribunal agreed with the expert opinion. However, it lowered the amount to CFA110,098,936, which was the original amount claimed. This is owing to the fact that the amount arrived at by the expert exceeded that which was claimed by B & B.[96] The tribunal further added interest to the award, which was to be calculated from the day that the taking took place. Although B & B requested an interest rate of 15 per cent, the tribunal awarded 10 per cent instead. The Congolese Government had used this interest rate in its counterclaims. Invoking its authority to decide the matter *ex aequo et bono*, the tribunal opined that a rate of 10 per cent was equitable under the circumstances.[97] This is still consistent with the US State Department's position on future profits as it acknowledges that, although the general rule should be to include future profits, it may not always be practicable if this amount is indeterminable.[98]

This position could be contrasted with the later case of *Société Ouest Africaine des Bétons Industriels (SOABI) v Senegal*.[99] In this case the ICSID tribunal did include lost future profits in its award, despite the fact that SOABI had not yet started making profits. The *SOABI* case is very much consistent with earlier non-ICSID cases of *Delagoa Bay and East African Railway*[100] and *Sapphire International*.[101] In *Delagoa*,

---

93 ibid 752, para 4.4 and 758, para 4.65.
94 ibid 759, para 4.75.
95 ibid 760, para 4.78.
96 ibid 760, para 4.79.
97 ibid 762, para 4.98.
98 Smith (n 16) 519; Gann (n 20) 625.
99 *Société Ouest Africaine des Bétons Industriels (SOABI) v State of Senegal* (1988) 2 ICSID Rep 164.
100 *United States and Great Britain v Portugal* (1900) quoted in Marjorie M. Whiteman, *Damages in International Law: Volume 3* (United States Government Printing Office 1943) 1694, 1697.
101 *Sapphire International* (n 65) 187–88.

88   Resource nationalism in international investment law

the Portuguese Government had annulled a railroad concession before the railroad had begun to operate.[102] This fact notwithstanding, the tribunal still opined that *lucrum cessans* were payable. Similarly, in the case of *Sapphire International* the tribunal held that the claimant was entitled to lost profits despite the fact that the area in dispute had not yet been prospected.[103] Since *SOABI*, however, subsequent ICSID tribunals have been reluctant to award lost profits in instances where there is no proven track record of profitability.[104] In this sense, it is an unusual case.[105]

In recent years, the state has invoked the 'abuse of rights' doctrine in order to deny the claimant investor lost profits.[106] This was illustrated in the controversial case of *Himpurna California Energy Ltd v PT (Persero) Perushaan Listruik Negara*.[107] This case concerned Himpurna, which had entered into a contract with Perushaan Listruik Negara (PLN), which was the Indonesian state owned electricity company. Under this agreement Himpurna was to generate electricity and then sell it to PLN who, in turn, would supply it to the Indonesian public. When PLN failed to purchase electricity generated by Himpurna the latter initiated arbitral proceedings. It claimed that PLN had breached their contract, which resulted in damages amounting to US$2.3 billion. This figure not only included damages for *damnum emergens*, which consisted of the initial investment plus interest but it also included *lucrum cessans*, which consisted of Himpurna's expected future profits.

In determining this issue, the arbitral tribunal applied the Indonesian Civil Code, which was the applicable substantive law. It noted that, according to Article 1217 of the Indonesian Civil Code, damages may include 'the loss which the creditor has suffered and the profit he has been made to forego'.[108] When it came to determining *damnum emergens*, the tribunal held that Himpurna was entitled to be reimbursed for money that it spent in reliance on the contract.[109]

As *damnum emergens*, Himpurna was thus awarded a sum of US$273,757,306, which consisted of US$254,502,586 in historical costs and US$19,254,720 in order to reflect the current value.[110] On the issue of *lucrum cessans*, the arbitral tribunal noted that this was well recognized by Article 1246 of the Indonesian Civil Code. However, the tribunal also noted that:

> the Code goes on to set out limiting factors which, again, are quite familiar. Art. 1247 (congruent with Art. 1152 of the *Code civil*) restricts recovery to damages

---

102 Whiteman (n 100) 1697.
103 Note 65 at 190.
104 See *Tecnicas Medioambientales Tecmed SA v United Mexican States* (2004) 43 ILM 133, 183; see also *Wena Hotels Ltd v Arab Republic of Egypt* (2000) 6 ICSID Rep 67; *Biloune and Marine Drive Complex Ltd v Ghana Investments Centre and the Government of Ghana* (1990) 95 ILR 183.
105 McLachlan, Shore and Weiniger (n 31) 325.
106 John Y. Gotanda, 'Recovering Lost Profits in International Disputes' (2005) 36 *Georgetown Journal of International Law* 61, 95–99.
107 (2000) 25 YB Comm Arb 13.
108 ibid 70–71.
109 ibid 78–79.
110 ibid 83.

Compensation under international investment law   89

foreseeable at the time of contracting; and Art. 1248 (congruent with Art. 1284 of the *Code civil*) requires that damages be the 'immediate and direct result of the breach'.[111]

Although the tribunal was of the view that Himpurna was in principle entitled to lost future profits, it ruled that these profits should not be calculated in a way that would effectively impoverish the host state. To do so, in the opinion of the tribunal, would militate against the abuse of rights doctrine under which the parties have an obligation to observe good faith as they exercise their rights. Thus, under this doctrine the claimant was barred from its right to full benefit from a bargain. The tribunal further stated that:

> this is a case where the doctrine of abuse of right must be applied in favour of PLN to prevent the claimant's undoubtedly legitimate rights from being extended beyond tolerable norms, on the ground that it would be intolerable in the present case to uphold claims for lost profits from investment not yet incurred.[112]

The tribunal refused to calculate lost profits 'as though the claimant had an unfettered right to create ever-increasing losses for the State of Indonesia (and its people) by generating energy without any regard to whether or not PLN had any use for it'.[113] The tribunal would have come to the same conclusion if this right had been derived from an explicit term of the contract.[114] The tribunal awarded Himpurna the sum of US$117,244,000 in lost profits. This constituted less than 10 per cent of the amount that Himpurna claimed.[115] The tribunal arrived at this figure by determining the after-tax net cash flow projections and then capping this figure at 36 per cent, which it then discounted to the present value at a rate of 19 per cent.[116]

The abuse of rights doctrine was also recognized in *Patuha Power Ltd v PT (Persero) Perusahaan Listruik Negara*. The arbitral tribunal in this case, once again applying the abuse of rights doctrine, denied a claim for lost profits. This was in light of the prevailing economic circumstances in Indonesia at the time.[117]

The outcome of these two cases can be contrasted with the case of *Karaha Bodas Co. v Perusahaan Pertambangan Minyak Das Gas Bumi Negara*.[118] In this case,

---

111 ibid 84.
112 ibid 93.
113 ibid 90.
114 ibid.
115 ibid 103.
116 ibid.
117 *Patuha Power Ltd v PT (Persero) Perusahaan Listruik Negara* in Mark Kantor, 'The Limits of Arbitration' (2004) 2 *Transnational Dispute Management* www.transnational-dispute-management.com/article. asp?key=89 (last accessed 5 June 2015).
118 364 F.3d 274, 282–85 (5th Cir. 2004).

90 Resource nationalism in international investment law

Karaha Bodas had entered into an agreement with Pertamina, which was the Indonesian state owned oil company. Karaha was to finance, build and operate geothermal facilities. Pertamina was then to purchase the energy that would be generated by Karaha. Owing to the country's financial crisis, Pertamina was unable to purchase the energy and, in consequence of this, Karaha Bodas initiated arbitral proceedings. The tribunal held that Pertamina had breached its contract with Karaha and thus awarded the latter a sum of US$111.1 million for lost expenditures and an additional US$150 million for lost profits.[119] The abuse of rights doctrine was not discussed.[120]

Karaha Bodas sought recognition and enforcement of the award in the United States. Enforcement of the award had been ordered by the United States District Court for the Southern District of Texas and affirmed by the United States Court of Appeals for the Fifth Circuit. In both instances, Pertamina claimed that the award should not be enforced on the basis that it was contrary to public policy. Pertamina contended that construction on the project was not complete and the Indonesian economy was in ruins. For this reason, awarding lost future profits would amount to an abuse of rights, which, in turn, violated United States public policy.[121]

This argument was rejected by both courts. The Court of Appeals particularly noted that the abuse of rights doctrine was not well established under American law. In addition, the abuse of rights doctrine only applied in cases where either (1) the overriding motive for the action is to cause harm, (2) the action is unreasonable, that is to say there is no legitimate interest in the exercise of the right and this exercise harms another or (3) the right is exercised for a reason other than for which it exists.[122] Because none of these factors was present in the instant case, the doctrine of abuse of rights did not apply. It would thus appear from these cases that the abuse of rights doctrine will only be applied if it is recognized under the substantive law chosen by the parties.

From the foregoing, it is clear that there is a duty to pay compensation. Although there are currently two compensation standards, it would appear from the case law that lost future profits are often paid to the investor, even if the tribunal does adopt the appropriate compensation standard. Moreover, international investment law makes no distinction between lawful and unlawful takings when awarding lost profits. Due regard must be given to future revenues that the investor would have generated. Not doing so would be to 'confiscate a portion of his property without compensation'.[123] Although the abuse of rights doctrine has been invoked in

---

119 Louis T. Wells, 'Double Dipping in the Arbitration Awards? An Economist Questions Damages Awarded to Karaha Bodas Company in Indonesia' (2003) 19 *Arbitration International* 471, 472.
120 ibid.
121 *Karaha Bodas v Perusahaan Pertambangan Minyak*, 190 F. Supp. 2d 936, 955 (S.D. Tex. 2001).
122 *Karaha Bodas v Perusahaan Pertambangan Minyak*, 364 F.3d 274, 306 (5th Cir. 2004).
123 Lieblich (n 64) 47–48.

Compensation under international investment law 91

curbing the amount of lost profits to which the investor is entitled, it would appear that this doctrine will only be applied if it is recognized under the substantive law chosen by the parties.

4.3 The efficient breach theory under international investment law

The efficient breach theory espouses that 'a party should be allowed to breach a contract and pay damages, if doing so would be more economically efficient than performing under the contract'.[124] The aim of contract law under this theory is to promote efficient behaviour. When the parties enter into a mutually beneficial agreement they are making each other better off.[125] The idea here is the promotion of 'welfare'[126] or 'wealth maximisation'.[127] The theory operates under the umbrella of 'utilitarianism', which propounds the view that the law exists to promote the greatest good for the greatest number.[128] Although there are various other utilitarian justifications for contract law, the efficient breach is the most prominent of these.[129]

The term 'efficiency' is seen through the prism of two schools of thought: 'Pareto efficiency' on the one hand and 'Kaldor-Hicks efficiency' on the other.[130] Pareto efficiency is divided into two categories. The first is Pareto optimality. Under Pareto optimality, behaviour is said to be efficient if one party's welfare is enhanced, but at the expense of another.[131] The second is Pareto superiority. Under this standard, a rule is said to be efficient if no person is made worse off by it but at least one person benefits from it.[132]

Under Kaldor-Hicks efficiency, a rule is efficient if the benefits a party obtains from a rule are far greater than the losses incurred by those that might be harmed by it. In other words a transaction is efficient even if it produces winners and losers. The only proviso is that winners gain more than the losers lose.[133] Under Kaldor-Hicks efficiency, compensation is not paid to the losers in such

---

124 Bryan A. Garner (ed), *Black's Law Dictionary* (West 2009) 592.
125 See Charles Fried, 'Contract As Promise Thirty Years On' (2012) 45 *Suffolk University Law Review* 961, 964.
126 Richard A. Posner, *The Economics of Justice* (Harvard University Press 1981) 61.
127 See Louis Kaplow and Steven Shavell, 'Fairness Versus Welfare' (2001) 114 *Harvard Law Review* 961.
128 See J.H. Burns and H.L.A. Hart (eds), *The Collected Works of Jeremy Bentham* (London 1977) 393.
129 See generally Stephen A. Smith, *Contract Theory* (Clarendon Press 2004) 136–40.
130 Richard S. Markowitz, 'Constructive Critique of the Traditional Definition and Use of the Concept of the Effect of a Choice on Allocative (Economic) Efficiency: Why the Kaldor-Hicks Test, the Coase Theorem, and Virtually all Law-and-Economics Welfare Arguments are Wrong' (1993) *University of Illinois Law Review* 485, 489.
131 Jules L. Coleman, 'Efficiency, Utility, and Wealth Maximization' (1980) 8 *Hofstra Law Review* 509, 512–13.
132 ibid 513.
133 Posner and Sykes (n 9) 13.

a situation. The criterion is satisfied 'as long as the monetised value of the health gains for the winners is greater than the monetized loss of health for the losers'.[134] If the transaction was costless and full compensation was given to the losers, then the transaction becomes Pareto superior instead of Kaldor-Hicks efficient. Because of this, it has been argued that Kaldor-Hicks efficiency is a 'potential Pareto-superior' standard.[135] The difficulty with this proposition lies in the fact that the loser does not receive compensation. As a consequence of this, some individuals are inevitably left worse off and, as such, this falls short of the conditions prescribed under Pareto superiority.[136]

The Pareto superiority position is the more widely utilized standard in defining efficiency, according to the efficient breach theory.[137] This is owing to the fact that self-interested persons would not object to its use. This is because few people would object to policies that would make at least one person better off without anyone else having to suffer in the process.[138] Moreover, it has been observed that:

> Exchanges among knowledgeable, rational persons in a free market are generally Pareto superior; rational individuals do not strike bargains with one another unless each perceives it to be in his or her own interest to do so. A successful exchange between such parties is, therefore, one in which the value to each of what he or she relinquishes is perceived as less than the value of what each receives in return. Such exchanges make no individual worse off; often they improve the lot of all concerned. Pareto superiority is connected in this way to the ideal of a free-exchange market.[139]

Kaldor-Hicks efficiency, on the other hand, requires a more complex evaluation of interpersonal comparisons of welfare. Whereas with Pareto efficiency, all one has to ask here is simply whether everyone did or would agree to it.[140]

The implications of the foregoing are very important when it comes to remedies under contract law. One of the means through which the law promotes efficiency is through its remedy of damages. The dominant remedy under the common law world is damages and not specific performance.[141] If the promisor breaches an agreement, then he or she is under an obligation to compensate the other party for that breach.[142] In some instances, it might not be economical to induce the

---

134 ibid.
135 Guido Calabresi and Philip Bobbit, *Tragic Choices* (WW Norton & Company 1978) 85–86.
136 See Coleman (n 131) 513.
137 ibid 520.
138 ibid 516.
139 ibid 516–17.
140 Smith (n 129) 110–11.
141 See Edwin Peel, *Treitel: The Law of Contract* (13th edn, Sweet & Maxwell 2011) 988, 1099.
142 Robert Upex and Geoffrey Bennett, *Davies on Contract* (10th edn, Sweet & Maxwell 2008) 288–89. See also Oliver W. Holmes, *The Common Law* (Macmillan 1882) 300–301. See also Oliver W. Holmes, 'The Path of the Law' (1897) 10 *Harvard Law Review* 457.

Compensation under international investment law   93

promisor to complete performance of a contract.[143] An example of such a situation is explained succinctly by Posner, who states:

> Suppose I sign a contract to deliver 100,000 custom-ground widgets at 10¢ apiece to A for use in his boiler factory. After I have delivered 10,000, B comes to me, explains that he desperately needs 25,000 custom-ground widgets at once since otherwise he will be forced to close his pianola factory at great cost, and offers me 15¢ apiece for them. I sell him the widgets and as a result do not complete timely delivery to A, causing him to lose $1,000 in profits. Having obtained an additional profit of $1,250 on the sale to B, I am better off even after reimbursing A for his loss, and B is also better off. The breach is therefore Pareto superior. True had I refused to sell to B he could have gone to A and negotiated an assignment to him of part of A's contract to me. But this would have introduced an additional step, with additional transaction costs – and high ones, because it would be a bilateral monopoly negotiation.[144]

In such an instance, efficiency would encourage the parties to repudiate their obligations 'where the promisor is able to profit from his default after placing his promisee in as good a position as he would have occupied had performance been rendered'.[145] The object of contract law is, therefore, to give the promisor an incentive to fulfil its contractual obligations 'unless the result would be an inefficient use of resources'.[146]

The efficient breach theory is not a 'prescriptive recommendation to act wrongfully', as suggested by some antagonists.[147] Nor does it immorally enrich a party that breaches a contract as charged by others.[148] An act is only immoral if it is done without taking cognizance of the wellbeing and interests of others.[149] The wellbeing of the disappointed promisee is addressed under the efficient breach theory by prescribing that the disappointed promisee must be paid damages, including the expected future profits from a particular transaction.[150] This effectively places the disappointed promisee in the position he or she otherwise

---

143 Richard A. Posner, *Economic Analysis of Law* (8th edn, Wolters Kluwer 2011) 150.
144 ibid 151.
145 Robert Birmingham, 'Breach of Contract, Damage Measures, and Economic Efficiency' (1970) 24 *Rutgers Law Review* 273, 284.
146 Posner, *Economic Analysis of Law* (n 143) 150.
147 Seana V. Shiffrin, 'The Divergence of Contract and Promise' (2007) 120 *Harvard Law Review* 708, 733.
148 See Daniel Friedman, 'The Efficient Breach Fallacy' (1989) 18 *Journal of Legal Studies* 1; see Shiffrin (n 147) 708 but cf. Daniel Markovits and Alan Schwartz, 'The Myth of Efficient Breach: New Defenses of the Expectation Interest' (2011) *Virginia Law Review* 1939, 1948. See also Avery Katz, 'Virtue Ethics and Efficient Breach' (2012) 45 *Suffolk University Law Review* 777, 784–85.
149 Charles Fried, 'The Convergence of Contract and Promise' (2007) 120 *Harvard Law Review Forum* 1, 3.
150 Posner, *Economic Analysis of Law* (n 143) 150–51.

would have been in had the breach not taken place. Once restored to this position, the disappointed promisee is rendered indifferent to whether the promisor completes the contract or not. It also gives the promisor an incentive to fulfil his or her promise unless breaching the contract will benefit the latter in some way even after having paid lost profits.[151]

As in the domestic contract law of common law jurisdictions, the dominant remedy in international investment law is compensation and not specific performance. There are advantages to specific performance.[152] However, under international investment law compensation is a more practical option because specific performance would be harder to enforce. This was certainly illustrated in *LIAMCO v Libya*, where the tribunal rejected outright LIAMCO's claims for specific performance. The tribunal opined that such a remedy would be impossible to implement and was therefore impractical. In addition, such an award would militate against the power of a state to nationalize. Provided the nationalization would be non-discriminatory and not accompanied by a wrongful act, it was not unlawful as such. For this reason the tribunal refused to undo the act of nationalization and the specific performance remedy was rejected.[153]

On a general level, international investment law does promote efficiency by addressing the risks of long-term investment projects.[154] This is owing to the rules and devices that exist to prevent the host state from taking advantage of the investor, once the investment has been sunk.[155] Under the obsolescing bargain model, it has been seen that once the investor enters the host state and commences operations, the latter is in a position to diminish the value of the former's investments by expropriating the investor's property, taxing it heavily or imposing other heavy regulatory burdens.[156] Protections are certainly made available through the contract between the host state and the investor, national law and the various sources of international law, including bilateral investment treaties (BITs).[157]

---

151 ibid.
152 Friedman (n 148) 7. See also Melvin A. Eisenberg, 'Actual and Virtual Specific Performance, the Theory of Efficient Breach, and the Indifference Principle in Contract Law' (2005) 94 *California Law Review* 975 and Richard R.W. Brooks, 'The Efficient Performance Hypothesis' (2006) 116 *Yale Law Journal* 571. But cf. Jody S. Kraus, 'A Critique of the Efficient Performance Hypothesis' (2007) 116 *Yale Law Journal Pocket Part* 423.
153 *LIAMCO v Libya* (n 75) 197–99 but cf. *Texaco v Libya* (1978) 17 ILM 1. See also Haliburton Fales, 'A Comparison of Compensation for Nationalization of Alien Property with Standards of Compensation under United States Domestic Law' (1983) 5 *Northwestern Journal of International Law & Business* 871, 888.
154 Rudolph Dolzer and Christoph Schreuer, *Principles of International Investment Law* (2nd edn, OUP 2012) 22.
155 Posner and Sykes (n 9) 288–97.
156 ibid 288. See also Edith Penrose, George Joffé and Paul Stevens, 'Nationalization of Foreign-owned Property for a Public Purpose: An Economic Perspective on Appropriate Compensation' (1992) 55 *Modern Law Review* 351, 354–55.
157 See generally Salacuse, *The Three Laws of International Investment: National, Contractual, and International Frameworks for Foreign Capital* (n 1).

Under the regime of international arbitration, an aggrieved investor can bring action against the host state in instances where it has violated an agreement. This allows the investor to bring action in a private and neutral forum rather than the national courts, which may raise issues of bias against the investor. Although some significant problems may arise, there are in place international conventions to enhance the enforceability of arbitral awards rendered.[158]

Under international investment law, if it is no longer efficient to comply with obligations, then it would be efficient to terminate the concession agreement.[159] The compensation regime under international investment law also promotes efficiency. As elucidated in the preceding section, in the event where a state does breach its contract with an investor, it is under a duty to pay compensation. As is the case in domestic law, compensation would entail restoring the investor to the position he or she would have been in had the breach not taken place. This includes payment of lost future profits.

Moreover, from the case law it has been seen that a state may unilaterally terminate a concession with a corporation once, or even before, operations have commenced. This could occur for example where a state nationalizes an oil company. In such a case, if the state still manages to make a profit, after compensating the oil company, inclusive of lost profits, then the state in the abstract has acted efficiently. This is because at least one party has made a gain and the other party loses nothing, thus falling within the parameters of Pareto efficiency. If the state cannot achieve that end, then this is an incentive not to cancel a concession with the investor.

It has been argued that 'an expropriation or nationalization spurned by an obsolescing bargain will realize a net loss'.[160] It is argued that such an action will result in economic harm to the investor. Foreign investors may also be reluctant to invest in a state that does not meet its contractual obligations. This effectively means that the state loses out in the long term, even if it will benefit in the short term. This is further compounded by the fact that nationalized entities tend not to be as efficient as privatized ones, owing to reduced levels of present and future investment, which leads to lower production that, in turn, has an adverse effect on the economy.[161]

This argument is misplaced, however, because the state will have to pay the investor lost future profits. From the investor's perspective it means that it has lost nothing because it is restored to the position it would have been in had the nationalization not taken place. Even if it did not, the investor still has access to such insurance facilities as MIGA, which covers various political risks.[162]

---

158 Posner and Sykes (n 9) 295.
159 Wells (n 119) 478.
160 Brandon Marsh, 'Preventing the Inevitable: The Benefits of Contractual Risk Engineering in the Light of Venezuela's Recent Oil Field Nationalization' (2008) 13 *Stanford Journal of Law Business & Finance* 453, 457–58.
161 ibid.
162 See S. Linn Williams, 'Political and Other Risk Insurance: OPIC, MIGA, EXIMBANK and Other Providers' (1993) 5 *Pace International Law Review* 59.

Moreover, as seen in Venezuela and other countries that have previously nationalized foreign owned entities, investors will still invest their capital in countries despite their history of terminating concession agreements.[163]

The final part of the argument above, however, touches upon a very pertinent point: the fact that economic efficiency is not necessarily as central to the objectives of the state as it is to private enterprises. This is because, whilst the latter will typically have profit-making as their main goal, the former does not have wealth maximization as its paramount consideration. In fact, the assumption of the efficient breach theory is that the parties to a contract are seeking to maximize wealth. Wealth maximization is defined in monetary terms.[164] Wealth maximization is seen as a factor determining whether a certain state of affairs is efficient or not.[165]

Although the state will weigh its options before it violates an agreement,[166] wealth maximization is often more a peripheral consideration. Nationalization, or termination of a concession, could take place when resource rich nations wish to make changes to their socio-economic system.[167] This duty to pay full market value, including lost future profits instead of paying book value, would effectively be a veto upon states to pursue this legitimate purpose.[168]

As will be noted in the next chapter, which is the case study on Zambia, when the Government of Zambia nationalized the copper mines in the 1970s for example, it did this for socio-economic reasons[169] and also to raise the standard of living of the poor. In addition to this, the government was concerned that the mining industry – which made up a large bulk of Zambia's economy – was dominated by two foreign companies: Anglo American and the Roan Selection Trust. It was concerned about Zambia's socio-economic interests being subservient to the commercial interests of these two mining companies. In 2008 the Government

---

163 See generally Paul Stevens, 'National Oil Companies and International Oil Companies in the Middle East: Under the Shadow of Government and the Resource Nationalism Cycle' (2008) 1 *Journal of World Energy Law & Business* 5.

164 See Richard A. Posner, 'Utilitarianism, Economics, and Legal Theory' (1979) 8 *Journal of Legal Studies* 103, 119, who says of wealth maximization: 'Wealth is the value in dollars or dollar equivalents (an important qualification, as we are about to see) of everything in society. It is measured by what people are willing to pay for something or, if they already own it, what they demand in money to give it up. The only kind of preference that counts in a system of wealth maximization is thus one that is backed up by money – in other words, that is registered in a market'.

165 Coleman (n 131) 523, 526.

166 Richard Morrison, 'Efficient Breach of International Agreements' (1994) 23 *Denver Journal of International Law & Policy* 183, 188.

167 Maarten H. Muller, 'Compensation for Nationalization: A North-South Dialogue' (1981) 19 *Columbia Journal of Transnational Law* 35, 45. See also Margot E. Salomon, 'From NIEO to Now and the Unfinishable Story of Economic Justice' (2013) 62 *International & Comparative Law Quarterly* 31, 36–46.

168 ibid.

169 Daniel Limpitlaw, 'Nationalization and Mining: Lessons from Zambia' (2011) 111 *Journal of the Southern African Institute of Mining and Metallurgy* 737, 737.

Compensation under international investment law   97

of Zambia once again cited socio-economic reasons when it introduced the windfall tax.[170]

When Venezuela nationalized its oil companies in the 1970s it also expressed concerns about the backbone of its economy being dominated by foreign owned interests.[171] Governments may also be seeking to correct what they perceive as a colonial wrong. This was certainly the case when the Zimbabwean Government expropriated foreign owned land.[172] Although the latter case does not deal with a concession per se, it accentuates the point that when a government expropriates property or breaches a concession its paramount concern is not wealth maximization. The fact that the state has to pay future profits may make it more onerous to pursue those goals. The state needs some form of flexibility when dealing with 'legitimate changes and circumstances'.[173] The rules as they stand do not permit the state that flexibility.

In sum, the efficient breach theory advances the view that parties should be allowed to breach a contract and pay damages, in lieu of performance, if doing so would be economically efficient. Damages would also include lost future profits. Under international investment law, compensation rather than specific performance is the dominant remedy. Once the state breaches an agreement it is under a duty to pay compensation to the investor. If the state breaches an agreement, compensates the investor and still makes a profit after doing so, it could be argued that the state has acted efficiently. In this respect, the rules on compensation may fall squarely within the parameters of the efficient breach theory.

However, the limitation of the efficient breach theory is that it fails to take cognizance of the fact that not all the parties to a contract are necessarily concerned with wealth maximization. Thus, whilst international investment law does promote efficiency, it does not promote sufficient flexibility to protect the investor whilst taking cognizance of the fact that the host state has legitimate public purposes to pursue. It is for this reason that this book recommends flexibility in concession agreements, which could be fostered through the insertion of renegotiation clauses into concession agreements.

4.4 Conclusion

It could thus be concluded that once the state unilaterally abrogates its contractual obligations, it is under a duty to compensate the investor. The purpose of this is to restore the investor to the position the latter would have been in had the breach not taken place. This would include not only *damnum emergens* but also *lucrum cessans*.

---

170 See ch 5.
171 Felix P. Rossi-Guerrero, 'The Transition from Private to Public Control in the Venezuelan Petroleum Industry' (1976) 9 *Vanderbilt Journal of Transnational Law* 475, 482.
172 See Dunia Zongwe, 'The Contribution of *Campbell v Zimbabwe* to the Foreign Investment Law on Expropriations' (2010) 2 *Namibia Law Journal* 31.
173 Posner and Sykes (n 9) 289.

It has also been seen that these are awarded whether the taking is deemed legal or illegal under the auspices of international investment law. In this sense, the rules of compensation promote efficiency in that they prevent the government from nationalizing unless it can compensate the investor, including for loss of future profits, and then make some money on top of that. The difficulty with payment of future profits in the state's case, however, is that it makes it more onerous to achieve the socio-economic goals it wishes to pursue as a result of the breach. With a loss of future profits, it makes it difficult for the state to pursue public purposes. This pursuit of public purposes is a legitimate state objective and prerogative, which distinguishes states from commercial actors such as investors.

There is therefore a limitation in the efficient breach theory, in that it focuses more on wealth maximization; that is to say, it presupposes that contract law governs the activities of profit-maximizing market participants. This is not quite the case in international investment law. On the one hand, there is a private party looking to make a profit but, on the other hand, we have the state whose objectives are seldom commercial. In this sense, one might argue that international investment law is efficient, but it does not necessarily provide sufficient flexibility to the state, which seeks to pursue legitimate public objectives when it breaches agreements. It is for this reason that in this book I advocate the insertion of renegotiation clauses into concession agreements. This book recommends that, in addition to stabilization clauses, the parties to the concession should consider inserting renegotiation clauses. It has been seen that the advanced stages of the resource nationalism cycle invariably manifest when the host state's natural resources experience a windfall.

From this and preceding chapters, it has been seen that it is not in the interests of the investor to have a contract that is too rigid as this cannot endure during the advanced stages of the resource nationalism cycle. Further, it is not in the interests of the state simply to abrogate the contract unilaterally, because of the potentially colossal pecuniary consequences. Renegotiation clauses foster a flexible relationship under which the parties can return to the renegotiating table in instances where circumstances have changed. This concept will be further explored in the next chapter, which consists of a case study on Zambia.

Chapter 5

The resource nationalism cycle in Zambia

5.1 Introduction

Zambia is a southern African country with a population of just over 13 million.[1] She is one of the world's major copper producers whose economy is pegged primarily on copper.[2] Because she is a mono-economy the people of Zambia have often looked to this national asset as a vehicle that can facilitate the development of the country. Mining in Zambia is not only of economic significance; it also has political and social importance.[3]

Copper mining in Zambia has undergone three transitions since the first major mining operations commenced in the 1920s.[4] The first stage was during the era of colonialism and the immediate aftermath of independence. During this period the mining industry was dominated by the Roan Selection Trust (RST) and the Anglo American Corporation. The second stage occurred when the Government of Zambia nationalized these two corporations and formed Zambia Consolidated Copper Mines Limited (ZCCM).[5] This was done under the tenets of President Kaunda's philosophy of 'humanism', which dictated that the state is to look after every Zambian citizen.

Contemporaneously, Zambia also became a 'one-party participatory democracy', with Kaunda's United National Independence Party (UNIP) being the only legal political party.[6] A depreciation in copper prices led to the decline of the

---

1 See *2010 Census of Population and Housing* (Zambia Central Statistical Office 2011) 2 http://unstats.un.org/unsd/demographic/sources/census/2010_phc/Zambia/PreliminaryReport.pdf (last accessed 8 June 2015).
2 Andrew Sardanis, *A Venture in Africa: The Challenges of African Business* (IB Tauris 2007) 244.
3 Muna Ndulo, 'Mining Legislation and Mineral Development in Zambia' (1986) 19 *Cornell International Law Journal* 1, 5.
4 Antony Martin, *Mining Their Own Business: Zambia's Struggle Against Western Control* (Hutchinson 1972) 30.
5 Savior Mwambwa, Aaron Griffiths and Andreas Kahler, *A Fool's Paradise? Zambia's Mining Tax Regime* (Centre for Trade Policy and Development 2010) 5.
6 Bizeck Phiri, 'Colonial Legacy and the Role of Society in the Creation and Demise of Autocracy in Zambia, 1964–1991' (2001) 10(2) *Nordic Journal of African Studies* 224, 225.

mining industry under government control. ZCCM went from being Zambia's prized asset to being a loss-making burden on the treasury.[7] This led to pressure on the Zambian Government, from the IMF and the World Bank, to privatize the mines owned by ZCCM.[8] Privatization was thus the third stage in the evolution of the Zambian mining industry.

Zambia had returned to multiparty democracy in 1990 and, a year later, the opposition Movement for Multiparty Democracy (MMD) came to power. The new government liberalized the economy and the mines were privatized. Owing to external pressure to privatize these assets expeditiously, various tax incentives were proposed in order to attract foreign mining companies. These incentives were especially necessary owing to the low price of copper on the London Metal Exchange (LME). To foster the privatization of its mining industry, the Government of Zambia signed a number of development agreements with foreign investors. These agreements granted generous terms to the investors by fixing the royalty rate for copper at 0.6 per cent, which was far below the royalty rate of 3 per cent stipulated in the now repealed Mines and Minerals Act 1995. In addition, the corporate tax rate was to be 25 per cent. Furthermore, the development agreements also contained stabilization clauses, which prohibited the Government of Zambia from altering the fiscal regime prescribed in the agreements.

Subsequent to the privatization of the mines, the copper prices increased dramatically. Despite this fact, Zambia gained very little in terms of tax revenues. For example, Zambia only received royalties of US$20 million from combined gross proceeds of US$3.4 billion. This was largely as a result of the low royalty rate stipulated in the development agreements.[9] This was further compounded by the fact that privatization led to mass retrenchments, cavalier disregard of safety and national labour laws, environmental degradation and a general reduction in the living standards of those living in mining towns.[10]

The aim of this chapter is to look at the resource nationalism cycle in Zambia. Section 5.2 of this chapter will give a history and general background of the mining industry in Zambia. Section 5.3 will then look at the advantages of privatization, as well as its disadvantages, which eventually led to increased political pressure and the subsequent introduction of the windfall tax. Finally, section 5.4 of this chapter will consist of a conclusion summing up its findings.

---

7 Christian von Soest, 'How Does Neopatrimonialism Affect the African State's Revenues? The Case of Tax Collection in Zambia' (2007) 45 *Journal of Modern African Studies* 621, 636.

8 John Lungu, 'Copper Mining Agreements in Zambia: Renegotiation or Law Reform?' (2008) 117 *Review of African Political Economy* 403, 405.

9 Evaristus Oshionebo, 'Stabilization Clauses in Natural Resource Extraction Contracts: Legal, Economic and Social Implications for Developing Countries' (2010) 10 *Asper Review of International Business & Trade Law* 1, 18.

10 Alastair Fraser and John Lungu, *For Whom the Windfalls: Winners and Losers in the Privatisation of Zambia's Copper Mines* (Civil Society Trade Network of Zambia 2006) 32–53.

5.2 The evolution of mining in Zambia

The Copperbelt, which is located on the border of Zambia and the Democratic Republic of Congo, is one of the world's largest sources of copper ore.[11] Copper mining has dominated the Zambian economy since the first commercial mine was opened at Roan Antelope (now Luanshya) in 1928.[12] At the time, Zambia was known as Northern Rhodesia. The general economic structure prescribed by the colonial government was that Northern Rhodesia's mineral wealth was to be used to finance the 'much more significant industrial, social, educational and governmental infrastructure in Southern Rhodesia'.[13]

Zambia attained independence from Britain in 1964. During the first decade of her independence, Zambia's copper reserves were still controlled by two foreign mining companies, namely the Anglo American Corporation (AAC) and the Roan Selection Trust (RST). There were concerns that these two corporations had not reinvested in mining operations and were externalizing profits, to the detriment of the people of Zambia. The discontent this caused led to President Kenneth Kaunda adopting various economic reforms, which culminated in the nationalization of Zambia's copper mines.[14] The nationalized mines were amalgamated under a single state owned corporation called Zambia Consolidated Copper Mines Limited (ZCCM). At the same time, Zambia also became a one-party state.[15]

With the revenues earned from ZCCM the government was able to pursue various socio-economic and developmental agendas. However, this was to be short-lived. After the fuel crisis of the 1970s the price of copper plummeted, which precipitated the decline of the Zambian economy.[16] In order to remain afloat, the Zambian Government obtained aid from the International Monetary Fund (IMF) and the World Bank. A second oil crisis and the continued depreciation of copper led to a debt crisis in Zambia. In order for the Zambian Government to continue receiving aid, the IMF and the World Bank insisted that the Government of Zambia privatize its mines and other state entities. This section will give an overview of the copper industry in Zambia, and also aims to discuss the three evolutionary processes the copper industry in Zambia has undergone since its very inception.

5.2.1 Commercial mining in Northern Rhodesia

As evidenced by various archaeological findings in prehistoric burial grounds, copper mining has existed in South–Central Africa for centuries. It was not only

---

11 ibid 7.
12 ibid. See also Martin (n 4) 54–55.
13 Fraser and Lungu (n 10).
14 Andrew A. Beveridge, *African Businessmen and Development in Zambia* (Princeton 1979) 46–54.
15 Neo Simutanyi, 'The Politics of Constitutional Reform in Zambia: From Executive Dominance to Public Participation?' in Danwood M. Chirwa and Lia Nijzink (eds), *Accountable Government in Africa: Perspectives from Public Law and Political Studies* (United Nations 2012) 26, 30.
16 Lungu, 'Copper Mining Agreements in Zambia: Renegotiation or Law Reform?' (n 8) 405.

102 Resource nationalism in international investment law

used to make ornaments but also as a medium for trade.[17] The existence of copper in South–Central Africa was first made known by missionaries, explorers and traders in the 1880s during the infamous 'Scramble for Africa', where the continent was arbitrarily divided between the European powers. It was during this period that Cecil Rhodes sought to increase British influence in Africa by building a railway line that went from Cape Town in South Africa to Cairo in Egypt. This venture, he postulated, would be financed by Africa's mineral wealth rather than the British Government. To foster this, a royal charter was granted to Rhodes's British South Africa Company in 1889, which authorized the company to act on behalf of the British Government.[18]

In order to access mineral reserves, the British South Africa Company (BSAC) obtained various concessions from Paramount Chief Lewanika of Barotseland, in the Western Province of Zambia.[19] The chief claimed within his jurisdiction large tracts of land, and had also made various treaties with other chiefs in North Eastern Rhodesia. As a result of these concessions, the BSAC was able to assert ownership of all minerals throughout Zambia. It could essentially do what it wished with these minerals and could also 'levy royalties on all minerals won by whoever won them'.[20] The legitimacy of all the treaties and concessions formalized by the BSAC is of course questionable, largely owing to the fact that the chiefs it entered into the agreements with did not always have jurisdiction over the areas claimed.[21]

Furthermore, the concept of individual ownership of land was 'foreign to native ideas'.[22] Land belonged to the community and not to the individual and certainly not to the chief. The only role of the chief was as a custodian or caretaker of the land on behalf of the tribal community. Although chiefs were only loosely referred to as the 'owners' of the land, none of the tribes possessed a chief who had the right to dispose of land. Chiefs had the authority to permit people to settle on the land within their chiefdom and to cultivate it.[23] However, under customary law this did not connote that the settler then became the owner of the land.[24]

Subsequent to the concessions being granted, various prospectors came to the country, with the first short-lived commercial copper mines opened at Kansanshi in 1908 and Sable Antelope in 1911. The first concentrate was produced at Bwana

17 See *Zambia's Mining Industry: The First 50 Years* (Roan Consolidated Mining Ltd 1978) 15–16.
18 Chipasha C. Luchembe, 'Legacy of Late Nineteenth Century Capitalism: The Cases of W.R. Grace and C.J. Rhodes' (1996) 10 *Botswana Journal of African Studies* 40, 55.
19 Francis L. Coleman, *The Northern Rhodesia Copperbelt 1899–1962* (Manchester University Press 1971) 4–5.
20 Muna Ndulo, *Mining Rights in Zambia* (Kenneth Kaunda Foundation 1988) 36.
21 M.L.O. Faber, 'The Recovery of the Mineral Rights' in M.L.O. Faber and J.G. Potter (eds), *Towards Economic Independence: Papers on the Nationalization of the Copper Industry in Zambia* (Cambridge University Press 1971) 40, 51.
22 *Sobhuza II v Miller and Others* [1926] AC 518, 525 (Viscount Haldane).
23 Mphanza P. Mvunga, *Land Law and Policy in Zambia* (Institute for African Studies 1982) 22–23. See also *Mwiinda v Gwaba* (1974) ZR 188, 193.
24 Ndulo, *Mining Rights in Zambia* (n 20) 76–95.

Mukubwa in 1913. The first statute governing mining in Northern Rhodesia was the Mining Ordinance of 1912. This provided regulations under which the BSAC could regulate the mining rights it granted. It enabled any company simply to pay a small fee and search for minerals in any part of Northern Rhodesia that had not already been allocated by the BSAC.[25]

In 1922 the BSAC decided to open the country to large-scale prospecting companies.[26] Concurrently, a new colonial office had been established, although under a settlement the BSAC was allowed to retain its mineral rights even though it had to pay a royalty to the office.[27] Although the Great Depression had an impact on the mining industry this brief slump was later reversed by a commodity boom spurred by high demand resulting from the Second World War and post-war reconstruction and industrialization.[28]

A concatenation of circumstances eventually culminated in the mining industry being dominated by two foreign mining companies: the Roan Selection Trust and the Anglo American Corporation. By the time of nationalization the Roan Selection Trust had rights to the following mines: Luanshya, Chambishi, Kalulushi, Nkana and Mufulira. The Anglo American Corporation held Nchanga, Konkola, Chingola, Nampundwe and Chililabombwe. Most of these names will re-emerge as we discuss the process of privatization. The demand for labour around these mines led to the emergence of towns in what is now known as the Copperbelt Province of Zambia.

Much of the wealth that was generated from the production of copper was diverted from the Government of Northern Rhodesia. Because the BSAC owned the mineral rights, it had therefore received the considerable amount of £135 million from royalties by 1964.[29] Moreover, the BSAC's headquarters were located in London. Thus the British Government also received a considerable amount in taxes. Moreover, the actual taxes levied by the Northern Rhodesian Government remained low mainly due to the influence exerted on the aforementioned government by the mining companies.[30]

The Central African Federation was established in 1953.[31] This federation consisted of Northern Rhodesia, Southern Rhodesia and Nyasaland (now known as Zambia, Zimbabwe and Malawi respectively). Under the terms of the Central African Federation, all income received from the territories was pooled. Northern

---

25 Cf. Ndulo, 'Mining Legislation and Mineral Development in Zambia' (n 3) 7.
26 Lawrence Butler, *Copper Empire: Mining and the Colonial State in Northern Rhodesia, c. 1930–64* (Palgrave 2007) 15.
27 Ndulo, 'Mining Legislation and Mineral Development in Zambia' (n 3) 7.
28 Cf. Butler (n 26) 60–193,
29 Christopher Ushewokunze, 'The Legal Framework of Copper Production in Zambia' (1974) 6 *Zambia Law Journal* 75, 79.
30 ibid.
31 Alastair Fraser, 'Introduction: Boom and Bust on the Zambian Copperbelt' in Alastair Fraser and Miles Larmer (eds), *Zambia, Mining, and Neoliberalism Boom and Bust on the Globalized Copperbelt* (Palgrave Macmillan 2011) 1, 5.

Rhodesia received a very small proportion of this. It was understood at the time that the purpose of Northern Rhodesia was to be a source of mineral wealth that would in turn support the infrastructure of Southern Rhodesia. The mining activities on the Copperbelt virtually converted large tracts of bush into cities. Having looked at the history of Northern Rhodesia and its eventual purpose within the Federation of Rhodesia and Nyasaland, it can be seen that the *raison d'être* of Zambia was copper mining. It could thus be argued that the seeds of Zambia's status as a mono-economy were sown as far back as the early 1920s when full scale commercial copper mining had commenced.[32]

5.2.2 Independence and nationalization of the mines

Zambia attained her independence on 24 October 1964. Owing to her copper wealth she was one of the most prosperous countries in sub-Saharan Africa.[33] In fact, as a result of high copper prices and revenues, Zambia was classified as a middle income country in 1969.[34] President Kenneth Kaunda and his United National Independence Party (UNIP) had propounded some very ambitious plans for the development of Zambia.[35] These plans were contingent upon the government's revenues from Zambia's copper reserves, which had enjoyed favourable world prices in the 1960s.[36] The major concern at the time was that no new mines were being developed and the interests of the Zambian public were being made subservient to the interests of private mining companies. These sentiments preceded the government's decision to nationalize the mines in 1969.[37]

Following the independence of most African countries in the 1960s and 1970s, there was a general paradigmatic shift in the economic philosophy of the country. A number of newly emancipated countries began to follow a form of African socialism means of obtaining their economic independence from their former colonial masters who were inclined to the tenets of capitalism. Tanzania's policies were guided by the policy of *Ujamaa*[38] and Nkrumah's Ghana was guided by consciencism.[39] Zambia was no exception to this trend and adopted a form of

---

32 Cf. Fraser and Lungu (n 10) 7.
33 *United Nations Conference on Trade and Development: Investment Policy Review Zambia* (UN 2006), UNCTAD/ITE/IPC/2006/14, 3.
34 Cf. Lungu, 'Copper Mining Agreements in Zambia: Renegotiation or Law Reform?' (n 8) 404.
35 See generally *First National Development Plan 1966–1970* (Office of National Development and Planning, Lusaka, July 1966).
36 Cf. Fraser and Lungu (n 10) 7.
37 Muna Ndulo, 'The Nationalization of the Zambian Copper Industry' (1974) 6 *Zambia Law Journal* 55, 55.
38 See Julius K. Nyerere, *Ujamaa: Essays on Socialism* (OUP 1968).
39 See Kwame Nkrumah, *Consciencism: Philosophy and Ideology for Decolonisation and Development With Particular Reference to the African Revolution* (Heinemann 1964); Steven Metz, 'The Socialist Theories of Nkrumah and Nyerere' (1982) 20 *Journal of Modern African Studies* 377; Bonny Ibhawo and J.I. Dibua, 'Deconstructing Ujamaa: The Legacy of Julius Nyerere in the Quest for Social and Economic Development in Africa' (2003) 8 *African Journal of Political Science* 59.

socialism known as humanism.[40] This philosophy essentially prescribed that it was the government's responsibility to look after every Zambian citizen.[41]

Under the tenets of humanism, Zambia also became a one-party state.[42] Writing in 1966, President Kaunda explained that multiparty democracy was not necessary because most liberating governments had been voted in overwhelmingly by the people and as such had the mandate to govern. This signified that the government had the trust of the people to guide the new nation. In such circumstances an opposition party was unnecessary and was nothing more than a means of accommodating theorists who believed that a 'government-in-waiting' was necessary. In addition to this, all that the opposition did was cause division, which would have led to the anarchy seen in other newly independent states of the time such as Congo, Sudan and Pakistan.[43] Anarchy in Kaunda's view would simply paralyse every aspect of the nation. He summed up this theory in one line: 'The great enemy of freedom is not totalitarianism but chaos'.[44]

As noted above, there were many concerns about the structure of the mining industry in Zambia, which had remained unchanged since independence. Central to these concerns was the fact that the mining industry was dominated by two foreign corporations: Anglo American Corporation (AAC) and the Roan Selection Trust (RST). The perception was that these two corporations were making significant profits from the favourable copper prices. Despite this fact they had not developed any new mines.

These concerns were highlighted by President Kaunda in 1968. During his Mulungushi reforms speech the president expressed his disappointment about the 'virtual lack of mining development since independence'.[45] The government had acquired the BSAC's mining rights on the eve of independence, which meant it was receiving royalties from Anglo American Corporation and Roan Selection Trust.[46] The mining companies expressed a concern that the current royalties system was an obstacle to investment.[47] President Kaunda responded to this claim:

> Let me also say that I do not agree with the mining companies that royalties have been the obstacle to the development of the industry. I have been following their accounts and I know very well that they could have embarked

---

40 Kenneth D. Kaunda and Colin M. Moss, *A Humanist in Africa* (Longman 1966).

41 Carol Graham, *Safety Nets, Politics and the Poor* (The Brookings Institution 1994) 164.

42 Miles Larmer, 'Enemies Within? Opposition to the Zambian One-party State 1972–1980' in Jan-Bart Gewald, Marja Hinfelaar and Giacomo Macola (eds), *One Zambia, Many Histories* (Library of Congress 2008) 98, 98.

43 Cf. Kaunda and Moss (n 40) 107.

44 ibid 108.

45 Andrew Sardanis, *Africa Another Side of the Coin: Northern Rhodesia's Final Years and Zambia's Nationhood* (IB Tauris 2011) 229.

46 Ndulo, 'Mining Legislation and Mineral Development in Zambia' (n 3) 13.

47 Alastair Fraser, 'Introduction: Boom and Bust on the Zambian Copperbelt' in Alastair Fraser and Miles Larmer (eds), *Zambia, Mining, and Neoliberalism Boom and Bust on the Globalized Copperbelt* (Palgrave Macmillan 2011) 1, 8.

upon further expansion if they chose to devote part of their profits for this purpose. Instead of re-investing they have been distributing over 80 per cent of their profits every year as dividends.[48]

In 1969 the government announced that the mines would be nationalized. The two mining companies were forced to give 51 per cent of their stakes in the mines to the Government of the Republic of Zambia. It is argued that, at the time, the president opted to nationalize because he was under political pressure.[49] The fact that his vice president, Simon Mwansa Kapwepwe announced his resignation at the time, in the wake of a leadership struggle within UNIP, lends credence to this claim. However, one might argue that this was merely a factor and not a determinant. Conceivably, from Kenneth Kaunda's Mulungushi Reform speech, we can see that nationalism was also a contributing factor.

It was noted that the mining industry was mainly in the hands of two foreign companies. Since the Zambian economy was mainly reliant on copper, it meant that national interests would be superseded by foreign ones. Moreover, racial discrimination was rife in what was still a mainly white dominated industry. It was very rare to find indigenous Zambian citizens at the upper echelons of management. Even when they did reach management levels, the Zambian would become an outcast among his expatriate colleagues.[50] His performance would be undermined and he would be disgraced in front of subordinates.[51] Moreover, there was still a disparity in the conditions of service given to expatriates and those given to Zambians.[52]

The nationalization of the mining industry was facilitated first through amending the Constitutional provision that prohibited the government from compulsorily acquiring private assets. Once the Constitution had been amended, the government passed the Mines and Minerals Act 1969. Under this Act the government was not only able to take over the undeveloped mines; it was also able to acquire 51 per cent of shares in the mining companies, thus giving it control over the national mining industry.[53] The nationalized mining companies were compensated and were to participate in dividends over a period of eight to twelve years.[54] They were thus compensated for lost future profits.

The nationalized companies were later amalgamated to form Zambia Consolidated Copper Mines Limited (ZCCM) in 1982. Nationalizing the mining

---

48 Cf. Sardanis (n 45) 229.
49 J.G. Potter, 'The 51 Per Cent Nationalization of the Zambian Copper Mines' in M.L.O. Faber and J.G. Potter (eds), *Towards Economic Independence: Papers on the Nationalization of the Copper Industry in Zambia* (Cambridge University Press 1971) 91, 95.
50 Michael Burawoy, *The Colour of Class on the Copper Mines: From African Advancement to Zambianization* (Manchester University Press 1971) 38.
51 ibid.
52 ibid 39–41.
53 Cf. Ndulo, 'Mining Legislation and Mineral Development in Zambia' (n 3) 11.
54 Ndulo, 'The Nationalization of the Zambian Copper Industry' (n 37) 56–59.

companies did much to reduce the 'deeply ingrained suspicion of foreign economic domination'.[55] Whilst under state control the mines played a very key role in the lives of many Zambian people, particularly those living on the Copperbelt. As Fraser and Lungu note:

> ZCCM was seen as a reflection of the State's developmental philosophy and supplied amenities much wider in scope than those offered during the colonial period, including free education for miners' children, alongside subsidised housing and food, electricity, water and transport. ZCCM literally operated a 'cradle to grave' welfare policy, even subsidising burial arrangements for the dead. Although the system is often referred to as 'paternalistic', it should be remembered that these services were not all initiatives from the top-down. In many cases improvements in terms and conditions of living quarters were demanded by the powerful Mineworkers Union of Zambia.[56]

In addition, the mines provided various services to the community as a whole. For example, it was the mining companies that maintained the roads. They also provided various social amenities such as bars, cafeterias and sports clubs. Furthermore, the income from miners helped to foster local entrepreneurship by enabling people to set up supermarkets and farms for the supply of food to miners. Moreover, the mining companies built and maintained hospitals which provided services for both employees of the mines and the wider community alike.[57] The government also implemented a process of 'Zambianization' in which Zambian citizens were placed in the senior management of ZCCM rather than expatriates.[58]

The social advantages associated with the mines were contingent upon the price of copper remaining high. Even in 1969 as the nationalizations were taking place *Time Magazine* warned that:

> Kaunda's action entails serious risks for his country. Zambia has neither the capital nor the skills to run the mines by itself. Kaunda must rely heavily on both the companies and their remaining 5,000 white miners to keep operations going. Only the steadily rising price of copper, now at a high of $740 per pound, has enabled Zambia to maintain a favourable balance of payments in recent years. Any decline in copper prices as a result of an end of the war in Vietnam, the discovery of new sources, or the increased use of other minerals, would hit Zambia hard.[59]

---

55 Cf. Ndulo, *Mining Rights in Zambia* (n 20) 202.

56 Fraser and Lungu (n 10) 8.

57 ibid.

58 See generally Muna Ndulo, 'The Requirement of Domestic Participation in New Mining Ventures in Zambia' (1977) 7 *Georgia Journal of International and Comparative Law* 579.

59 *Time Magazine*, 'Mining: Nationalization in Zambia' (22 August 1969) http://www.time.com/time/magazine/article/0,9171,898567,00.html (last accessed 8 June 2015).

World events were soon to have an impact on this lifestyle that many Zambians had taken for granted. The first major event that took place was the oil crisis of 1974. Simultaneously, the price of copper collapsed. With reduced copper revenues the Government of Zambia was forced to borrow money in order to maintain the lifestyle that it had created during the boom years. It was effectively borrowing money to subsidize consumption. After the second oil crisis, which took place in 1979, interest rates escalated leaving Zambia in a severe debt crisis. This coupled with continued depreciation of copper prices led to Zambia going from a middle-income nation to one of the poorest in the world.[60]

The hardest hit were the people of Zambia that the policy of humanism had sought to benefit. Certainly, at the time of independence, humanism worked and living conditions did improve for the large majority, because funds were readily available. However, as soon as a downturn occurred these improvements quickly disappeared.[61] The situation was further exacerbated by the fact that during the economic crisis a great deal of money was being pulled out of the mines with very little of it being reinvested. This meant that there was less exploration and drilling going on and as such no new mines were opened after 1979. According to statistics, production decreased from a staggering 750,000 tonnes in 1973 to just 257,000 tonnes in 2000. The mines were making losses to the extent that the government had to borrow money to pay salaries. It was clear that in order to revive the mining industry foreign capital would be needed.[62]

As a result of the slump in copper prices, by 1994 Zambia had become the 25th poorest country in the world.[63] The economic decline led to popular discontent in the 1980s. The UNIP Government was perceived as having failed to formulate a coherent plan to combat the worsening economic crisis, which in turn undermined its legitimacy and credibility.[64] This popular discontent, coupled with an attempted coup, led to the government amending the Constitution and permitting the formation of other political parties.[65] Zambia thus returned to multiparty democracy in 1990.[66] The main opposition was the Movement for Multiparty Democracy (MMD), whose leader Frederick Chiluba had dismissed humanism as 'ruse behind which there is nothing of substance'.[67] The MMD promised to liberalize the economy and privatize the mines.

---

60 James Ferguson, *Expectations of Modernity: Myths and Meanings of Urban Life on the Zambian Copperbelt* (University of California Press 1999) 6–7.
61 Carol Graham, *Safety Nets, Politics and the Poor* (The Brookings Institution 1994) 164.
62 John Lungu, *The Politics of Reforming Zambia's Mining Tax Regime* (Southern Africa Resource Watch 2009) 16.
63 Ferguson (n 60) 6.
64 Carolyn Baylies and Morris Szeftel, 'The Fall and Rise of Multiparty Politics in Zambia' (1992) 54 *Review of African Political Economy* 75, 76.
65 Cf. Sardanis (n 45) 303.
66 Michael Bratton, 'Zambia Starts Over' (1992) 3 *Journal of Democracy* 81, 86.
67 Cf. Baylies and Szeftel (n 64) 86.

5.2.3 Privatization of the mines

A limited privatization programme commenced in 1990 under President Kenneth Kaunda. This was largely as a result of pressure from the IMF and the World Bank.[68] The World Bank had begun to exert pressure on the Kaunda administration as far back as 1983 when it introduced its first structural adjustment programme. From then on, the IMF and the World Bank had a great say on Zambia's economic policies. Zambia saw the folly of resisting the two institutions when it attempted to divorce the IMF in 1987. During that year the government through its 'New Economic Recovery Programme' had attempted to limit its debt-service payment to 10 per cent of net export earnings, which was lower than the IMF's preferred rate.

As a result Zambia's donors cut off their assistance to the state. Zambia continued to accumulate arrears with no actual income. As Fraser and Lungu put it: 'Within eighteen months the donors had made their point: the price of future support would be compliance with donor priorities'.[69] The government thus re-engaged with the IMF and the World Bank and took various required measures such as devaluing the currency, removing price controls and removing food subsidies.[70]

Once Zambia had taken these measures the donors came back in. However, by then President Kaunda and UNIP had lost the 1991 General Election to the MMD. Its leader Frederick Chiluba defeated President Kaunda in 1991 with 76 per cent of the national vote, whilst his party the MMD took 125 of the 150 seats in Parliament.[71] Among many of its promises the MMD under its manifesto undertook to liberalize the economy once it took office.[72] This programme had been endorsed by the Mineworkers' Union of Zambia, whose members had suffered badly as a result of the decline of the mines since nationalization. They saw liberalization as a means through which new investment could be attracted to the ailing industry.[73]

Subsequent to MMD's victory, donors poured a great deal of aid money into Zambia.[74] Many conditions had been attached to this aid, one of which was the privatization of 280 parastatal corporations. The major process of privatization thus commenced with the enactment of the Privatisation Act 1992.[75] By June 1996 the government had succeeded in selling 137 government owned corporations.

---

68 John Craig, 'Putting Privatisation Into Practice: The Case of Zambia Consolidated Copper Mines Ltd' (2001) 3 *Journal of Modern African Studies* 389, 391.
69 Cf. Fraser and Lungu (n 10) 9.
70 ibid.
71 See generally Baylies and Szeftel (n 64) 76.
72 Lungu, *The Politics of Reforming Zambia's Mining Tax Regime* (n 62) 16.
73 Cf. Fraser and Lungu (n 10) 9.
74 See generally Lise Rakner, Nicolas van de Walle and Dominic Mulaisho, 'Zambia' in Shantayanan Devarajan, David R. Dollar and Torgny Holmgren (eds), *Aid and Reform in Africa: Volume 1* (World Bank 2001).
75 Cf. Lungu, *The Politics of Reforming Zambia's Mining Tax Regime* (n 62) 13.

The World Bank later recommended the process as a model for other countries to follow because of the expedience, thoroughness and transparency with which it had been conducted.[76] Campbell and Bhatia particularly noted that: 'Zambia was the one country case study in which not one interview revealed any concern about the transparency of the process; detractors based their opposition to the program on the perceived effect on employment, not on the way the process was handled'.[77]

The process may have been thorough and expedient; however, it was certainly not transparent but a vehicle through which corrupt MMD officials including President Chiluba himself conducted what Transparency International called a 'looting exercise' in which they simply grabbed assets.[78] The Privatisation Act neither precluded government officials from acquiring a company nor did it require them to declare their intention to bid. This was one of the factors that facilitated corruption during the privatization process and ultimately demonstrates that the process was not transparent at all.[79]

The mines under ZCCM, which were seen as the 'crown jewels of the privatisation process',[80] went under extensive changes during the privatization process. There were several options considered when it came to the privatization of ZCCM. One of the options considered was the takeover of ZCCM as a whole by a transnational mining company. In fact, the Anglo American Corporation showed great interest in this regard. This was also supported by the Mineworkers Union of Zambia who were concerned about workers conditions being significantly degraded by intra-company competition.[81]

However, there were concerns about the implications of selling off ZCCM as a whole. One of these concerns was that if a foreign corporation were to monopolize the nation's prime asset then Zambia's developmental interests would become subsidiary to those of the Anglo American Corporation. This option was also considered potentially insalubrious because at the time various changes had been taking place in a recently liberated South Africa. The concern was that the Anglo American Corporation would be so preoccupied with those changes that it would be 'unlikely to commit the scale of resources required to rehabilitate existing operations and develop new mines'.[82]

The first concern highlighted was certainly later confirmed by the Anglo American Corporation's actions in 2002. It had eventually bought Konkola Copper Mines (KCM). However, it saw the venture as unprofitable owing to low

---

76 Oliver Campbell and Anita Bhatia, *Privatization in Africa* (World Bank 1998) 111.
77 ibid 156.
78 See John Craig, 'Evaluating Privatization in Zambia: A Tale of Two Processes' (2000) 27 *Review of African Political Economy* 357, 361.
79 Cf. Fraser and Lungu (n 10) 10.
80 Cf Lungu, 'Copper Mining Agreements in Zambia: Renegotiation or Law Reform?' (n 8) 405.
81 ibid 406,
82 Cf. Craig (n 78) 394,

copper prices and opted to pull out.[83] Hypothetically, if it had bought ZCCM as a whole and later chosen to abandon the project as it did with KCM, this would have led to economic collapse. Thus it could be argued that Zambia may very well have dodged a bullet by rejecting the option of selling ZCCM as a whole to Anglo American, or any corporation for that matter.

The alternative option considered and later adopted was to unbundle ZCCM and sell it piecemeal to different private investors, as recommended by the German firm Kienbaum Development Services GmbH.[84] Each of the mining divisions was to become a separate mining company. The majority interest in these companies was to be sold to private investors, whilst ZCCM would retain a minority interest and supply technical and support services. This solution fostered the potential to attract foreign capital from a number of foreign mining companies to resuscitate the ailing mining industry, whilst also averting the possibility of domination by one single multinational corporation. Although ultimately adopted this option was not immediately welcomed. Anglo American was certainly opposed to this option because of concerns that its minority share in ZCCM would be translated into minority shares in the smaller companies once sold off. This would leave it with control in none of them. The process of unbundling in Anglo American's view also lacked any commercial sense.

One might argue that Anglo American's concerns were not well founded. With reference to its first concern, it was already a minority shareholder anyway, exerting very little influence on mining policy in any event. Thus, it is perplexing that it would expect any more than it already had under the previous economic regime. Secondly, whilst the possibility of the disintegration of the company may have adversely affected the combined value of the assets it equally did not make business sense to have more profitable mines subsidizing the less profitable ones. Ultimately, one needs to keep in mind that Anglo American Corporation had a financial interest in opposing the unbundling of ZCCM. Again, this simply confirms the suspicion that had it dominated the mining industry, its interests would have taken precedence over national interests which, quite understandably, was not a very attractive option. As a result of the concerns highlighted by the Anglo American Corporation and others the government decided to explore the issue further.[85]

The other option considered was to keep ZCCM intact and float its shares on the stock exchange. This was very similar to what Ghana did with its Ashanti Goldfields in 1994, where it reduced its equity share by floating its shares on both the London and Ghanaian stock exchanges.[86] This option would help ZCCM in that it avoided the need to unbundle the corporation and at the same time

---

83 See 'Anglo American Quits Zambia' BBC News (Tuesday 20 August 2002) http://news.bbc.co. uk/1/hi/business/2205509.stm (last accessed 8 June 2015).
84 Craig (n 78) 394.
85 ibid 395.
86 See Antoinette Handley, 'Business, Government and the Privatisation of the Ashanti Goldfields Company in Ghana' (2007) 41 *Canadian Journal of African Studies* 1, 8–14.

averted the possibility of domination by a foreign mining company. The plan would involve obtaining additional financing and concentrate capital expenditure on the most profitable units of ZCCM. It would then sell off the least profitable units such as Chambishi and Kansanshi Mine.

The difficulty with this plan, however, is that it was not clear whether it would raise as much capital as it needed to resuscitate the mining industry. This was owing to the fact that at the time, even with a very optimistic valuation, the Chambishi Mine was not expected to raise more than US$50 million and Kansanshi was expected to raise even less. Furthermore, the option of putting ZCCM in even more debt was not particularly attractive and this was further compounded by the fact that floating the government's shareholding interests at current equity prices was unlikely to raise any more than US$30 million.

There was also the concern that further changes of ownership would require the agreement of Anglo American. Of course, the possibility of finding an investor at all was questionable. Before Ghana floated its shares in Ashanti Goldfields, it had made undertaken some extensive rehabilitation work on the project and, as a result, management gained the confidence of foreign investors. This is in contrast to ZCCM, which had not carried out any rehabilitation work. For this reason the possibility of obtaining an investor was questionable in any event.

Ultimately, the most viable option was the unbundling of ZCCM. The mines were broken down into seven. The first set of mines, and the largest, were the Nkana Mine which was packaged along with the Mufulira Mine and, concentrating and treating assets, became Mopani Copper Mines Plc (MCM). The Glencore Group had the largest share, taking on 73.1 per cent, whilst First Quantum Minerals Ltd would take on 16.9 per cent and ZCCM-IH (as it was now known) would have the remaining 10 per cent.

Zambia had also qualified in 1996 for the World Bank's Heavily Indebted Poor Countries (HIPC) initiative. This essentially meant that Zambia would be entitled to debt relief if she cleared certain hurdles. Under this scheme Zambia received even more pressure to privatize the mines. In addition, Zambia was required to establish a policy that was investor friendly. In order to facilitate investment Zambia passed the Mines and Minerals Act 1995 and the Investment Act 1993.[87] The latter Act repealed and replaced the Investment Act of 1991. The 1991 Act had established the Zambian Investment Centre, which was created to foster the process of investing in Zambia listed in Part III of the new Act. The said institution would continue under the 1993 Act.[88] The 1993 Act also created tax incentives,[89] removed exchange controls and provided various protections against

---

87 See Kenneth K. Mwenda, 'Legal Aspects of Foreign Direct Investment in Zambia' (1999) 6(4) *Murdoch University Electronic Journal of Law* http://www.murdoch.edu.au/elaw/issues/v6n4/mwenda64nf.html. Please note that the 1993 Act was eventually repealed and replaced by the Zambia Development Agency Act.
88 Section 4 of the Investment Act 1993.
89 See generally sections 24, 25, 26 and 31 of the Investment Act 1993.

The resource nationalism cycle in Zambia 113

forced acquisition of private corporations.[90] Moreover, corporations were now enabled to externalize funds with no government interference.[91] In addition to this, the Constitution of Zambia also provided that compensation would be paid, in instances where private property was seized. Article 16(1) of the Constitution states:

> Except as provided in this Article, property of any description shall not be compulsorily taken possession of, and interest in or right over property of any description shall not be compulsorily acquired, unless by or under the authority of an Act of Parliament which provides for payment of adequate compensation for the property or interest or right to be taken possession of or acquired.

The Mines and Minerals Act 1995 also provided incentives for mining in Zambia. In addition to this it also permitted government officials to enter into development agreements with multinational corporations. Under these agreements the government was able to give additional tax incentives, including paying lower royalties and corporate tax.[92] The development agreements fostered the sale of the mines to multinational corporations. Rothschild and Clifford Chance had advised the government to undertake the sale of the mines in two phases. Under phase one the government was to sell a majority of its shareholdings in ZCCM to multinational corporations and to hold on to a minority of its shares under a company called ZCCM Investment Holdings (ZCCM-IH). Under stage two the government was to sell all of its shares in ZCCM-IH to the Zambian public. Stage two is yet to come to fruition.[93]

In total, ZCCM was divided into seven bundles and sold off to multinational mining companies. The mines at Nchanga, Konkola and Nampundwe became Konkola Copper Mines (KCM). Initially this was held by the Anglo American Corporation, which chose to exercise its pre-emptive rights during the privatization process and took 65 per cent of KCM. It was to develop the new Konkola Deep Mining Project (KDMP). However, in 2002 it decided to pull out of Zambia because, in its view, KDMP would not generate as much money in the short term. KCM thus reverted to state ownership. As a result of this the country's biggest asset was almost brought to a halt. The newly elected President Levy Mwanawasa, also of the MMD, immediately sought out other investors for the project. In 2004 the MMD sold 51 per cent of interests in KCM to Vedanta at what can only be described as a knockdown price of US$25 million.

To a certain extent this decision would haunt the Mwanawasa administration because, within a year, copper prices increased dramatically. According to the

---

90 Section 35 of the Investment Act 1993.
91 Section 36 of the Investment Act 1993.
92 Section 9 of the Mines and Minerals Act 1995.
93 Cf. Lungu, 'Copper Mining Agreements in Zambia: Renegotiation or Law Reform?' (n 8) 407.

London Metal Exchange the price of copper stood at US$2500 per ton at the beginning of 2004 and rose up to just over US$5000 per ton in 2005.[94] Thus, within a year Vedanta had recouped its initial US$25 million investment.[95] The Mwanawasa administration was intensely criticised because of this. However, I would argue that history will judge the parties more favourably. Put into context, KCM was one of Zambia's most productive mining companies. Without the investment in the copper mine it could not run and if it did not run this would have had severe repercussions for Zambia as a whole. The fact that Mwanawasa was a newly elected president in a fledgling African democracy would have further magnified the need to get this right. This would have called for some tough decision-making. He did not possess the luxury of hindsight that we do today. For this reason I believe that history will judge his decision more favourably.

The smaller facilities located at Baluba and Luanshya, along with the Mulayashi greenfield site, were combined to form the Roan Antelope Mining Corporation of Zambia (RAMCOZ). This was eventually bought by the J&W Group and Enya Holdings BV from Switzerland and was renamed Luanshya Mines Plc. In addition to this, these companies also purchased the smelter at Chambishi, along with the acid and cobalt plants, and the Nkana slag dumps were sold together to form Chambishi Metals Plc. The mine at Chambishi was sold separately from the smelter and other assets to form Chambishi Mines Plc. This was purchased by a Chinese mining company called Non-Ferrous Metals Co. The mine at Kansanshi, and an acid plant were juxtaposed to form Bwana Mukubwa Mines Ltd. This was purchased by First Quantum Minerals Ltd from Canada. Finally, the mine at Kalulushi became Chibuluma Mines Plc, which was purchased by Metorex from South Africa.[96]

This section has demonstrated that mining in Zambia has gone through three waves. The first wave commenced when the mines were first established to 1969. During this phase mining in Zambia was dominated by the Roan Selection Trust (RST) and the Anglo American Corporation (AAC). The second phase took place between 1969 and 1997 when the government of Zambia nationalized the mining companies and eventually merged them into one single corporation called ZCCM. The final phase took place after 1997 when ZCCM was split into seven different units, which were all sold to multinational mining companies.

5.3 The resource nationalism cycle in Zambia: from privatization to the windfall tax

This section illustrates the cyclical nature of resource nationalism in Zambia. When the Government of Zambia was seeking to attract foreign direct investment

---

94 London Metal Exchange http://www.lme.com/copper_graphs.asp (last accessed 8 June 2015).
95 Fraser and Lungu (n 10) 13.
96 Lungu, 'Copper Mining Agreements in Zambia: Renegotiation or Law Reform?' (n 8) 406.

The resource nationalism cycle in Zambia   115

in its mining sector, it granted very liberal terms to the foreign investors.[97] Once the investment had been sunk, the copper price experienced a sustained upward trend. It was during this period that pressure from civi society and opposition political parties heightened. It was argued that, due to the low taxation on copper mines, Zambia was not maximizing the benefits of high copper prices.

This popular discontent was reflected in the 2006 General Election, when the Patriotic Front led by Michael Sata gained massive support in the urban areas and won every seat there. The Patriotic Front campaigned on a promise that it would increase mining taxes. Although the MMD ultimately won the election, this and other factors caused the MMD to rethink the preferential tax regime that the foreign mining companies had previously enjoyed. Therefore, the MMD proceeded to introduce the windfall tax in 2008.

This section illustrates that various factors contributed to this. The first was the high copper prices, the political pressure and the fact that the MMD had a majority in Parliament. According to the Electoral Commission of Zambia, during the 2006 General Election, the MMD won 73 seats out of 148 contested seats. In addition, the MMD also won the presidency. Constitutionally, the president is allowed to appoint eight members of Parliament. This would give the MMD a majority in the legislature.[98]

5.3.1 Entering into agreements

As highlighted in the preceding sections, the copper mining industry was first in the hands of private individuals and then nationalized to form ZCCM. When the latter began to operate at a loss, the Government of Zambia proceeded to privatize that entity. To facilitate the process of privatization the government had signed various development agreements with multinational corporations. These development agreements were entered into under the auspices of the Mines and Minerals Act 1995. In order to explore the legality of the windfall tax one must look to the development agreements between the government and the multinational mining companies. Development agreements were defined in the Mines and Minerals Act 1995[99] as 'an agreement entered into under section nine in relation to a large-scale mining licence'. Section 9 of the Act states as follows:

> (1) For the purpose of encouraging and protecting large-scale investments in the mining sector in Zambia, the Minister may, on behalf of the Republic, enter into an agreement relating to the grant of a large-scale mining licence.

---

97 Christopher Adam and Anthony M. Simpasa, 'Harnessing Resource Revenues for Prosperity in Zambia' (OxCarre Research Paper 36, Revised Draft) 25–27 http://www.oxcarre.ox.ac.uk/images/stories/papers/RevenueWatch/oxcarrerp201036.pdf (last accessed 8 June 2015).

98 Electoral Commission of Zambia http://www.elections.org.zm/past_election_results.php (last accessed 8 June 2015).

99 Chapter 218 of the Laws of Zambia (now repealed).

(2) An agreement referred to in subsection (1) shall be known as a development agreement, and may contain provisions, which notwithstanding the provisions of any law or regulation shall be binding on the Republic. . . .

Ministers were thus granted the authority by Parliament to enter into development agreements with mining companies. It is also clear that the provisions were binding on the Republic of Zambia. All of the agreements contained tax stability clauses and some of them contained generally worded stabilization clauses in addition to the tax stability clauses. An example of the wording of the general stabilization clause is contained in the development agreement with Konkola Copper Mines. It stated as follows:

> GRZ further undertakes, during the Stability Period, it shall not by general or special legislation or by administrative measures or decree or by any other action or omission whatsoever (other than an act of nationalisation such as is referred to in Clause [. . .]) ('GRZ Action') vary, amend, cancel or terminate this Agreement or the rights and obligations of the Parties under this Agreement, or cause this Agreement or the said rights and obligations to be varied, amended, cancelled or terminated, or prevent or hinder performance of this Agreement by any party thereto, provided always that this Agreement and the rights and obligations of the Parties under this Agreement may be varied, amended, cancelled or terminated as expressly provided herein. GRZ undertakes that KCM and its officers, directors, employees and shareholders shall be held free and made exempt from any GRZ Action or any change in the law of Zambia which would, but for such freedom or exemption, adversely affect KCM's rights under, or KCM's ability to comply with its obligations under, this Agreement.

The tax stability clauses, which all the contracts contained, were more specific. In these agreements the government undertook not to increase taxes including corporate tax and royalties, for a stability period of 15–20 years, in a way that would have a 'material adverse effect' on the distributable profits of the foreign owned mining companies.[100] The government was, at least in the abstract, precluded from increasing taxes and introducing any new taxes for a period of 15 years, which was to constitute the tax stability period.[101]

There has been much speculation as to why the Government of Zambia entered into these asymmetrical agreements in the first place.[102] The answer may lie in the fact that Zambia was trying to attract much needed investment. At the time,

---

100 See for example the Mopani Copper Mines Development Agreement http://www.minewatch zambia.com/agreements.html (last accessed 8 June 2015).
101 Oshionebo (n 9) 18.
102 Lungu, *The Politics of Reforming Zambia's Mining Tax Regime* (n 62) 16.

The resource nationalism cycle in Zambia 117

copper prices were low and the mines were operating at a loss. The government provided incentives owing to the lacklustre response from multinational corporations during the privatization process. The government was thus left in the precarious position of providing tax incentives or simply closing the mines.[103]

According to the former Minister of Finance, Edith Nawakwi, the mines at the time were making losses of up to US\$1 million a day. The mines were headed for shutdown and, in order to stay afloat and pay salaries to workers, the government had to borrow large sums. In order to turn the mines around, huge sums of money needed to be raised and the government was in no position to do this. For this reason, foreign direct investment was needed and in order to attract this investment it needed to accept the terms of these contracts, pernicious as they may have seemed.

Moreover, it must be remembered that the government was also under pressure from the World Bank and the IMF to privatize the mines so that it could qualify for debt relief. To borrow the words of Edith Nawakwi: 'it was like somebody was pointing a gun to your head'.[104] There are also suggestions that ministers may have benefited from secret deals.

What is clear, however, is that the development agreements were asymmetrical and by 2008 the Government of Zambia sought to rectify this through further agreements and by increasing taxes. In his 2008 budget speech the then Minister of Finance, Ng'andu Magande announced that there would be a new tax regime governing the mines in which copper revenues would 'adequately contribute to the advancement and the social and economic welfare of the people of Zambia'.[105]

5.3.2 The shortcomings of privatization

There were several advantages associated with the privatization process. These advantages are perhaps best summed up by the Permanent Secretary of the Ministry of Mines who noted that: 'It has been very, very successful. Closed mines have opened up, new mines are coming up and the existing mines were limping and they are [now] all doing very well'.[106] One very notable advantage was the presence of new foreign capital. It must be recalled that under ZCCM the mines were stalling and this was further compounded by low copper prices. The process of privatization ensured the flow of foreign capital, which in turn was used to resuscitate an ailing industry. Even the heavily critical Mineworkers' Union of

---

103 See the Ministerial Statement on the Status of Mining Taxation by the Hon. Situmbeko Musokotwane, http://www.parliament.gov.zm/index.php?option=com_docman&task=doc_view&gid=770 (last accessed 8 June 2015).

104 Edith Nawakwi quoted in Lungu, *The Politics of Reforming Zambia's Mining Tax Regime* (n 62) 16.

105 Budget Address by The Hon. Ng'andu P. Magande, MP Minister of Finance and National Planning: Delivered to the National Assembly on 25 January 2008 http://www.parliament.gov.zm/index.php?option=com_docman&task=doc_view&gid=242 (last accessed 8 June 2015).

106 Interview with Leonard Nkhata quoted in Fraser and Lungu (n 10) 19.

Zambia was forced to concede that: '[s]ince 1998 we have close to US$1.4 billion which has gone into the mining industry, into refurbishment of plants, and purchases of spares and machinery. So one sees that privatization addressed capitalization, the issue of refurbishing and the issue of exploration and drilling. It has shown in the increased copper production'.[107] Because the mines were rehabilitating a previously stagnant industry it could be argued that the government had achieved one of its intended objectives through the process of privatization.

Tied to rehabilitation of the mines was increased production. As has been noted, copper production in 1982 was 591,853 tons. This dropped to 415,645 tons in 1989, before eventually declining to just over 250,000 before the process of privatization had been finalized. According to the Zambian Chamber of Mines, production began to rebound. For example, in 2001 production increased to 300,000 tons per year and this steadily increased to just above 450,000 tons in 2005. By 2009 this had increased dramatically to more than 650,000 and leapt to 850,000 in 2011. These statistics prove that mining companies had become more productive once they had been privatized as opposed to when they were under government control. Moreover, new mines began to open up for the first time in 25 years.[108] Among these were Lumwana Mine, which is fully functional and the Trident Mine, which was under construction at the time of writing. These are both located in the Northwestern Province of Zambia.

There were also, however, some notable disadvantages. Although privatization recapitalized the industry there were also mass redundancies. In 1976, 62,222 were employed by the mining industry. Despite the decline in the industry employment generally stood at 56,582 in 1991. By the time the process of privatization had been finalized, jobs in the mining industry were slashed to 19,145 in 2001, although this did increase slightly to 19,900 in 2004. Many workers were made redundant by the process of privatization. When the multinational mining companies were moving in they had told the government they wanted no liability in paying pensions or other retrenchment packages. These responsibilities were thus left at the door of government. The difficulty, however, is that at the time the government treasury did not have very much money. The IMF and the World Bank had asked the government to focus more on debt service when framing the budget. As a result it became very onerous on the government to pay pensions. This again led to resentment by the general populace, who saw the mining companies as a foreign force that had come into the country, was making profits and causing mass unemployment. In short, the Zambian people felt that foreigners were taking a huge advantage much to the detriment of the people.

Tied to the issue of employment is the propensity of mining companies to employ people on fixed-term contracts, which have no security or pension attached to them. They also tend to sub-contract the work out. Although the

107 Interview with Charles Muchimba quoted in Fraser and Lungu (n 10) 19.
108 ibid 20–21.

general safety record on mines has improved since privatization this is actually not the case for staff that are sub-contracted. This is particularly evident for contractors who work in mine development, which entails preparing new tunnels for mining. Under the 'support compliance' regulations, contractors are precluded from asking miners to work in an unsupported roof span of more than two metres when developing a new tunnel. This is to avert the possibility of rock falls. Because contractors are paid by the metre it is not uncommon to find a situation whereby workers develop as much as 20 metres without protection. Rock falls are actually a very common problem in mining companies as a result.[109]

Privatization also had a large impact on the community as a whole in the mining towns. Most families in Zambia still relied primarily on one cash income, which typically came from the father.[110] A majority of the miners, being men, were unemployed, leaving many families without a steady income. This was further compounded by the fact that the schooling and health facilities provided by the mines under ZCCM were also scrapped, making life more onerous for the people living in the mining towns. Furthermore, as a result of mass pollution caused by the mines, people were unable to grow their own food to sustain themselves. Excess sulphur dioxide emissions caused by smelting led to acid rain, which destroyed the crops. Without a steady income, people could not buy food and the very little they could grow was being destroyed.[111]

In addition, the sulphur dioxide emissions caused respiratory diseases.[112] Moreover, the mines discharged much of their waste into the rivers. Poorer communities who had no access to piped water often had to draw their water directly from the river. This water was used not only for drinking but also for crops. Thus the emission of waste in rivers was as a result of this very hazardous. For those that had access to piped water, the local authorities had to spend more and more money on purifying the water. This ultimately meant raising the water rates, again making life more onerous for the people living in mining towns. This caused even more resentment.[113]

Much of this resentment was targeted at the Chinese investors whose state owned company Non-Ferrous Company Africa (NFCA) owns the Chambishi Mine.[114] Of the 2100 people employed, only 52 were Zambian unionized employees on permanent contracts.[115] In addition, 687 were on fixed-term

---

109 Cf. Fraser and Lungu (n 10) 24.
110 ibid 32.
111 ibid 33.
112 ibid.
113 ibid.
114 Pengtao Li, 'The Myth and Reality of Chinese Investors: A Case Study of Chinese Investment in Zambia's Copper Industry' (2010) *Southern African Institute of International Affairs*, Occasional Paper Number 62 at 9 http://www.eisourcebook.org/cms/June%202013/Myth%20&%20Reality%20 of%20Chinese%20Investors,%20Zambian%20Copper%20Case%20Study.pdf (last accessed 8 June 2015).
115 Fraser and Lungu (n 10) 48–49.

contracts, whilst 1093 were employed indirectly through two Chinese sub-contracting firms. The subcontracted workers earned as little as K120,000–K150,000. According to the exchange rate at the time they were essentially earning between US$40 and US$50 per month.[116]

In addition, NFCA employed 180 Chinese employees, who were all on permanent contracts. There was a senior management team consisting of 12 people.[117] Eleven of them were Chinese and only one was Zambian. This was at variance with the development agreement in which NFCA undertook to 'take all reasonable efforts in its recruitment and employment of employees in its professional, managerial, engineering and scientific grades . . . to bring to the attention of such qualified Zambians, positions available within NFCA'.[118] Having more expatriates than Zambians at the upper echelons of management is a common occurrence amongst foreign owned mining companies.

Healthcare is rather difficult to access in the town of Chambishi. The 52 members of staff on permanent salaries and their dependants are able to access this. However, the non-permanent staff also have access but may only nominate one person of their choice. This can be problematic for people who have families. The development agreements do oblige NFCA to provide healthcare to its employees and their families; however, the corporation argues that contractual members of staff are technically not employees of the company.[119]

One of the other impacts in Chambishi is the growth of informal settlements. When privatizing, ZCCM sold all of its houses to sitting employees. However, because many of them had no formal employment they were forced to move and rent their houses out so they could have some sort of an income. They would then move to shanty towns. The municipal council used to service water and sewerage in these areas. It relied primarily on ZCCM for financing to do this. This financing was withdrawn as a result of privatization. Because most people living in Chambishi were unemployed and very poor it meant the council could not collect user fees. This loss of finance coupled with the overcrowding meant that the council had more obligations and less money to fulfil them with. Services were thus frequently suspended and there was no money to invest in further infrastructure to deal with the overcrowding.[120]

The Chambishi disaster of 2005 did much to fan the anti-Chinese sentiment.[121] This disaster involved an accident at the explosives manufacturing plant BGRIMM, which was a subsidiary of NFC Africa.[122] Fifty-two people died. It emerged in the

---

116 ibid 49.
117 ibid.
118 Clause 6.8 of the development agreement between the Government of Zambia and Non-Ferrous Metals http://minewatchzambia.blogspot.co.uk/ (last accessed 8 June 2015).
119 Fraser and Lungu (n 10) 50.
120 Cf. ibid 51.
121 Li (n 114) 9.
122 ibid.

aftermath that the company had been breaching labour regulations and had not maintained an adequate record of the workers at the plant.[123]

It must be emphasized, however, that these challenges caused by privatization are not limited to Chinese companies. The pollution for example highlighted above is perpetrated by Vedanta, which is an Indian company. It is also clear that, as far as senior management is concerned, most of the other companies which are Swiss, British, South African and Canadian owned are also guilty of employing a disproportionate number of expatriates. Thus, levelling resentment solely at Chinese investors is somewhat questionable.

Because the privatized mines were all foreign owned there was the other challenge of externalization of profits. Once the mines had made their profits the money would leave the country without having any tangible impact on the local economy. Because the mines are now in private hands it essentially means that the government no longer directly gains any income from sales and profits accrued by the mines. This means that it has to rely solely on taxation. The difficulty with this is the tax holiday that all the mining companies received during the process of privatization.

5.3.2.1 Introduction of the windfall tax

5.3.2.1.1 LOW TAXATION AND HIGH COPPER PRICES

One of the factors contributing to the resource nationalism cycle in Zambia was the sustained upward trend of world copper prices. This and the tax incentives granted to mining companies meant that the government was losing out on substantial revenue. The mineral royalty, as provided in the development agreements, stood at 0.6 per cent, which was significantly lower than the 3 per cent provided for by the Mines and Minerals Act 1995.[124] Moreover, company income tax under the development agreements stood at 25 per cent of gross income. This was lower than the 35 per cent ordinarily charged to other corporations in other industries. These preferential tax rates were thus introduced as a means of encouraging otherwise disinterested investors to pour their capital into Zambia.[125]

The World Bank described the contribution of mining revenues to the treasury as 'extremely small'.[126] The Marginal Effective Tax Rate (METR) calculated by the World Bank stood at zero per cent 'because of the relatively low tax rates and significant incentives' that the mining sector enjoyed. This can be contrasted with

---

123 Dag Haglund, 'Regulating FDI in Weak African States: A Case Study of Chinese Copper Mining in Zambia' (2008) 46 *The Journal of Modern African Studies* 547, 556.
124 See generally the repealed Mines and Minerals Act 1995, Chapter 218 of the Laws of Zambia. See also Lungu, 'Copper Mining Agreements in Zambia: Renegotiation or Law Reform?' (n 8) 407.
125 *United Nations Conference on Trade and Development Investment Policy Review Zambia* (UN 2006) 21–22.
126 *Zambia: Sectoral Study of the Effective Tax Burden* (December 2004) Foreign Investment and Advisory Service (FIAS), a joint service of the World Bank and IFC, 39 http://siteresources.worldbank.org/EXTEXPCOMNET/Resources/2463593-1213973103977/10_Zambia.pdf (last accessed 8 June 2015).

122 Resource nationalism in international investment law

other sectors of the economy. Tourism for example had an METR of 0–10 per cent, whereas small business was 25–35 per cent, and the financial sector was 25–35 per cent. Comparatively, therefore, the mining industry brought in very little revenue.[127]

World copper prices experienced a surge. By 2006 they had increased to more than US$8000 per ton. By 2005, First Quantum Minerals Ltd was making net earnings of US$152.8 million. This can be contrasted with its earnings of US$4.6 million in 2003.[128] Similarly, Konkola Copper Mines made US$206 million in 2006, which is almost quadruple the US$52 million it made in 2005.[129] In addition to this, it was reported that Zambia actually had the lowest copper revenue in comparison not only to its counterparts in Africa but also around the world. For example Chile, in the 2005/2006 fiscal year, made US$8 billion from copper in sharp contrast to Zambia, which only made US$10 million.[130] It had become apparent that the prevailing tax regime at the time was not providing sufficient revenue to the government. In order to maximize the revenues generated, the government would have to raise taxes.

Moreover, despite the rise in copper prices Zambia was still a shadow of its former self during the ZCCM days. This led to a prevailing feeling of resentment because the perceived profits that the multinational mining companies were making were not directly benefiting the people of Zambia.

5.3.2.1.2 POLITICAL INFLUENCE

The Zambian Government also came under extreme political pressure to maximize the amount of revenue from the surge in copper prices. Not only was the government being pressured by civil society but it was also being pressured by opposition political parties to renegotiate the development agreements. In addition to this, it came under pressure from external groups such as Scottish Catholic International Aid Fund (SCAIF) and Christian Aid and Action for Southern Africa (ACTSA).[131] Zambia conducts tripartite elections every five years.[132] The people of Zambia vote directly for their president.[133] At the same time they also vote for their members of Parliament and city councillors.[134]

---

127 ibid vii–xi.
128 First Quantum Minerals Ltd, *Annual Report* 2005 http://www.first-quantum.com/files/doc_financials/2005AR.pdf (last accessed 8 June 2015).
129 Vedanta Resources Plc, Annual Report 2006 http://www.vedantaresources.com/uploads/vedanta2006annualreportv1.pdf (last accessed 8 June 2015).
130 Joan Chirwa, 'Be Open on Mine Taxes, Sichinga Advises Govt' (2008) *Business Post* (1 April 2008), cited in Lungu, 'Copper Mining Agreements in Zambia: Renegotiation or Law Reform?' (n 8) 409.
131 Lungu, *The Politics of Reforming Zambia's Mining Tax Regime* (n 62) 18.
132 Electoral Commission of Zambia website (n 98).
133 Muna Ndulo, 'The Democratization Process and Structural Adjustment in Africa' (2003) 10 *Indiana Journal of Global and Legal Studies* 315, 356; art 34, Constitution of Zambia.
134 Electoral Commission of Zambia website (n 98).

Public resentment of perceived exploitation from foreign mining companies was perhaps reflected in the General Election of 2006. Although the sitting MMD Government ultimately won the 2006 election, it did lose all urban seats on the Copperbelt and in Lusaka. The opposition Patriotic Front did well in those areas. In its manifesto it promised to increase mineral taxes and reduce personal taxes on mine workers. These promises seem to have resonated well with most of the urban workers, who conceived that the MMD had sold out the country to foreign mining companies, at the expense of the welfare of the people of Zambia.[135]

The MMD won the presidential election of 2006. In addition, it won 73 seats out of 150. It only maintained its majority in Parliament because the President has the Constitutional right to appoint eight members of Parliament.[136] The Patriotic Front, on the other hand, gained 43 seats, up from two in the previous Parliament.[137] The MMD Government could not ignore the significant gains that the opposition had made in Parliament. The Government of Zambia decided to reconsider the taxation regime that the mining companies had enjoyed. The government had initially set up a team to renegotiate the terms of the development agreements, with the aid of the World Bank. However, this process was never undertaken. Instead, in a bid to reassert the sovereignty of Zambia and emboldened by support from the opposition and civil society alike, the government proceeded to terminate all contracts unilaterally. The paradigmatic shift in government policy is encapsulated in a statement by the then Deputy Minister of Finance, Jonas Shakafuswa, who stated that:

> Our colleagues should understand that the Zambian people are in a hurry to develop and they should not frustrate this because this decision was made by the government based on the wishes of the Zambian people. . . . So if they decide to resist these changes, they will be leaving a bad legacy not only for themselves but for all international companies. And remember, these changes are a call of the people, so if they want to frustrate this decision, then they will face the wrath of Zambian people.[138]

A new fiscal and regulatory regime was thus implemented in 2008. This system was intended to 'ensure that the tax regime remains stable and robust' and 'works efficiently and effectively for both high and low metal prices as well as high and low cost operating mines'.[139] The overall objective of the government of the day was to have an effective tax rate of no more than 47 per cent on the mining sector.

---

135 Lungu, *The Politics of Reforming Zambia's Mining Tax Regime* (n 62) 19.
136 Jeremy Gould, 'Zambia's 2006 Elections: the Ethnicization of Politics?' (2007) 1 *The Nordic Africa Institute* 5–9. See also art 63(1)(b) and art 68(1) of the Constitution of Zambia.
137 Gould (n 136).
138 Hon. Jonas Shakafuswa MP, quoted in Fraser (n 47) 20.
139 Situmbeko Musokotwane (n 103) 2.

In order to foster this, the government nullified all development agreements that had been signed by passing the Mines and Minerals Development Act No. 7 of 2008. Section 160(1) of this Act stated that: '[a] development agreement which is in existence before the commencement of this Act shall . . . cease to be binding on the Republic from the commencement of this Act'.

A plethora of new measures were introduced under the new fiscal regime. The government increased the corporate tax rate from 25 per cent to 35 per cent. The government also increased the mineral royalty rate from 0.6 per cent to 3 per cent. In addition, a variable windfall tax was introduced on various metals including copper. The windfall tax was triggered at various levels. For copper, the windfall tax would be 25 per cent in instances where the price per tonne was US$2500 to US$3000; 50 per cent when the price was between US$3000 and US$3500 per tonne; and 75 per cent when the price exceeded US$3500 per tonne. It was projected by the Ministry of Finance that these measures would bring in an additional US$415 million from the mining industry in 2008.[140]

The mining companies resisted these changes, because they rendered operations more onerous. It was noted by the Minister of Finance that the windfall tax had some major flaws and was very weak in its design.[141] As a result, the effective tax rate was actually higher than that intended. The effective tax rate for high cost mines ranged between 64 and 96 per cent. For low cost mines it ranged between 57 and 64 per cent. This was clearly above the rate intended by the government, which was up to 47 per cent. The Minister of Finance, Dr Situmbeko Musokotwane MP further stated that:

> the marginal tax rates, particularly for high costs mines, were very high, in some cases even higher than 100 percent. This simply meant that for every 1 dollar increase in the price above the highest trigger level of copper price, a mining company had to pay taxes of more than one dollar. Additionally, the design of the windfall tax in the Zambian case was defective and not consistent with international practice as it was based on revenue as opposed to profit. It therefore did not take into account the cost of production. Sir, in countries with similar taxes, they are always profit based.[142]

It would thus appear that the fiscal system that followed the unilateral cancellation of the mining agreements discussed was deeply flawed. The effective tax rate on mining companies not only rendered operations more onerous and expensive but, as a result of this, some mining companies resisted the windfall tax altogether.

140 Lungu, *The Politics of Reforming Zambia's Mining Tax Regime* (n 62) 19.
141 Ministerial Statement on the Status of Mining Taxation http://www.parliament.gov.zm/index.php?option=com_docman&task=doc_view&gid=770 (last accessed 8 June 2015).
142 ibid.

The legality of the windfall tax was also questioned. This is owing to the fact that the government increased taxes during the stability period, which was clearly prohibited by all the contracts. As we have seen in previous chapters, the breach of stabilization clauses certainly renders the state liable to pay some form of monetary compensation to the injured investor.[143] This will certainly include the payment of *damnum emergens* and the payment of lost future profits (*lucrum cessans*). The amount payable will obviously be determined by an arbitral tribunal, should the mining companies elect to initiate proceedings, as First Quantum has done.[144]

In 2009, world copper prices fell as a result of the effects of the global financial crisis.[145] As a consequence of this, the mining companies announced that there would be major job losses in the mining sector.[146] The government was thus compelled to announce several concessions to the mining sector. This included abandoning the windfall tax. Some have argued that this was done in exchange for the mining companies accepting the initial cancellation of the development agreements.[147]

5.3.3 Lessons for Zambia

As has been seen from this section and those preceding it, Zambia is a good example of the cyclical nature of resource nationalism. At independence in 1964 its mines were privately owned. Wishing to maximize the benefits from this, the host state decided to nationalize the mines in 1969 by taking up 51 per cent shares in the mines held by the Roan Selection Trust and Anglo American Corporation Ltd. This represented the first wave of the resource nationalism cycle in Zambia. Subsequent to negotiations the Government of Zambia compensated the mines.[148]

The amount of compensation payable was determined by negotiation and not by a court or arbitral tribunal. The Roan Selection Trust was paid a sum of K84.15 million, which was to be paid in US dollars.[149] The Anglo American Corporation Ltd, on the other hand, was to be paid a sum of K125.766 million, also to be paid in US dollars. The price of the assets was based on the book value as at 31 December 1969. In terms of how the government would pay, it was agreed that payments would be rendered out of future profits made by the government. This meant that the Government of Zambia was to meet the payments from the dividends on its 51 per cent share in the companies.[150]

---

143 Oshionebo (n 9) 33.
144 'First Quantum Minerals Drops Lawsuit Against Zambian Government Filed in UK' *Lusaka Times* http://www.lusakatimes.com/2014/03/02/first-quantum-minerals-drops-lawsuit-zambian-government-filed-uk/ (last accessed 12 June 2015).
145 Mwambwa, Griffiths and Kahler (n 5) 7.
146 ibid.
147 ibid.
148 Ndulo, 'The Nationalization of the Zambian Copper Industry' (n 39) 56.
149 ibid 58.
150 ibid.

Through mismanagement, a slump in the price of copper and other factors, the mines became less profitable. In order to resuscitate them, foreign direct investment was sought and fostered through the privatization programme and the entering into of agreements between the Government of Zambia and foreign mining companies. These agreements contained stabilization clauses and tax stability clauses, which were to run for 15–20 years. In other words, the government had expressly undertaken not to raise taxes unilaterally or to do anything that would have a material adverse effect on the commercial interests of the mines for the stipulated period. When the price of copper appreciated, the government sought to maximize the benefits accruing from this. Thus, it terminated all agreements and increased corporate taxes and royalties and also introduced a windfall tax. This second wave of the resource nationalism cycle in Zambia represented a breach of the government's contractual obligations.

Breach of contracts containing stabilization clauses will render the government liable to compensate the investor. There is a plethora of jurisprudence which shows that arbitral tribunals respect the sanctity of contracts and will not allow host states unilaterally to abrogate contracts containing these clauses.[151] Despite this fact, however, we have seen from Zambia and other case studies that governments still tend to abrogate such rigid contracts unilaterally, in the advanced stages of the resource nationalism cycle. This is because they wish to maximize the revenue they could potentially gain from high prices. They will often be under intense political pressure to do so, as seen from the Zambian case study. Governments could either raise taxes or nationalize the foreign investors' assets altogether. The former of these was what transpired in Zambia.

The difficulty, however, is that should the investor sue the Government of Zambia, the latter will almost certainly have to compensate the investor. From the findings in the previous chapter, it is clear that the compensation package will include compensation indemnifying the mining companies not only for their sunk costs but also for *lucrum cessans* or lost future profits.[152] This is a reflection of the fact that tribunals respect the sanctity of contracts and it is thus reflected in their compensation awards. Moreover, arbitral tribunals seek to restore the investor to the position the latter would have been in had the breach not taken place.[153]

Should this occur, this will lead to a loss of revenue for the Zambian Government. The inflexibility this leads to precludes the Government of Zambia from exercising its legitimate public functions. However, to rule otherwise will also have an impact on the legitimate expectations of the investor. The reality, however, is that the prices of natural resources are mercurial and are subject to change over time. This factor will necessitate entering into flexible contracts so that the state and the investor can episodically revisit the terms of the concession as and when

---

151 See ch 3 of this book.
152 See ch 4, particularly at 117–37.
153 See *Sapphire International Petroleum Ltd v National Iranian Oil Co.* (1967) 36 ILR 136, 185–86.

circumstances change.[154] This can be accomplished through the insertion of renegotiation clauses into the contract.[155]

In the absence of renegotiation clauses, the Republic of Zambia could also rely on its obligation to uphold international environmental standards. In light of the environmental degradation that occurred in cities such as Chingola, the government retains the ability to regulate the environment despite the existence of stabilization clauses in the concession agreements.[156] Under international law, this could potentially be done by pursuing two avenues: (1) by limiting the scope of the stabilization clause to areas that do not directly or indirectly conflict with international law; or (2) by taking an evolutionary approach vis-à-vis the content and interpretation of the stabilization clause.[157]

The host state could limit the scope of the stabilization clause through express or implied 'compliance with international law'.[158] This option has often been discussed in relation to stabilization clauses and the application of human rights standards by the host state. It is argued that state sovereignty is limited by the obligation of the host state to observe human rights. Therefore, as the host state enters into a concession with an investor, it cannot undertake to impair the rights of individuals or groups that might be affected by the investment project.[159] For this reason, it is contended that stabilization clauses are valid but their scope is restricted in that they can neither impair the rights of third parties nor can they prevent the host state from progressively realizing human rights.[160]

This reasoning can be extended to other international law obligations. One of these is to observe international environmental standards.[161] Given this fact, the Government of Zambia could pass laws that are in line with its international environmental obligations. This would not violate the stabilization clauses contained in the concession agreements, first, because most of the terminated agreements referred mainly to tax. Secondly, even with the generally worded clauses, we have seen that where they conflict with Zambia's international obligations, the latter take precedence.

The second avenue that could be pursued is taking the evolutionary approach. This may be achieved by allowing the evolution of social and environmental

---

154 Lungu, 'Copper Mining Agreements in Zambia: Renegotiation or Law Reform?' (n 8) 413.
155 See Talal Abdulla Al-Emadi, 'The Renegotiating Clause in Petroleum International Joint Venture Agreements' (2012) Oxford Student Legal Studies Paper No. 04/2012 http://papers.ssrn.com/sol3/papers.cfm?abstract_id=2073340 (last accessed 8 June 2015).
156 See generally Lorenzo Cotula, 'Reconciling Regulatory Stability and Evolution of Environmental Standards in Investment Contracts: Towards a Rethink of Stabilization Clauses' (2008) 1 *Journal of World Energy Law & Business* 158.
157 Lorenzo Cotula, 'Regulatory Takings, Stabilization Clauses and Sustainable Development' (2008) *OECD Global Forum on International Investment* 13 http://www.oecd.org/investment/globalforum/40311122.pdf (last accessed 8 June 2015).
158 ibid.
159 ibid.
160 ibid.
161 ibid 14.

128 Resource nationalism in international investment law

standards within the concession agreement itself. This approach would relate more to the content and interpretation of the stabilization clause itself, rather than its scope.[162] This would involve interpreting the clauses in a way that recognizes changes in social and environmental standards.

In the *Gabčíkovo-Nagymaros*[163] case, the International Court of Justice held that although new norms of international environmental law do not undermine treaty obligations that are already in existence, such developments must be taken into account in the implementation of existing obligations. Such reasoning could be applied to contractual obligations as well. That is to say that existing contractual obligations should be implemented in a way that takes into account developments in international law. Such a concept is not alien to international investment law. As seen in *The American Independent Oil Company (AMINOIL) v Kuwait*,[164] the concession in this case had progressively undergone various changes, to which the investor had readily acquiesced. This effectively changed the character of the contract. Thus, the contract had lost its 'former absolute character'.[165]

In sum, in the absence of renegotiation clauses, if the Republic of Zambia wishes to alter its legislation in a way that does not contravene the stabilization clauses, it could argue that it has the right to regulate the environment, in light of the environmental degradation caused by the mines. It is argued above that this could be possible through two means: (1) limiting the scope of the stabilization clause; or (2) interpreting the stabilization clause in a way that takes into account the evolution of international environmental law norms. It would be of more utility to have renegotiation clauses, however, in order to facilitate flexibility and consequently a long-lasting, cooperative relationship between the host state and the investor. Such a relationship would enable both parties to come together episodically and reconsider the terms of the contract in a way that takes into account the investor's legitimate expectations and the host state's right to pursue its legitimate public functions.

5.4 Conclusion

The mining industry in Zambia has gone through several transitions since its inception when the first European explorers began operations more than a century ago. It is apparent that their sole focus was on copper mining, much to the detriment of other sectors of the economy. Thus, the sole driving force of the Zambian economy was mining, making Zambia a mono-economy. Those controlling the mines thus controlled the economy. At independence those controlling the mines were foreign mining companies, much to the discomfort of the government at the time, which proceeded to nationalize the mines.

---

162 ibid 16.
163 *Case Concerning the Gabčíkovo-Nagymaros Project (Hungary v Slovakia)* [1997] ICJ Rep 92.
164 [1982] ILM 976.
165 ibid para 101.

Owing to a combination of mismanagement and a slump in the copper prices the mining companies became less productive. This led to an unprecedented stagnation in the economy. This was compounded by the fact that the government had to borrow money in order to keep the country running. With virtually no money coming in the country was plunged deeper and deeper into debt. The government was eventually pressurized by the IMF and the World Bank to privatize most government owned companies, including the mines.

The multinational mining companies were granted tax incentives owing to the very low world copper prices that would have compounded the profitability of these ventures. However, as soon as operations commenced the copper prices rebounded to unprecedented levels. Meanwhile, mass lay-offs and environmental degradation led to resentments. Furthermore, there were concerns that the amount of profits the mines were making was not commensurate with the benefit to national development. This led to increased political pressure on the government to introduce a windfall tax on mining companies, to increase the mining royalty and the corporate tax. The concession agreements contained tax stability clauses, which stipulated that the government was not to increase taxes for a period of 15 years. The government nonetheless increased the corporate tax, introduced a windfall tax on copper and increased the mineral royalty. From what we have seen in the previous chapter on stabilization clauses, such an action would render the Government of Zambia susceptible to compensating the investor.

The case study of the windfall tax illustrates the adverse effects of inserting stabilization clauses into concession agreements. We have seen that, without the prior agreement of the investor, the host state is prohibited from taking any legislative or administrative measures to raise revenues. If it does, this will have pecuniary consequences. If it does not, however, this also leads to a loss of revenue. This precludes the host state from undertaking legitimate public functions. On the other hand, if stabilization clauses were ineffective this would also affect the legitimate expectations of the investor. What is needed is a clause that is sufficiently flexible in that it will protect the investor's legitimate expectations and the legitimate public functions of the state. Such a balance can be accomplished through the insertion of renegotiation clauses into concession agreements. This will be the recommendation in the final chapter of this book.

Chapter 6

Flexibility through renegotiation clauses

6.1 Introduction

From the preceding chapters it has been seen that investors have genuine concerns about protecting their investments and will often insert stabilization clauses into their contracts as a buffer against state interference with their investment. When states do prematurely terminate concessions, they are under a duty to compensate the investor. This includes paying compensation for loss of future profits.

As seen in Chapter 4, this ensures efficiency. However, it does not allow the state sufficient flexibility to pursue legitimate public purposes. The Zambian case study in the preceding chapter provides an illustration of such pursuit. The rigidity of contracts containing stabilization clauses has proven to be a 'major source of conflict between host governments of developing countries and transnational corporations derives'.[1] The investor requires stability and predictability in the contract on the one hand and the state requires flexibility on the other.

As a consequence of this, I submit that additional mechanisms are required in order to guarantee the long-term subsistence of development agreements and concessions alike. Such a mechanism would preserve the sovereign prerogatives of the state, whilst protecting the legitimate commercial expectations of the investor.[2] In this chapter, I propose that this additional contractual mechanism can come in the form of a renegotiation clause, which enables the parties to review and renegotiate certain terms either at specific intervals or at the occurrence of certain trigger events.[3] The insertion of such a clause enables the parties to avoid the inflexibility that is typically associated with contracts that contain stabilization clauses.[4]

Renegotiations may also occur outside the existing contractual framework. These can be more onerous because they are typically 'undertaken in apparent

---

1 Samuel Asante, 'Stability of Contractual Relations in Transnational Investment Process' (1979) 28 *International and Comparative Law Quarterly* 401, 404.
2 Sangwani Ng'ambi, 'Stabilization Clauses and the Zambian Windfall Tax' (2010) 1 *Zambia Social Science Journal* 107, 116.
3 See Jeswald W. Salacuse, 'Renegotiating International Project Agreements' (2000) 24 *Fordham International Law Journal* 1319, 1321.
4 Peter Muchlinski, *Multinational Enterprises and the Law* (2nd edn, OUP 2007) 584.

violation of the contract or at least in the absence of a specific clause authorizing a renegotiation'.[5] Certainly, when a change of circumstances renders the contract onerous or economically impossible to perform, then the parties may be discharged from the contract under some jurisdictions, the courts may direct the parties to renegotiate in others, or the courts may have the powers to adapt the contract on the parties' behalf. The course of action taken depends largely on the scope of the court's jurisdiction as provided for under its national laws.

Section 6.2 seeks to define renegotiation clauses and examine some reasons behind the parties' desire to renegotiate. Section 6.3 will discuss the principle of *rebus sic stantibus* as the means through which the parties may seek to renegotiate or be discharged from their contract in the event of unforeseeable changed circumstances. Section 6.4 will discuss a renegotiation process, which does contain a clause and will recommend a clause that deals specifically with windfall profits. Finally, in section 6.5 I will be summarizing my findings.

6.2 Renegotiation clauses defined

Renegotiation clauses are contractual mechanisms that give the parties the option to review, discuss and adapt the terms of a contract. These typically take effect either upon the occurrence of a triggering event or during specific intervals.[6] If the triggering event has the effect of altering the contractual equilibrium that exists between the parties, then there exists the possibility of adapting the contract. This is provided that the parties agree to such adaptation or provided that the clause itself prescribes adaptation by a third party. The legal validity of these clauses is undisputed because they are inserted by the free will of the parties.[7]

The insertion of a renegotiation clause will facilitate what is referred to as intra-contract renegotiations.[8] This is because they occur within the framework of the agreement itself. This can be contrasted with extra-contract renegotiation, which as the name implies occurs outside the framework of the existing concession agreement. These types of renegotiations would have occurred during the renegotiation of the various mineral concessions in the 1960s and 1970s. The fundamental feature of these renegotiations is that one party was requesting the alteration of pre-existing contractual obligations, even though there was no provision for this in the agreement itself.[9] The third type of renegotiation is referred to as post-contract renegotiation. These types of renegotiations occur upon the expiration of the

---

5 Salacuse, 'Renegotiating International Project Agreements' (n 3) 1321.
6 See also John Y. Gotanda, 'Renegotiation and Adaptation Clauses in International Contracts Revisited' (2003) 36 *Vanderbilt Journal of Transnational Law* 1461, 1462.
7 Abdullah Al Faruque, 'Renegotiation and Adaptation of Petroleum Contracts: The Quest for Equilibrium and Stability' (2008) 9 *Journal of World Investment and Trade* 113, 129.
8 Jeswald W. Salacuse, *The Three Laws of International Investment: National, Contractual, and International Frameworks for Foreign Capital* (OUP 2013) 277.
9 ibid.

contract. Although the parties, in the abstract, are relieved of their obligations once the contract has elapsed, they may nonetheless attempt to renew their relationship.[10]

Renegotiation clauses can be contrasted with stabilization clauses. In the latter case the aim is to freeze the law so as to 'keep the original balance alive throughout the contract', whereas in the former case the aim is to keep the relationship alive by 'requiring the parties to strike a new balance wherever there are circumstances justifying a change in the original obligations of the contract'.[11]

The difficulty with rigid contractual arrangements, whether fiscal or otherwise, is that they cannot 'realistically persist in the face of the dynamic economic changes at the global and national level over ten years'.[12] The contractual framework should reflect this and acknowledge that the possibility of change is a normal and integral feature of international business.[13] This could be accomplished through the insertion of renegotiation clauses in the contract.

Although it is understandable that the investor would need some form of stability in its contracts, this position cannot be sustained in the long run. Renegotiation, on the other hand, does not undermine the stability of concession agreements. It actually provides a form of insurance against the resource nationalism cycle. Governments are more likely to react adversely if they realise that the contract emphatically excludes the possibility of future revision.[14] There would be far less inclination to nationalize or take any other draconian measures if the terms of the agreement episodically could be revisited, reopened and revised. Asante observes:

> If periodical review is recognized as a realistic feature of the investment process, financiers could take it into account in determining the financing agreements, and the renegotiation could be so timed as to coincide with the year in which the investor would have recouped his investment. Thereafter, both parties could agree on a reasonable rate of return for the investor.[15]

Despite their differences, the two clauses can coexist within the same contract.[16] The combination may seem incongruous. However, the advantage of having the clause lies in the fact that governments and corporations alike are then under an obligation to renegotiate the contract in good faith, with the aim of restoring the contractual equilibrium.

---

10 ibid 276–77.
11 M. Sornarajah, *The Settlement of Foreign Investment Disputes* (Kluwer 2000) 53.
12 Asante, 'Stability of Contractual Relations in the Transnational Investment Process' (n 1) 411.
13 ibid.
14 ibid 412.
15 ibid.
16 Thomas W. Wälde and George Ndi, 'Stabilizing International Investment Commitments: International Law Versus Contract Interpretation' (1996) 31 *Texas International Law Journal* 215, 265–66.

The need to renegotiate is influenced by a plethora of factors. These all seem to emanate from the fact that concessions are long-term agreements which, as a general rule, will run for a period exceeding 10 years. Indeed, some may even run for 60 years, as was the case in *The American Independent Oil Company (AMINOIL) v Kuwait*.[17] Regardless of the timeframe, it is within the realm of contemplation that episodically a concatenation of circumstances will necessitate the revisiting of certain contractual provisions.[18] Such a situation for example may be precipitated by a sudden windfall in commodity prices. As evidenced in previous chapters there may be a perception, whether misconceived or not, that multinational corporations are externalizing more profits from the natural resources of the host state than they are actually bringing in. This can further be compounded in instances where the state is in a relatively weaker bargaining position than the corporation.[19]

The perceived unfairness of this may lead to political strife, which in turn may lead to two potential consequences. If a friendly host government, which may have previously granted favourable terms to the investor, is in power it may wish to revisit the terms of the concession. The incentives received by multinational corporations may possibly be reduced or even revoked so that the party in power may maintain its political hegemony. This is so as to obtain an equitable share of the profits generated by the multinational corporation as a result of the windfall. Such a move would be calculated to pacify an agitated people, which in turn would generate the political mileage needed for the government of the day to maintain its political hegemony.

The second potential consequence is that the political strife may lead to a change of government through democratic or, indeed, extra-democratic means.[20] In such an instance the new government may seek to renegotiate the terms of the contract so as to reach a more equitable tax regime. Failure to renegotiate with an overzealous government may potentially lead to the outright nationalization of the investor's assets. The renegotiation clause acts as a buffer against such extreme consequences by aiding the parties in reaching an equitable solution 'which eventually facilitates stability in the contractual relationship by promoting confidence, trust and reliability between them'.[21] By inserting renegotiation clauses, the parties are minimizing the chances of a conflict occurring.[22]

---

17 (1982) 21 ILM 976.
18 Al Faruque, 'Renegotiation and Adaptation of Petroleum Contracts: The Quest for Equilibrium and Stability' (n 7) 115.
19 ibid 117.
20 See Paul Stevens, 'National Oil Companies and International Oil Companies in the Middle East: Under the Shadow of Government and the Resource Nationalism Cycle' (2008) 1 *Journal of World Energy Law & Business* 5, 6.
21 Al Faruque 'Renegotiation and Adaptation of Petroleum Contracts: The Quest for Equilibrium and Stability' (n 7) 133.
22 See also Gotanda, 'Renegotiation and Adaptation Clauses in International Investment Contracts, Revisited' (n 6) 1469.

It has further been advanced that culture is an influencing factor. Perceptions of how business ought to be conducted vary from culture to culture. Invariably, the business practices of capital exporting nations will be very different from those of the capital importing ones. As a result of this, differences may arise and it may be necessary to renegotiate the terms of the contract. It is argued that there is a divide between East and West in terms of how business is conducted. In the East, particularly Asia, businesses typically seek to avoid conflict and endeavour to keep the contract alive despite times of adversity.[23] In the East, contracts are seen as fluid and implicitly can be renegotiated upon the occurrence of unforeseen events. This is in contrast to their Western counterparts, who take a more rigid approach to contracts.[24] In view of this, renegotiation clauses are seen as a 'middle ground between total contractual rigidity, on the one hand, and complete relational flexibility on the other'.[25]

This perceived divide between East and West can be questioned, however.[26] It is argued that when determining the impact that culture has on renegotiation, categorizing the regions in this manner is too simplistic and assumes that the 'culture in each category is homogenous'.[27] This assumption is erroneous because it ignores the variations that exist between the countries in these regions, such as the geographical location, historical developments and stages of economic development.[28] For this reason, if we are to examine the impact of culture we must analyse this on two levels of culture: national and organizational.[29]

On a national level, the heterogeneous nature of culture within national boundaries renders it dangerous to 'draw conclusions based on national culture without considering differences within a nation such as those arising from organizations and individuals'.[30] This position can be contrasted with an alternative view, which defines culture as 'the collective programming of the mind which distinguishes the members of one group from another'.[31] The difficulty with this latter position is that it is too narrow because it only looks at culture from a national perspective and, as a result, assumes 'culture is homogenous within national boundaries'.[32]

---

23 Sornarajah, *Settlement of Foreign Investment Disputes* (n 11) 54.
24 Salacuse, 'Renegotiating International Project Agreements' (n 3) 1515–16.
25 Salacuse, *The Three Laws of International Investment: National, Contractual, and International Frameworks for Foreign Capital* (n 8) 283.
26 Talal A. Al-Emadi and Maryam A. Al-Asmakh, 'Cultural Differences and Their Impact: Some Brief Comments' (2006) 5 *Chinese Journal of International Law* 807.
27 ibid 808.
28 Edward E. Chamisa, 'The Relevance and Observance of IASC Standards in Developing Countries and the Particular Case of Zimbabwe' (2000) 35 *International Journal of Accounting* 267, 270.
29 Al-Emadi and Al-Asmakh (n 26) 808.
30 ibid 809.
31 Geet Hofstede, *Cultures Consequences: International Differences in Work-Related Values* (Sage Publications 1984) 25.
32 Al-Emadi and Al-Asmakh (n 26) 809.

Looking at culture from an organizational point of view enables us to understand that culture is influenced by 'various local cultures each with their own distinctive values'.[33] This would suggest that, whilst there may be a dominant culture within the organization, it still comprises various other local cultures which may exist within the organization. It is the attributes of people and not the organizational structure that influences organizational behaviour.[34] Organizations should also be viewed as 'containing patterned behaviour of interdependent parts including interdependent people'.[35] One is thus left with an organization with many types of people, who possess myriad competencies. However, there also exists an organizational culture under which the people therein, despite their differences, share 'common organizational attributes'.[36] The approach of looking at the organizational culture is advantageous in their view, as it acknowledges the fact that an organization consists of people that come from various backgrounds and exert their own culture to influence organizational behaviour.[37]

Stabilization clauses on their own cannot withstand the realities associated with long-term contracts.[38] No one questions the necessity of inserting some form of protective clause into the concession agreements.[39] However, the vicissitudes of the natural resource industry are a good enough reason to provide for some form of flexibility in long-term agreements through renegotiation clauses. This facilitates renegotiations that can be conducted in instances where there are windfall profits or, indeed, in instances where the economic situation has become so onerous to the investor that it needs to revise certain contractual terms to stay afloat. It is in the interests of the parties to renegotiate the contract as their relationship is an interdependent one and their interests inextricably linked.[40]

6.3 Contracts without a renegotiation clause

Even in the absence of a renegotiation clause in a long-term agreement, there may still be alternative avenues through which the host state may realize flexibility in its agreements. The host state could achieve this by relying on the principle of

---

33 Maryam Alavi, Timothy R. Kayworth and Dorothy E. Leidner, 'An Empirical Examination of the Influence of Organisational Culture on Knowledge Management Practices' (2005) 22 *Journal of Management Information Systems* 191, 195.
34 Al-Emadi and Al-Asmakh (n 26) 810.
35 ibid.
36 ibid.
37 ibid.
38 See S.K. Chatterjee, 'The Stabilization Clause Myth in Investment Agreements' (1988) 5 *Journal of International Arbitration* 97.
39 See George K. Foster, 'Managing Expropriation Risks in the Energy Sector: Steps for Foreign Investors to Minimise their Exposure and Maximise Prospects for Recovery When Takings Occur' (2005) 23 *Journal of Energy & Natural Resources Law* 36.
40 Al Faruque, 'Renegotiation and Adaptation of Petroleum Contracts: The Quest for Equilibrium and Stability' (n 7) 132.

rebus sic stantibus or changed circumstances.[41] Section 6.3 will examine the principle of *rebus sic stantibus*. Under this rule there may be an obligation to renegotiate if there is a change of circumstances. However, this depends largely on the legal system. The principle of *rebus sic stantibus* entails that in the event of an unforeseen change of circumstances that destroys the economic viability of a contract the parties may be permitted to renegotiate the contract or refer the matter to a tribunal for amendment[42] or termination.

The principle of *rebus sic stantibus* is not diametrically opposed to *pacta sunt servanda*. In fact it is argued that the two principles complement each other like two sides of a coin. The former simply tempers the rigidity of the latter by ensuring that contracts are enforced in a more equitable and dynamic manner.[43] From the case law examined in this section, it will be seen that *pacta sunt servanda* is still respected; however, it is universally understood by international law and leading systems of national law that unforeseen circumstances may necessitate the renegotiation, adaptation or outright termination of contracts.

The principle of changed circumstances infers that, in instances where changed circumstances adversely affect the economic viability of a contract, there may be a duty to renegotiate. However, in order to activate and depend on this principle, there must either be a contractual term to this effect or the applicable law must provide for it.[44] Application of the doctrine varies from jurisdiction to jurisdiction. Two factors, however, do bring some form of commonality. First, the courts in most jurisdiction respect the fact that *pacta sunt servanda* is the overriding policy of contract law. Secondly, whilst the courts recognize that *rebus sic stantibus* is one of the exceptions to this rule, they are only willing to apply it in limited circumstances, thus averting the potential for misuse of the principle.[45] The approach of the courts is best summed up by Arbitrator Lalive in *Indian Cement Co v Pakistani Bank*,[46] where he opined that:

> The principle '*Rebus sic stantibus*' is universally considered as being of strict and narrow interpretation, as a dangerous exception to the principle of sanctity of contracts. Whatever opinion or interpretation lawyers of different countries

---

41 Hadiza T. Mato, 'The Role of Stability and Renegotiation in Transnational Petroleum Agreements' (2012) 5 *Journal of Politics and Law* 33, 35.

42 See *Establishment of Middle East Country X v South Asian Construction Co.* (1987) 12 YCA 97, 109. This can be contrasted with the position in *AMCO Asia v Indonesia* (1984) 23 ILM 351 and *Hungarian State Enterprise v Yugoslav Crude Oil Pipeline* (1984) 9 YCA 69, 70.

43 Hasan S. Zakariya, 'Changed Circumstances and the Continued Validity of Mineral Development Contracts' in Kamal Hossain (ed), *Legal Aspects of the New International Economic Order* (Frances Pinter 1980) 263, 275.

44 Klaus P. Berger, 'Renegotiation and Adaptation of International Investment Contracts: The Role of Contract Drafters and Arbitrators' (2003) 36 *Vanderbilt Journal of Transnational Law* 1347, 1350.

45 Norbert Horn, 'Changes in Circumstances and the Revision of Contracts in some European Laws and International Law' in Nobert Horn (ed), *Adaptation and Renegotiation of Contracts in International Trade and Finance* (Kluwer 1995) 29.

46 ICC Case No. 1512.

may have about the 'concept' of changed circumstances as an excuse for non-performance, they will doubtless agree on the necessity to *limit* the application of the so-called 'doctrine *rebus sic stantibus*' (sometimes referred to as 'frustration', 'force majeure', '*imprevision*' and the like) to cases where compelling reasons justify it, having regard not only to the fundamental character of the changes, but also to the particular type of the contract involved, to the requirements of fairness and equity and to all circumstances of the case.[47]

The first part of this section will examine international law's recognition of the principle. It will then go on to discuss the varying approaches under the common law and civil law jurisdictions. This overview is necessary for the chances of adaptation depend largely on the idiosyncrasies of a particular jurisdiction and therefore the choice of law applicable to a contract plays a large part in this. The potential uncertainty this presents the parties with is a good reason for the insertion of renegotiation and adaptation clauses into concession agreements.

6.3.1 Rebus sic stantibus *under international law*

The principle of fundamental change of circumstances (*rebus sic stantibus*) is certainly one that is recognized under international law. This principle is found in Article 62 of the Vienna Convention on Treaties, which highlights the grounds upon which a state may withdraw from a treaty. Article 62(1) states that, provided the circumstances were unforeseen, a state may withdraw from a treaty in instances where '(a) the existence of those circumstances constituted an essential basis of the consent of the parties to be bound by the treaty; and (b) the effect of the change is radically to transform the extent of obligations still to be performed under the treaty'. Article 62(2) further provides that the principle may not be invoked in instances where the treaty establishes a boundary or where the fundamental change is a direct consequence of a breach committed by the invoking party.

In the *Gabčíkovo–Nagymaros* case the International Court of Justice (ICJ) opined that it was only willing to apply the doctrine of *rebus sic stantibus* where the fundamental change of circumstances was unforeseen. These circumstances must go to the root of the treaty itself. The ICJ further added that, because the wording of Article 62 of the Vienna Convention on the Law of Treaties was negative and conditional, the ICJ also ruled that the doctrine of fundamental change of circumstances can only be applied in exceptional cases.[48]

The ICJ ultimately left it to the parties to go back and negotiate in good faith the means through which they were going to achieve the objectives of the Treaty they had entered into. We can thus see that even under international law the

---

47 ibid 128–29.
48 *Case Concerning the Gabčíkovo–Nagymaros Project* (Hungary/Slovakia), Judgment of 25 September 1997, para 104 http://www.icj-cij.org/docket/files/92/7375.pdf (last accessed 9 June 2015).

principle of sanctity of contracts is respected. The courts do recognize that a change of circumstances can indeed excuse the parties from performing a contract. However, this is applied in limited circumstances and the courts certainly will not engage in the modification or alteration of agreements between two parties.

Clearly the preceding case relates more to treaties than it does to contracts between multinational corporations and the host government. Although it is only in draft form, the sentiments expressed in the UN Draft Code of Conduct for Transnational Corporations do provide an indication of the potential direction that the United Nations may eventually go with the principle of *rebus sic stantibus*. Article 5 of the draft code states that a transnational corporation should respond positively to requests for renegotiation of agreements in instances

> marked by duress, or clear inequality between the parties, or where the conditions upon which such a contract was based have fundamentally changed, causing thereby unforeseen major distortions in the relations between the parties and thus rendering the contract unfair or oppressive to either of the parties. Aiming at ensuring fairness to all parties concerned, review or renegotiation in such situations should be undertaken in accordance with applicable legal principles and generally recognised legal practices.[49]

Further evidence of this principle is also found under the UNIDROIT Principles of International Commercial Contracts.[50] These Principles, whilst recognising *pacta sunt servanda*, state that it is not an absolute rule. Article 6.2.2 states that there is an obligation to perform despite the hardship unless 'the occurrence of events fundamentally alters the equilibrium of the contract either because the cost of a party's performance has increased or because the value of the performance a party receives has diminished'. The events must occur after the conclusion of the contract.

Furthermore, the events must not have reasonably been taken into account at the conclusion of the contract and they must be beyond the control of the party seeking excuse. Paragraph (d) further provides that the party should not have assumed the risk of events. The commentary sheds more light on what this actually means. It says that even though certain risks may not have been undertaken expressly, the element of risk may be implied from the very nature of the contract. A person who enters into a speculative transaction is deemed to assume a certain degree of risk even though he or she is not fully aware of them at the time that the contract is being concluded.[51]

---

49 UNDECOSOC 1979 Transnational Corporations: Codes of Conduct, Formulations by the Chairman, Article 5, reprinted in Norbert Horn (ed), *Legal Problems of Codes of Conduct for Multinational Enterprises* (Kluwer 1980) 493–94.

50 http://www.unidroit.org/english/principles/contracts/principles2010/integralversionprinciples 2010-e.pdf (last accessed 9 June 2015).

51 UNIDROIT Principles 216.

In the event of hardship, Article 6.2.3 provides that the disadvantaged party is 'entitled to request renegotiations'. Such a request must be made without undue delay and should state the grounds upon which it is made. Paragraph (2) provides that this request for renegotiation does not in itself give the disadvantaged party the right to withhold performance. Paragraph (3) states that, in an event where the parties fail to arrive at an agreement, they may take the matter to court. Paragraph (4) lays down that, where the courts do find hardship, they may if reasonable either terminate the contract or adapt it 'with a view to restoring its equilibrium'.

Article 7.1.7 provides for instances of force majeure. Paragraph 1 states that non-performance of a contract is excused if the party in breach can prove that it was as a result of an impediment beyond his or her control and as a result could not reasonably be expected to have taken that impediment at the time that the contract was being concluded nor could the party have avoided or overcome this impediment or its consequences. If the impediment is only temporary then the party is only excused for a reasonable period of time. The reasonableness of such a timeframe depends on 'the effect of the impediment on the performance of the contract'.[52] Indeed, there is also a duty to notify the other party of this impediment and its effect on the ability to perform. Failure to give such notification within a reasonable timeframe may render the party in breach liable for any damages resulting from this.[53]

Excuse for non-performance is also recognized under Article 79(1) of the Convention on the International Sale of Goods (CISG), which provides that a party may escape liability for failure to perform his or her obligations if that party can prove that this was as a result of an impediment beyond his or her control and that could not have reasonably been taken into account at the time the contract was being concluded. Furthermore, the party must be unable to avoid or overcome its consequences.

In *Scafom International BV v Lorraine Tubes*, the Belgian Supreme Court interpreted this as including force majeure. Thus, if there is an unforeseen change of circumstances that leads to the alteration of the contractual equilibrium, then this might under limited circumstances enable the parties to extricate themselves from performance of their contractual obligations.[54] The Convention leaves the parties to adopt any remedy apart from the payment of damages.[55] From this it could be inferred that renegotiation and adaptation is within the scope of the parties' prerogatives. However, this is a mere inference and is by no means a certain avenue to pursue because it depends on the parties' willingness to do so and it depends on the courts' willingness to enforce the contract.

---

52 Article 7.1.7(2).
53 Article 7.1.7(3).
54 Anna Veneziano, 'UNIDROIT Principles and CISG: Change of Circumstances and Duty to Renegotiate according to the Belgian Supreme Court' (2010) 15 *Uniform Law Review* 137, 139.
55 Lukanda Kapwadi, 'Renegotiating a Long Term Investment Contract: The Case of Mining Contracts in DRC' (LLM Thesis, University of Pretoria 2012) 42.

140 Resource nationalism in international investment law

6.3.2 Common law systems

The general position under the common law is that the parties are bound by the terms of the contract. However, English common law also recognizes that there may be instances where a change of circumstances renders the contract impossible to perform. In such an event the contract is said to be frustrated. As was stated by Lord Simon in *National Carriers Ltd v Panalpina (Northern) Ltd*:[56]

> Frustration of a contract takes place when there supervenes an event (without default of either party and for which the contract makes no sufficient provision) which so significantly changes the nature (not merely the expense or onerousness) of the outstanding contractual rights and/or obligations from what the parties could reasonably have contemplated at the time of its execution that it would be unjust to hold them to the literal sense of its stipulations in the new circumstances . . .[57]

The doctrine of frustration discharges the parties from any duty to perform.[58] This event, however, should not be self-induced.[59] In addition, it must have been unforeseeable.[60] It should be noted at this point, however, that the doctrine of frustration, like *rebus sic stantibus*, is only applied in limited circumstances. Moreover, it is established that the mere fact that commercial realities have changed leading to increased costs or an adverse effect on one party's profit-making capacity does not in itself amount to a frustrating event.[61] Furthermore, the court does not have the power to modify or amend the contract in the event that it does find that the contract has been frustrated. All the court can do is discharge the parties of any pre-existing duty to perform.[62]

The English position can be contrasted with the slightly more liberal approach of the United States.[63] Section 2-615 of the Uniform Commercial Code recognizes the principle of 'commercial impracticability'.[64] This doctrine allows the parties to request a renegotiation in instances where circumstances have altered so radically that performance of the contract is no longer economically viable.[65]

---

56 *National Carriers Ltd v Panalpina (Northern) Ltd* [1981] AC 675.
57 ibid 700.
58 See generally Patrick Atiyah, *An Introduction to the Law of Contract* (6th edn, OUP 2005) and Sir David Hughes Parry, *Sanctity of Contracts in English Law* (Stevens 1959) 47.
59 See *Maritime National Fish v Ocean Trawlers* [1935] AC 524.
60 See *Walton Harvey Ltd v Walker & Homfrays Ltd* [1931] 1 Ch 274.
61 *Tennants (Lancashire) Ltd v C S Wilson & Co Ltd* [1917] AC 495 (HL); *Davis Contractors Ltd v Fareham Urban District Council* [1956] AC 696 (HL); *Tsakiroglou & Co Ltd v Noblee Thorl GmbH* [1962] AC 93 (HL).
62 G.H. Treitel, *Frustration and Force Majeure* (Sweet & Maxwell 1994) 498.
63 Zeyad Al Qurashi, 'Renegotiation of International Petroleum Agreements' (2005) 22 *Journal of International Arbitration* 261, 271.
64 See also section 268(2) of the Restatement (Second) of Contracts.
65 Abba Kolo and Thomas W. Wälde, 'Renegotiation and Contract Adaptation in International Investment Projects: Applicable Legal Principles and Industry Practices' (2000) 1 *Journal of World Investment and Trade* 5, 35.

Indeed, the change of circumstances must be unanticipated at the time that the original contract was being signed and must be financially damaging to the party requesting it, with the possibility of even driving that party to bankruptcy.[66] Although the position in the United States is slightly wider than under English common law we can see that it is still very narrow.

6.3.3 Civil law systems

Judges under the civil law systems appear to be slightly more empowered than their common law counterparts. The general rule is that *pacta sunt servanda* is the prevailing principle when contracting under the civil law. However, this rule only subsists if the underlying circumstances that were 'essential in the conclusion of the agreement' continue to exist.[67] The principle of *rebus sic stantibus* gained particular traction in the aftermath of the devastation caused by the wars in Europe.[68] The courts saw no justification for holding the parties to contracts that were deemed impossible to perform. It does not follow, of course, that the parties are permitted an easy escape from their contracts. Certain conditions do need to be met and these are encapsulated in the German principle of *Störung der Geschäftsgrundlage* and the French principle of *imprévison.*[69]

Paragraph 313 of the German Civil Code propounds the principle of *Störung der Geschäftsgrundlage*. Under this principle, the parties are no longer bound to their contractual obligations in instances where unforeseen events have led to a drastic alteration of the essential circumstances that subsisted when the contract was formalized. The disrupted economic equilibrium should be so unbalanced that the contract no longer has any real value to the affected party. Originally, the German Civil Code did not actually contain a provision that expressly dealt with the issue of changed circumstances. The German courts thus interpreted paragraph 242 of their Civil Code, which imposes a general duty of good faith on contracting parties, so as to read into it the principle of *Wegfall der Geschäftsgrundlage.*[70] It was advanced that compelling a party to complete a contract when circumstances had changed radically and unforeseeably, would be against good faith.

However, in 2002, the provisions of the Civil Code were revised and, as such, a new provision was included.[71] Paragraph 313 of the Civil Code was entitled *Störung*

---

66 See *Aluminum Co. of America v Essex Group, Inc.*, 449 F. Supp. 53 (W.D. Pa. 1980).
67 Kolo and Wälde (n 65) 36.
68 Peter J. Mezzacano, 'Force Majeure, Impossibility, Frustration and the Like: Excuses for Non-performance; the Historical Origins and Development of an Autonomous Commercial Norm in the CISG' (2011) *Nordic Journal of Commercial Law* 1, 38.
69 Kolo and Wälde (n 65) 36.
70 Basil S. Markesinis, Hannes Unberath and Angus Johnston, *The German Law of Contract: A Comparative Treatise* (2nd edn, Hart Publishing 2006) 336–41. See also Mezzacano (n 68) 48; Rainer Geiger, 'The Unilateral Change of Economic Development Agreements' (1974) 23 *International and Comparative Law Quarterly* 78, 93; Kolo and Wälde (n 65) 36.
71 Markesinis ibid 324.

142 Resource nationalism in international investment law

der Geschäftsgrundlage. Earlier interpretations of paragraph 242 are thus codified in the new provision. In contrast to their common law counterparts, the German courts do not only have the power to terminate a contract; they can also adapt it in instances of changed circumstances as codified in paragraph 313 of the German Civil Code.[72]

The principle of *rebus sic stantibus* is also found in the French doctrine of *imprévison*.[73] It is implied from this theory that contracts between the French Government (or an emanation of the same) can only subsist as long as the fundamental circumstances contemplated by the parties are still in existence.[74] In order for *imprévison* to arise, two essential requirements must be met: 'the change of contractual circumstances must not be due to any fault on behalf of the debtor and the contract must not contain any provisions related to the adaptation (indexing or renegotiation) to the new circumstances'.[75]

However, this principle in the French context emanates from French administrative law and applies only to administrative contracts concluded with the French Government.[76] It does not apply to civil contracts and the French courts have episodically resisted any attempts to extend it to such contracts. This was clearly illustrated in the *Canal de Craponne* case, where the Cour de Cassation held that: 'The courts cannot – even in the interest of equity – take into consideration the time and circumstances in order to modify these agreements, and to substitute new clauses for those which have been freely accepted by the parties'.[77] This, it would appear, is in sharp contrast to the German position. Despite the French reluctance to apply this principle to civil contracts it has been adopted by various other civil law jurisdictions such as Poland, Italy, Greece and Egypt.[78]

6.3.4 Hardship clauses

The parties could also rely on hardship clauses, if these are contained in the concession agreement. These are utilized for different purposes in contracts. Typically, however, the purpose of these clauses is to deal with any potential hardships that may arise that are beyond the contemplation or control of the parties. When such eventualities arise, it gives the parties the right to request the suspension or termination of the contract.[79] An example of a hardship clause is the ICC Model Hardship Clause:

---

72 Mezzacano (n 68) 48.
73 See Geiger (n 70) 94–99 and Barry Nicholas, *The French Law of Contract* (2nd edn, OUP 1992) 208–210.
74 Sidonia Culda, 'The Theory of Imprevision' (2010) 52 *Fiat Iustitia* 41, 42.
75 ibid.
76 Zakariya (n 43) 271 and Culda (n 74) 46.
77 Kapwadi (n 55) 39.
78 See art 269 of the Polish Civil Code of 1932, arts 1467–69 of the Italian Civil Code of 1946, art 388 of the Greek Civil Code and art 147 of the Egyptian Civil Code.
79 H Konarski, 'Force Majeure and Hardship Clauses in International Contractual Practice' (2003) 4 *International Business Law Journal* 405, 405–407.

Flexibility through renegotiation clauses   143

1. A party to a contract is bound to perform its contractual duties even if its events have rendered performance more onerous than could reasonably have been anticipated at the time of the conclusion of the contract.
2. Notwithstanding paragraph 1 of this Clause, where a party to a contract proves that:

   a) the continued performance of its contractual duties has become excessively onerous due to an event beyond its reasonable control which it could not reasonably have been expected to have taken into account at the time of the conclusion of the contract; and that
   b) it could not reasonably have avoided or overcome the event or its consequences, the parties are bound, within a reasonable time of the invocation of this Clause, to negotiate alternative contractual terms which reasonably allow for the consequences of the event.

3. Where paragraph 2 of this Clause applies, but where alternative contractual terms which reasonably allow for the consequences of the event are not agreed by the other party to the contract as provided in that paragraph, the party invoking this Clause is entitled to termination of the contract.[80]

It must be noted that these types of clauses are not so popular in concession agreements.[81] This is owing to the fact that investors feel that they lead to contractual instability and may provide an easy avenue through which the host state may evade its contractual responsibilities.[82] Because, in their view, the term hardship cannot be defined with great precision, such a clause may lead to a situation whereby the parties to the contract will excuse their non-performance of a contract, by invoking, inducing or advancing the most spurious of claims.[83] Such resistance has subsided somewhat over the years.[84] Hardship clauses are also problematic if they provide for termination of the concession when the hardship occurs. Termination is not an appropriate remedy for concession agreements. This is owing to the fact that the investor has, by the time the hardship takes place, invested considerable sums of money on the project and supporting infrastructure.[85]

Furthermore, *rebus sic stantibus* seems to apply more in instances where the parties are experiencing some sort of hardship or detriment arising from the changed circumstances. From the wording of the above-mentioned clauses and the general

---

80 *ICC Force Majeure Clause 2003* (ICC Publishing 2003) 15.
81 Stefan M. Kröll, 'The Renegotiation and Adaptation of Investment Contracts' in Norbert Horn and Stefan M. Kröll (eds), *Arbitrating Foreign Investment Disputes* (Kluwer Law International 2004) 425, 440.
82 ibid.
83 ibid.
84 ibid; *Lemire v Ukraine* (2002) YBCA 133, 136.
85 Kröll (n 81) 441.

principles applying to frustration, force majeure, *imprévision* and *Störung der Geschäftsgrundlage*, it seems that it only applies to instances where the parties are experiencing some sort of hardship. The purpose of this chapter is to propose ways in which renegotiation can be initiated in instances where multinational mining companies are accruing windfall profits as a result of commodity prices. For these reasons it is more prudent for the parties to insert renegotiation clauses in their contract.

The better way forward is for the state and the investor to renegotiate the terms of the contract. This enables both parties jointly to consider ways in which they could benefit from the surplus they can and will potentially earn from the rise in the price of a particular natural resource. Similarly, given the mercurial nature of natural resources, the parties may also jointly consider reducing taxes in instances where the price depreciates.

6.4 Contracts with a renegotiation clause

From the preceding section it is evident that if renegotiation is to occur it would be best for the parties to insert a clause to that effect into the contract. This is owing to the fact that, whilst the legal systems at both international and national level recognize the principle of *rebus sic stantibus*, they are only willing to apply it in limited circumstances so as to preserve the sanctity of contracts and other agreements entered into. Thus, it is by no means certain that the contracts will be adapted by the courts. Therefore, if we are to have any form of flexibility it must be in the form of a contractual clause permitting the renegotiation and adaptation of the terms of concession agreements. These clauses would be the mechanism through which renegotiation is facilitated between the host state and the investor.[86] An example is Article 34.12 of the Model Exploration and Production Sharing Agreement of 1994 of Qatar, which states:

> Whereas the financial position of the Contractor has been based, under the Agreement, on the laws and regulations in force at the Effective Date, it is agreed that, if any future law, decree or regulation affects Contractor's financial position, and in particular if the customs duties exceed . . . percent during the term of the Agreement, both parties shall enter into negotiations, in good faith, in order to reach an equitable solution that maintains the economic equilibrium of this Agreement. Failing to reach agreement on such equitable solution, the matter may be referred by either Party to arbitration pursuant to Article 31.[87]

---

86 Samuel K.B. Asante, 'The Concept of Stability of Contractual Relations in the Transnational Investment Process' in Kamal Hossain (ed), *Legal Aspects of the New International Economic Order* (Frances Pinter 1980) 255.

87 Piero Bernardini, 'The Renegotiation of the Investment Contract' (1998) 13 *Foreign Investment Law Journal* 411, 416.

Flexibility through renegotiation clauses 145

A number of issues arise from the renegotiation.[88] The first element is to identify the circumstances that will lead to a renegotiation. This is what is referred to as the trigger event. The second issue that arises is the effect that the trigger event should have on the contract. The third issue that needs to be identified is the objective of the renegotiation. In other words: what are the parties seeking to achieve through the negotiation? Once these factors have been established, clear guidelines on the procedure for the renegotiation need to be drawn up by the parties. Finally, there must be a solution stipulated in case the parties fail to reach an agreement. This would normally mean referral to a third party to review the matter and possibly alter the terms of the agreement.

6.4.1 Triggering event

The very first issue that must be identified is the event, or indeed concatenation of events, that will activate the process of renegotiation. This is referred to as the triggering event. Once the triggering event is identified, it will become the legal basis upon which the parties may then proceed to renegotiate.[89] As we have noted above, some clauses specify the precise events that will trigger a renegotiation. They may for example stipulate tax increases or the fluctuation or depreciation of commodity prices. An example of this is the Lasmo clause, which made reference to the introduction of 'new law(s) and/or regulation(s) . . . in Vietnam adversely affecting CONTRACTOR'S interest or any amendments to existing laws and/or regulations'.[90] Similarly, the Ghana/Shell clause states that: 'It is hereby agreed that if during the term of this Agreement there should occur such changes in the financial and economic circumstances relating to the petroleum industry'.[91]

Precision in the language will serve to narrow the instances in which renegotiation between the parties can be initiated. Other clauses may utilize such general terminology as 'a substantial change in the circumstances existing on the date of the agreement' or 'a change of circumstances', thus widening the scope of events that may trigger a renegotiation. Some clauses may not even mention a trigger event at all. An example of such a clause is the Ok Tedi clause, which utilizes more general terminology when it states that: 'The parties may from time to time by agreement in writing add to, substitute for, cancel or vary all or any of the provisions of this Agreement'.[92]

The advantage of having a narrowly defined clause is that the specificity contained therein leads to certainty, which is good for both the state and the

---

88 Piero Bernardini, 'Stabilization and Adaptation in Oil and Gas Investments' (2008) 1 *Journal of World Energy Law and Business* 98, 103.
89 Al Faruque, 'Renegotiation and Adaptation of Petroleum Contracts: The Quest for Equilibrium and Stability' (n 7) 122.
90 Berger (n 44) 1359.
91 ibid.
92 ibid.

146 Resource nationalism in international investment law

investor. This is owing to the fact that clearly defined events will, in theory, circumvent an opportunistic party from requesting renegotiation in instances outside the scope of the terms defined in the contract.[93] It is argued that difficulties typically arise in the event where the triggering event is not sufficiently defined in the concession agreement.[94] However, there is a danger that the terms can be so stringent that it leads to precisely the type of rigidity identified in stabilization clauses. A wide definition is advantageous in that it allows for some form of flexibility. However, there is also a danger that it can be so wide that it leads to uncertainty. This fact notwithstanding, a wider definition at least allows for the type of flexibility that in the long run will certainly protect the investor's interests, whilst protecting the state's sovereignty. Furthermore, it is rather difficult to envisage and thus account for every conceivable eventuality in the contract.[95] For this reason it is better to have a wide definition that will capture every reasonable eventuality that may not be envisaged by contractual draftspersons.

The possibility of either of the parties initiating vexatious renegotiations is averted by the fact that arbitral tribunals tend to define the triggering events very narrowly in any event.[96] Clearly, this will lead to some consternation on the part of both parties; however, 'express contractual language will not totally eliminate risk. There is virtually nothing that can accomplish this'.[97] The issue of certainty, however, can be addressed in section 6.4.2, which deals with the effects of the change on the contract and which is more important than the actual triggering event.

6.4.2 The effect of the change on the contract

Renegotiation and adaptation clauses should apply only in exceptional circumstances.[98] Again, this could be defined in the clause itself by determining the effect of the triggering event on the actual relationship of the parties. If the effect on the parties does not manifest, then again there is no legal basis for renegotiation. It could be drafted in a way that the triggering event causes a 'disproportionate prejudice', 'substantial detriment', 'substantial economic imbalance' on the parties' relationship or simply materially affects 'the economic and financial basis of the agreement'.[99] They could also use a term such as 'the consequences and effects

---

93 Al Faruque, 'Renegotiation and Adaptation of Petroleum Contracts: The Quest for Equilibrium and Stability' (n 7) 123.
94 Rudolph Dolzer and Christoph Schreuer, *Principles of International Investment Law* (2nd edn, OUP 2012) 85.
95 Bernardini, 'Stabilization and Adaptation in Oil and Gas Investments' (n 88) 103.
96 Zeyad A. Al Qurashi, 'Renegotiation of International Petroleum Agreements' (2005) 22 *Journal of International Arbitration*, 261, 290.
97 W. Fox, *International Commercial Agreements: A Primer on Drafting, Negotiating and Resolving Disputes* (Kluwer Law International 1998) 217.
98 Bernardini, 'Stabilization and Adaptation in Oil and Gas Investments' (n 88) 104.
99 ibid 105.

Flexibility through renegotiation clauses   147

of which are fundamentally different to what was contemplated by the parties at the time of entering the agreement'.[100] The Ghana/Shell clause stipulates that the triggering event must 'materially affect the fundamental economic and financial basis of this Agreement'.[101] Neither of the parties should be allowed to demand performance during renegotiation.

6.4.3 The objectives of the renegotiation

The precise obligations of the parties in the course of renegotiation must be defined.[102] Subjective wording such as 'removing the unfairness' or 'adopting an equitable revision' may be utilized.[103] Alternatively, an objective wording such as 'restoring the original contractual equilibrium' can also be used.[104] The Lasmo clause talks of making 'necessary changes to this Agreement to ensure that CONTRACTOR is restored to the same economic conditions which would have prevailed if the new law and/or regulation or amendment had not been introduced'.[105] The objectives of either party may be very different. As Al Faruque notes:

> The host government may seek to achieve diverse goals through a renegotiation of the petroleum contract – to gain greater control of the economy for the government and citizens; to secure an increase in revenue from the project; to promote economic self-reliance; to combat economic imperialism; to implement an ideology; to implement a policy of joint venture between foreign investors and state corporations; to obtain government control of major productive enterprises; to promote state monopolies; or to gain access to new technology, etc[106]

The investor may also have its own objectives during the renegotiation process. The investor's interests may lie in the economic viability of continuing with the contract in its original form. Tied to this, the investor will also be interested in restoring the equilibrium of the contract. Indeed, there may be cases where the investor discovers that a particular find is not as economically viable as initially anticipated. Perhaps the investor may also seek to renegotiate in instances where the price of a commodity has depreciated. Whatever the situation, just like the host state, the investor will require the terms of the contract to be renegotiated from time to time.[107]

---

100 ibid.
101 Berger (n 44) 1359.
102 Bernardini, 'The Renegotiation of the Investment Contract' (n 87) 419.
103 Bernardini, 'Stabilization and Adaptation in Oil and Gas Investments' (n 88) 105.
104 Model Production Sharing Agreement for Turkmenistan, ibid.
105 Berger (n 44) 1359.
106 Al Faruque, 'Renegotiation and Adaptation of Petroleum Contracts: The Quest for Equilibrium and Stability' (n 7) 118.
107 ibid.

148 Resource nationalism in international investment law

6.4.4 The procedure

The procedure for the renegotiations should clearly stipulate the parties' obligations.[108] Invariably, renegotiation clauses are cryptic on the factual obligations of the parties. How do the parties thus decipher what these are? It is suggested that, regardless of the formulation of the renegotiation clauses, the parties can decipher what their obligations are by looking at the inherent functions of the renegotiation clause. These are threefold. The first is to compel the parties to 'cooperate in the renegotiation procedure in an efficient manner'.[109] That is to say that the parties should act in a manner that is aimed at successfully reaching a solution. This means adopting a flexible attitude and consideration for the needs of the other party. These sentiments are shared by the tribunal in *AMINOIL v Kuwait*,[110] where the tribunal stated that:

> [Neither side has neglected] the general principles that ought to be observed in carrying out an obligation to negotiate, – that is to say, good faith as properly to be understood; sustained upkeep of the negotiations over a period appropriate to the circumstances; awareness of the interests of the other party; and a preserving quest for an acceptable compromise. [111]

The second function of the clauses is to adapt the contract to, and only to, the changed circumstances.[112] There is no justification for altering and restructuring the entire contract unless this is actually stipulated in the contract itself. The third function of these clauses is to 'maintain and control the commercial balance of the contract to adjust to changed circumstances'.[113] It should certainly not lead to a situation whereby one party seeks to exploit the other party's weakness so as to obtain a commercial advantage. Thus, the obligations of the parties during the renegotiation process are as follows:

> 1. Keeping to the negotiation framework set out by the clause, 2. Respecting the remaining provisions of the contract, 3. Having regard to the prior contractual practice between the parties . . . 5. Paying attention to the interests of the other side . . . 12. Giving appropriate reasons for one's own adjustment suggestions . . . 15. Making an effort to maintain the price-performance relationship taking into consideration the parameters regarded as relevant by the parties. . . . 16. Avoiding an unfair advantage or detriment to the other side ('no profit – no loss' principle).[114]

---

108 Bernardini, 'Stabilization and Adaptation in Oil and Gas Investments' (n 88) 105.
109 Berger (n 44) 1364.
110 Note 17.
111 ibid 1014.
112 Berger (n 44) 1365.
113 ibid 1365.
114 ibid 1365–66.

These factors can serve as a mere starting point in determining the parties' obligations in each case. However, this also has to be determined in conjunction with the actual wording of the renegotiation clause. Further consideration must be paid to the nature of the contract and the intention of the parties.[115]

6.4.5 Course of action should the renegotiation fail

If the parties do fail to reach an agreement there are two further problems. The first problem is that arbitrators are reluctant to adapt the contracts in instances where they do not have the authority to do so. The second problem may arise during ICSID arbitration. Because there needs to be an actual legal dispute, arbitrators may deny jurisdiction in the case at all. This is owing to the fact that failing to agree during the process of negotiation does not necessarily constitute a 'legal dispute' under ICSID.

6.4.5.1 Agreements to negotiate

There is a potential pitfall in having a renegotiation clause in the contract. The clause does impose a duty on the parties to negotiate in good faith. As emphasized in an unpublished award by the International Chamber of Commerce, there is 'a duty for the parties to accept and take actively part in the negotiation, with the will to reach an agreement . . . to respect the negotiation frame adopted by the parties agreement, without reopening the already contractually accepted provisions'.[116] These negotiations must be carried out in good faith and must be concluded within a reasonable period of time. Failure to do this may amount to breach of contract.[117]

However, even though there is a duty to negotiate, this does not mean that there is an actual obligation for the parties to come to an agreement subsequent to the renegotiation proceedings.[118] This was succinctly highlighted by the tribunal in *The American Independent Oil Co. (AMINOIL) v Kuwait*, which noted that: 'An obligation to negotiate is not an obligation to agree. Yet the obligation to negotiate is not devoid of content, and when it exists within a well-defined juridical framework it can well involve fairly precise requirements'.[119]

This position is also illustrated in the case of *Wintershall AG v Qatar*.[120] This case involved the Government of Qatar, which had entered into an exploration and

---

115 ibid 1366.
116 Unpublished ICC Award No. 4727 (1987) s 85, quoted in Wolfgang Peter, *Arbitration and Renegotiation of International Investment Agreements* (Kluwer Law International 1995) 246.
117 ibid.
118 Salacuse, 'Renegotiating International Project Agreements' (n 3) 1334. See also the cases of *Railway Traffic between Lithuania and Poland*, PCIJ Series A/B No. 42 at 116 and *North Sea Shelf Case* (1969) ICJ Rep 4, para 85 at 47.
119 *AMINOIL v Kuwait* (n 17) 1004.
120 (1989) 28 ILM 795.

production sharing agreement (EPSA) with Wintershall. Under this agreement, the Government of Qatar had granted Wintershall the exclusive right to explore, drill for and produce petroleum in a specified area offshore of Qatar. This contract, which commenced in 1973, was to subsist for a period of 30 years.

Under the agreement, Wintershall was required to relinquish 50 per cent of the specified area after a period of five years. It could, however, continue to exploit the other 50 per cent. After eight years, Wintershall was required to relinquish an additional 20 per cent of the specified area. This would leave the company with only 30 per cent. If no petroleum was found within a period of eight years, then the Government of Qatar had the option of terminating the agreement altogether. The agreement further stipulated that Wintershall was allowed to produce any non-associated natural gases that it discovered during the course of the contract. This was subject, however, to the parties entering into further agreements on the matter. In an event where the Government of Qatar felt that the production of this non-associated gas was not economical, Wintershall had the option of producing it on its own.

Wintershall had failed to find oil in commercial quantities. A factor contributing to this was a boundary dispute with Bahrain. Consequently, the Qatari Government prevented Wintershall from exploring in structure (A) of the contract area; an area that was most likely to contain oil. The five-year period elapsed and Wintershall had to cede 50 per cent of the specified area, in accordance with the terms of the agreement.

In 1980, Wintershall informed the Qatari Government that it had discovered a substantial amount of non-associated gas in the remaining 50 per cent of the specified area that it had been exploring. It intimated to the government that the utilization of this was economical. The parties engaged in various negotiations; however, no agreement was reached. Moreover, the Government of Qatar terminated the agreement in 1985. The parties did, however, engage in further negotiations for another year but still failed to arrive at an agreement. Wintershall thus initiated arbitral proceedings against the government. Wintershall alleged, first, that the government had expropriated its contractual rights by preventing it from exploring structure (A) of the specified area. Secondly, Wintershall alleged that the Qatari Government had breached its contractual obligations by failing to arrive at an agreement on the discovery of the non-associated gas.

The tribunal first held that the government had not expropriated Wintershall's contractual rights.[121] The tribunal further held that the Government of Qatar had not breached its obligations.[122] Indeed, the government did have a duty to negotiate in good faith and this duty had not been breached because it was 'clear that such a duty does not include an obligation on the part of the respondent to reach agreement with respect to the proposals made by the claimants'. The government's

121 ibid 809.
122 ibid.

· decision was dictated by 'normal commercial judgment' and was therefore justified. The refusals were made in good faith.[123]

It has been seen, therefore, that there is a duty for the parties to negotiate. However, from the case law it has been seen that there is no actual duty to reach an agreement per se. In the event that the parties do fail to reach an agreement, it is therefore recommended that the matter be referred to a third party such as an arbitrator. The renegotiation clause itself or the concession should provide for such a referral. The role of the arbitrator would be to examine the matter and then amend the concession on behalf of the state and the investor.

6.4.5.2 Adaptation of contracts under international commercial arbitration

When the parties fail to arrive at an agreement following a renegotiation, they could refer the matter to an arbitrator. The potential disputes that may arise are whether the prevailing circumstances meet the triggering conditions set out in the contract or the extent to which the contract should be adapted.[124] The parties could potentially initiate arbitration proceedings, provided of course that there is a clause to that effect in the contract, which there invariably is. In such an instance the arbitrator may then decide whether the conditions set out in the contract are met. In an instance where the arbitrator finds that the conditions have not been met, then in the abstract the agreement would continue in full force. I say in the abstract given the political realities of failure to adapt contracts that are perceived to be unfair.

If the arbitrator does indeed find that the conditions have been met, then three potential solutions could be propounded: (1) the arbitrator may ask the parties to go back and negotiate the terms of the contract based on his or her findings; (2) the arbitrator may simply terminate the agreement; or (3) the arbitrator may adapt the contract in a way that restores the contractual equilibrium.

The first two options are well within the scope of the arbitral tribunal's competence. However, whether an arbitral tribunal has the jurisdiction to amend or adapt a contract is questionable.[125] The powers of the tribunal are contingent on the authority it has been granted by the parties themselves. Arbitral tribunals that have not been granted the authority to amend a contract on behalf of the parties are generally reluctant to do so. For this reason the express consent of the parties is required before the arbitral tribunal can move to adapt a contract.[126] This was certainly the position of the arbitral tribunal in *AMINOIL*, which opined that:

> [T]here can be no doubt that, speaking generally, a tribunal cannot substitute itself for the parties in order to . . . modify a contract unless that right is

---

123 ibid 814–15.
124 Bernardini, 'Stabilization and Adaptation in Oil and Gas Investments' (n 88) 106.
125 F.A. Mann, 'The Aminoil Arbitration' (1984) 14 *British Yearbook of International Law* 213, 218.
126 Al-Faruque (n 7) 141.

conferred upon it by law, or by the express consent of the parties . . . arbitral tribunals cannot allow themselves to forget that their powers are restricted. It is not open to doubt that an arbitral tribunal – constituted on the basis of a 'compromissory' clause contained in the relevant agreement between the parties to the case . . . could not by way of modifying or completing a contract, prescribe how a provision [for the determination of the economic equilibrium] must be applied. For that, the consent of both the parties would be necessary.[127]

It would thus seem in order for the arbitral tribunal to modify the contract; this power would effectively have to be conferred upon the tribunal by the parties through the arbitration clause. It would appear that the authority granted by the parties may be sufficient in allowing the arbitrators to adapt a contract.

Under the *kompetenz-kompetenz* rule, arbitrators are able to determine their own jurisdiction.[128] That is to say, it is for the arbitral tribunal to decide whether or not it has the authority to determine a matter. Such authority derives from the arbitration clause itself, coupled with the substantive law elected by the parties. The issue of jurisdiction is particularly important because, if the arbitrators go beyond the scope of the powers conferred upon them, then this is a ground upon which the award may be refused recognition and enforcement.[129]

Once an award is rendered unenforceable by a competent authority under the law of the seat of the arbitration, it makes it difficult, although not impossible, to seek recognition and enforcement elsewhere. Article V(1)(e) of the New York Convention states that an award may be refused recognition and enforcement if it 'has been set aside or suspended by a competent authority of the country in which, or under the law of which, that award was made'.[130] As a result of this, potentially the parties may be foreclosed from seeking recognition and enforcement in other jurisdictions.[131]

The term 'in which or under the law of which' is somewhat ambiguous.[132] This is especially so in instances where the actual seat of the arbitration differs from the

---

127 *AMINOIL v Kuwait* (n 17) 1016. In this case art 9, which contained the renegotiation clause, stated as follows: 'If as a result of changes in the terms of concessions now in existence or as a result of the terms of concessions granted hereafter, an increase in benefits to Governments in the Middle East should come generally to be received by them, the Company shall consult with the Ruler whether in the light of all relevant circumstances, including the conditions in which operations are carried out, and taking into account all payments made, any alterations in the terms of the agreements between the Ruler and the Company would be equitable to the parties'.

128 See art 16(1) of the UNCITRAL Model Law on International Commercial Arbitration which states: 'The arbitral tribunal may rule on its own jurisdiction, including any objections with respect to the existence or validity of the arbitration agreement'. See also *Texaco v Libya* (n 23) paras 11–13. See also Tibor Várady, John J. Barceló III and Arthur T. von Mehren, *International Commercial Arbitration: A Transnational Perspective* (3rd edn, Thomson 2006) 113–21.

129 Article V(1)(c) New York Convention 1958.

130 Article V(1)(e) New York Convention 1958.

131 Luigi Russi, 'Chronicles of a Failure: From a Renegotiation Clause to Arbitration of Transnational Contracts' (2008) 24 *Connecticut Journal of International Law* 77, 96.

132 ibid.

Flexibility through renegotiation clauses   153

applicable procedural law. Suppose, for example, that the parties select country A as the seat of arbitration and the law of country B to govern proceedings. It may be possible for the arbitrator to adapt contracts under the law of country B but perhaps not possible to do so under the law of country A. The predicament here is that if the award is set aside by a court in country A it may be difficult to seek recognition and enforcement elsewhere because of the 'trump card' under Article V(1)(e) of the New York Convention. This can occur despite the fact that the procedural law selected by the parties does in fact permit adaptation. As such, this effectively frustrates the parties' choice of procedural law and leaves them with an unenforceable award, despite the fact that the parties have adhered strictly to this procedural law.[133]

This position is further compounded by the fact that the interpretation of the term 'foreign award' varies from jurisdiction to jurisdiction. This is because of the rather open ended definitions propounded under the New York Convention. On the one hand, Article I(1) states that foreign awards are those which either are 'made in the territory of a State other than the State where the recognition and enforcement of such awards are sought' or those which are 'not considered as domestic awards in the state where their recognition and enforcement are sought'. Thus, recognition and enforcement under Article V(1)(e) may be refused in two instances: if it has been annulled in the country where the award was made or annulled in the country under which the law governing the award was made.

This may lead to a plethora of unreasonable outcomes. Country A may consider awards rendered in its territory but under a different procedural law as 'non-domestic'. Country B, on the other hand, may consider all awards made within its jurisdiction as domestic, regardless of the applicable procedural law. Thus an award rendered in country A but under the procedural law of country B may be considered as 'non-domestic' by both.

Conversely, an award rendered in country B under the law of country A may be considered as domestic by both. Now, in the latter situation, supposing the award was upheld in country A but set aside in country B, recognition and enforcement may still be difficult to attain in other jurisdictions again despite strict adherence to the procedural law selected by the parties. Because of the confusion and fragmentation that this leads to, it should not be left to individual states to decide what is domestic and what is not.[134]

In order to determine whether an award is domestic or not it is proposed that the law should focus more on the procedural law and not on the seat of the arbitration.[135] Only the country whose law is chosen should be allowed to set aside the award. That way, the New York Convention is interpreted in accordance with the object and purpose of those that drafted it. The intention of the Convention

133 Russi (n 131) 96.
134 ibid 98.
135 ibid 99.

was to ensure that awards are recognized in as many jurisdictions as possible. The idea that we should focus on the procedural law is also endorsed in the American case of *Bergesen v Joseph Muller Corp.*[136] In this case the US District Court stated that: 'awards "not considered as domestic" denotes awards . . . made within the legal framework of another country'.[137]

6.4.5.3 Role of ICSID arbitrator

If the parties elect to settle the matter under ICSID, there are questions as to whether the arbitrator has the competence or jurisdiction to adapt the contract in instances of changed circumstances.[138] This is owing to Article 25 of the ICSID Convention, which discusses the jurisdiction of the ICSID Tribunal. That is to say, it is the provision which stipulates that: 'the limits within which the provisions of the Convention will apply and the facilities of the Centre will be available for conciliation and arbitration proceedings'.[139] Under Article 25(1) of the ICSID Convention, the tribunal's jurisdiction extends to 'any legal dispute arising directly out of an investment'.

Therefore, it is clear from the foregoing provision that the matter before a tribunal must constitute a 'legal dispute' in order for the tribunal to accept it. If it does not amount to a legal dispute, then this would be a ground upon which any award rendered can be annulled under Article 52(1)(b) of the ICSID Convention. That provision states that an award may be annulled where the tribunal manifestly exceeds its powers. Once this occurs, the award loses its binding force and, as a consequence, cannot be enforced in the territory of any contracting state.[140]

The question that therefore arises is whether a failure to reach an agreement on the revision of specific terms of the contract, subsequent to renegotiation proceedings, actually constitutes a legal dispute under the ICSID Convention. The difficulty is that the term has not been defined under the ICSID Convention. In defining the term 'legal dispute', ICSID tribunals have often relied on the definition propounded by the International Court of Justice (ICJ).[141] The ICJ states that a legal dispute occurs when there is 'a disagreement on a point of law or fact, a conflict of legal views or interests between parties'.[142] Attempts at clarifying what

---

136 710 F .2d 928 (2d Cir. 1983).
137 ibid 932.
138 Bernardini, 'The Renegotiation of the Investment Contract' (n 87) 423 and Kröll (n 81) 451–56.
139 International Bank for Reconstruction and Development, *Report of the Executive Directors, on the Convention on the Settlement of Investment Disputes Between States and Nationals of Other States* (18 March 1965) https://icsid.worldbank.org/ICSID/StaticFiles/basicdoc/partB.htm (last accessed 9 June 2015).
140 Article 53(1) ICSID Convention.
141 Christopher Schreuer, *The ICSID Convention: A Commentary* (Cambridge University Press 2001) 93 para 42. See for example *Maffezini v Spain* (2001) 16 ICSID Rev—FILJ 212, 245 paras 93–94.
142 *Mavrommatis Palestine Concessions (Greece v Great Britain)*, Judgment of 30 August 1924, *PCIJ* (Series A) No. 2 at 11. See also International Court of Justice, *Case concerning East Timor*, ICJ Reports 1995, 90 para 22.

Flexibility through renegotiation clauses 155

was intended by those that drafted the ICSID Convention were also made in the Report of the Executive Directors submitted to member governments in 1965. Here, it was stated that:

> The expression 'legal dispute' has been used to make clear that while conflicts of rights are within the jurisdiction of the Centre, mere conflicts of interest are not. The dispute must concern the existence or scope of a legal right or obligation, or the nature or extent of the reparation to be made for breach of a legal obligation.[143]

The views expressed in the report are accentuated by those of Delaume. In his view, reference to a legal dispute limits the scope of the arbitrator's jurisdiction to a review of the contractual rights and obligations of the parties in the light of the applicable law. In his view, issues such as non-performance or interpretation of the agreement would fall within the scope of the term 'legal dispute'. However, he goes on to say that: 'disputes regarding conflicts of interest between the parties, such as those involving the desirability of renegotiating the entire agreement or certain of its terms, would normally fall outside the scope of the Convention'.[144]

The consequences of this are far-reaching. It is clear that if the parties fail to agree that the conditions necessitating the renegotiation process have actually occurred, as set out in the clause, then this constitutes a legal dispute. This is owing to the fact that this is a disagreement concerning the legal rights and obligations of the parties. Thus, any dispute of the sort can be characterized as legal. In a similar vein, if following the unsuccessful renegotiation one party feels the contract should subsist under the old terms and another feels that it ought to be terminated, then this too may constitute a legal dispute. Where the difficulty comes, however, is if the parties fail to come to a consensual revision of the terms without fault on either side. In such a case, the arbitrator may be asked to intervene in a matter that does not exactly constitute a legal dispute.[145]

It is recommended, therefore, that if the parties are to choose ICSID as the means through which they will settle all disputes arising out of the contract, they should in addition to this allocate the responsibility of adaptation to a third party operating outside of the mechanisms established under the ICSID Convention.[146] The ICSID Convention itself remains applicable in all other respects of the dispute except adaptation. Thus, if a dispute arises the parties

---

143 Quoted in Bernardini, 'The Renegotiation of the Investment Contract' (n 87) 423. See also A.F.M. Maniruzzaman, 'The Pursuit of Stability in International Energy Investment Contracts: A Critical Appraisal of the Emerging Trends' (2008) 1 *Journal of World Energy Law and Business* 121, 133–34.

144 Georges R. Delaume, 'ICSID Arbitration: Practical Considerations' (1984) 1 *Journal of International Arbitration* 101, 116–117.

145 Bernardini, 'The Renegotiation of the Investment Contract' (n 87) 424.

146 ibid.

156 Resource nationalism in international investment law

still have recourse to the ICSID Tribunal.[147] The advantage of such an approach is that it averts problems of jurisdiction and affords the parties the necessary flexibility needed to draft a renegotiation provision that is congruous with the specific needs of the parties.

6.4.6 A Proposed renegotiation clause in the event of windfall profits

To foster renegotiation proceedings, it would therefore mean that there must be a renegotiation clause in the concession agreement. During the course of research for this book, the clauses found were typically those dealing with a change of circumstances which negate the economic viability of the contract. In theory, these cannot actually function in instances of windfall profits because the triggering events stipulated are typically meant to have an adverse effect on the actual contract. This is not the case where there is a windfall in the prices of the natural resources of the host state. In such a case, the investor actually benefits from the change of circumstances. Thus, the renegotiation clause inserted into the contract would have to reflect that fact. In Zambia's case, I would recommend the following renegotiation clause to be inserted into future agreements:

> Upon the occurrence of a substantial change in the circumstances that materially affects the fundamental economic and financial basis of this Agreement the parties will engage in negotiations in good faith in order to reach an equitable solution to the tax incentives outlined in this Agreement. Such negotiations shall begin immediately after one Party has delivered to the others written request for such negotiation. If within 15 (fifteen) business days following the date on which such notice is given the Parties cannot reach an equitable solution regarding the tax incentives, a dispute shall be declared and such dispute shall be submitted to arbitration in accordance with the provisions of the arbitration clause.

The benefit of using the term 'substantial change of circumstances' as the triggering event is that it is wide and therefore captures all unpredictable and unforeseen events or circumstances, which would otherwise be difficult to cater for or envisage in a long-term concession agreement. The person drafting the concession could then include 'windfall in copper prices' as part of the definition of substantial change in circumstances.

The host state could also leave it open-ended to include other 'reasonable unforeseen events', thus encompassing any factors that might adversely affect the investor. Although an open-ended renegotiation clause may lead to some form of uncertainty, it is ultimately beneficial because it is flexible. A rigid contract will simply serve to antagonize the parties, particularly the host state, which still has

---

147 Bernardini, 'Stabilization and Adaptation in Oil and Gas Investments' (n 88) 110.

many sovereign prerogatives at its disposal, which it could utilize at least in the short term, thus putting the investor at a disadvantage. Should the parties fail to reach an agreement, the clause stipulates that the matter ought to be referred to arbitration.

The renegotiation clause should thus be supplemented by an arbitration clause from which the tribunal will derive its authority to adapt the contract on behalf of the parties. One way the arbitrators may be given a free hand to decide to adapt contracts is by giving them the power to decide the matter *ex aequo et bono* (from equity and conscience or according to the right and good).[148] This frees the arbitrators from the 'constraints of the applicable law' and enables them to amend and adjust long-term contracts to changed circumstances. Another way this goal could be attained is by electing the procedural law of a jurisdiction that permits the adaptation of contractual provisions.

Examples of such jurisdictions include the Netherlands and Sweden. Article 1020, paragraph 4(c) of the Netherlands Arbitration Act provides that parties may submit a matter to the arbitrator and the latter is authorized to fill in the gaps of a contract or modify the legal relationship between the parties.[149] Similarly, the Swedish Arbitration Act states that: 'the filling of gaps in contracts can also be referred to arbitrators'.[150] Thus, the arbitration contained in the concession agreement should stipulate that the procedural law applicable is Dutch law or Swedish law. That would be a means through which the parties could resolve any issues of jurisdiction that may arise in the event that renegotiations fail and the parties have to submit the matter to arbitration.

The proposed solution is a feasible one in the light of political risk insurance. As has been seen in this and preceding chapters, stabilization clauses purport to prevent the host state from unilaterally abrogating concession agreements. It has, however, been seen that natural resources are mercurial and do episodically escalate, which is a factor contributing to the advanced stages of the resource nationalism cycle. The host state in such circumstances wishes to maximize the benefits of this windfall in profits that the investor is receiving. Host states are unlikely to abide by the terms of the contract if they are too rigid.

As noted by Joffé and others: 'Despite the inclusion in original contracts of stabilization clauses designed to anticipate and counter the risk implicit in the obsolescing bargain, this outcome is inevitable. Stabilization clauses have rarely been effective since producer governments still enforced changes in contractual terms to reflect their perception of their right to capture additional rent'.[151] For this

---

148 Berger (n 44) 1379.
149 English Translation of the Netherlands Arbitration Act 1986 http://www.dutchcivillaw.com/legislation/civilprocedure044.htm (last accessed 9 June 2015).
150 Swedish Arbitration Act, *Arbitration Institute of the Stockholm Chamber of Commerce* http://www.sccinstitute.com/?id=23746 (last accessed 9 June 2015).
151 G. Joffé, P. Stevens, T. George, J. Lux and C. Searle, 'Expropriation of Oil and Gas Investments: Historical, Legal and Economic Perspectives in a New Age of Resource Nationalism' (2009) 2 *Journal of World Energy and Business* 3, 22.

reason, stabilization clauses pose more of a risk to the investor than renegotiation clauses, which foster a long-term cooperative relationship between the investor and the state.

Agreements between the host state and the investor must be seen as susceptible to continuous adjustment rather than 'a body of fixed rights and obligations impervious to political, economic and social changes'.[152] Although such an approach may represent a departure from traditional doctrines, Anglo–American theory of contract has not always remained fossilized and inflexible. A departure from the traditional doctrine is in the common interest of both the investor and the host government.[153] This is owing to the fact that flexibility in the contract enables the parties to renegotiate the terms of the contract in a way that accommodates the legitimate public functions of the host state and the legitimate expectations of the investor. The cooperative relationship that this fosters makes it less likely for the host state to take resource nationalist actions, thus rendering the renegotiation clause less risky when assessing the project for insurance purposes.

6.5 Conclusion

It could thus be concluded that renegotiation and adaptation of contracts is certainly within the realms of possibility, even without a clause to that effect in the concession agreement. This is evidenced in the principle of *rebus sic stantibus*, which excuses the parties from performance in instances where the very root of the contract has been affected by a change of circumstances. This of course comes with the added proviso that this change was beyond the contemplation of the parties at the time that the contract was formalized. This principle is recognized by international law and most major legal systems that follow the common law and the civil law.

The difficulty with relying on the principle of *rebus sic stantibus* lies in the fact that it is applied only in limited circumstances, owing to the courts' respect for the sanctity of contracts. Furthermore, whilst some courts have the power to adjust the contracts in some jurisdictions, others do not, whilst some may simply terminate the contract altogether. These myriad possibilities and outcomes simply lead to uncertainty. This is further compounded by the fact that *rebus sic stantibus* applies solely to changed circumstances that are to the detriment of the parties.

This combined with the emphasis on *pacta sunt servanda* as an overriding principle in judicial decisions and legal instruments alike leads to the conclusion that inserting renegotiation and adaptation clauses into concession agreements may be

---

152 Samuel K.B. Asante, 'The Concept of Stability of Contractual Relations in the Transnational Investment Process' in Kamal Hossain (ed), *Legal Aspects of the New International Economic Order* (Frances Pinter 1980) 259.
153 ibid.

the best way forward. The renegotiation clause should also stipulate what must happen if the renegotiation process fails.

In this chapter I have recommended that, should the parties fail to come to an agreement subsequent to the renegotiation clause, then they should refer the matter to a tribunal. The arbitrator should also be given the power to adapt the terms of the contract. The tribunal can be given such authority by the parties, who should select the law of a jurisdiction that would grant the arbitrators the authority to adapt the terms of the contract on the parties' behalf. This is owing to the fact that authority to do so can only be derived from the contract itself. Without such authority, there is a possibility that the award can be set aside under the New York Convention, or annulled under the ICSID Convention. The flexibility facilitated by renegotiation and adaptation is necessary as it is the best means of simultaneously preserving the state's right to pursue legitimate public functions, whilst still protecting the legitimate expectations of the investor.

Chapter 7

Conclusion

The aim of this chapter is to summarize the main findings of this book. This book aimed to show that some form of flexibility is needed in concession agreements and this can be fostered through renegotiation clauses. This flexibility enables both the host state and the investor to renegotiate the terms of the contract as and when circumstances change, as they invariably will throughout the life of the contract. This is more likely to foster a long-term relationship and the cooperation of the government. A government is less likely to take a resource nationalist stance if it is able to renegotiate the contract intermittently. This can be contrasted with the insertion of stabilization clauses which are far too rigid and are less able to withstand the advanced stages of the resource nationalism cycle.

Chapter 2 of this book concerned the resource nationalism cycle. The chapter commenced by discussing what the term 'foreign direct investment' entailed. It was seen that in order for an entity to qualify as an investment, there must be an acquisition of a lasting interest, which must flow from one economy to another. In the case of minerals and petroleum such a process is fostered when the host state grants a concession to the investor. Under such concessions, the investor is given the right to explore and exploit the host state's natural resource. In return, the host state receives revenues in the form of royalties and taxes from the investor, typically at a preferential rate in order to attract investment.

Once the concession is signed, the investor will sink substantial resources into the host state, which in turn will enable the investor to explore and exploit natural resources in the host state. In order to recoup this investment, the investor will have to make a profit. Chapter 2 endeavoured to show, however, that in the long run the investment once sunk becomes susceptible to a plethora of political risks. In turn, these risks jeopardize the investor's prospect of making a profit. Such risks will typically manifest in the advanced stages of the resource nationalism cycle.

The resource nationalism cycle is one that begins at a point when a resource rich host state wishes to attract foreign direct investment. This is typically because it lacks the capacity to explore and exploit its vast natural resources. The government of the host state will thus take a stance which is geared towards liberalizing the economy. This means various incentives, including fiscal incentives such as lower taxes and royalties, which will in turn render investing in the host state more profitable and attractive to investors. The host state will usually offer this at a time when the prices of the natural resource are relatively low. The aim of the host state is to appear as a sufficiently attractive investment destination.

The difficulty arises once the investment has been sunk and the prices of natural resources begin to experience a sustained upward trend. The high prices might lead to a perception that the foreign investor is making a large profit at the expense of the host state. This may lead to political pressure on the host government to maximize its control over its natural resources. It is in such instances that the state has typically sought to exert greater control over its investment. In moderate cases, this may mean increasing taxes and in extreme cases it may lead to outright nationalization. Either situation will involve the revision of any fiscal incentives that the investor has been enjoying or the outright nationalization of the investor's assets.

In this sense, the resource nationalism cycle intersects with the obsolescing bargaining model. This model essentially espouses that the incentives offered in concession agreements are susceptible to later changes by the host government once the investment has been sunk. During the negotiation stages, the host state needs the foreign capital in order to explore and exploit its natural resources. In this sense, the host state is in a relatively weaker position than the investor, especially when the latter has alternative countries in which to invest its capital. The investor is thus in a position to make certain demands, including fiscal incentives, that the host state seemingly has no choice but to acquiesce in.

However, once the investment is sunk, the host state is in a stronger position than the investor because of the legislative and administrative prerogatives at its disposal. These prerogatives could be utilized in a way that adversely affect the investor's chances of making a profit. This may mean revoking the fiscal incentives that the investor has previously enjoyed. It may also lead to an outright nationalization, as highlighted above. Both outcomes jeopardize the investor's prospects of making a profit. This suggests that some form of protection is needed and this is something that the investor is in a position to demand during the negotiation stage, when it is the stronger party. To protect themselves from these risks, investors will take contractual and extra-contractual precautions.

As far as extra-contractual precautions are concerned, the investor may obtain investment insurance from MIGA, OPIC or any private investment insurance scheme. Through these the foreign investor is able to insure its investment against the political risks highlighted. In addition, the investor may insist on various contractual clauses, and will invariably insist that an arbitration clause is inserted. This is to ensure that any disputes arising between the host state and the investor may be heard by a neutral forum, operating outside the fray of national judicial mechanisms. Moreover, investors and their financiers typically insist on the insertion of stabilization clauses into the concession. These are clauses under which the state makes an express undertaking not to take any administrative or legislative action that will adversely affect the investor.

162 Resource nationalism in international investment law

The validity of stabilization clauses is upheld by arbitral tribunals; despite arguments raised they militate against the principle of permanent sovereignty over natural resources. Chapter 3 of this book showed that the principle of permanent sovereignty over natural resources is a legitimate one under international law. In fact, it is through this very principle that host states derive their authority to grant concessions to foreign investors.

Chapter 3 then looked at the academic debates and case law dealing with stabilization clauses. It was concluded that when states freely enter into agreements with foreign investors, they are bound by them. This is because arbitral tribunals respect the sanctity of contracts and often invoke the international law principle of *pacta sunt servanda* as the basis of their decisions. A host state cannot invoke the principle of permanent sovereignty over natural resources as an excuse for the unilateral termination of contracts containing stabilization clauses. It has been seen that arbitral tribunals typically reject this argument. Once a state breaches its concession agreements, there are pecuniary consequences and these were discussed in Chapter 4 of this book.

It is axiomatic that when a state terminates a contract with the investor, the former will have to indemnify the latter. There are two standards of compensation under international investment law: appropriate compensation and the 'Hull formula'. Under the former standard, compensation is determined on a case-by-case basis. Under the latter, it must be prompt, adequate and effective. Prompt means there should be no unwarranted delays in payment. Effective means that payment should be made in a freely convertible currency. Adequate means paying the investor the full market value of the nationalized asset. This also includes lost future profits. This book has demonstrated that, although there is no consensus as to which standard of compensation ought to apply under international investment law, it is clear that in either case arbitral tribunals have often included lost future profits as part of their compensation package. This is a necessary facet, because it ensures that the investor is restored to a position that the latter would have been in if the state had not unilaterally terminated the contract.

Under the efficient breach theory, a promisor is permitted to pay damages in lieu of performance if it would be efficient to do so. Efficiency under the Pareto definition means that at least one party should benefit from an action and no party should lose out. Thus, if the promisor makes a profit, after leaving the disappointed promisee in exactly the position he or she would have been in, then this would be efficient behaviour. This would include paying the disappointed promisee lost profits as well.

It could thus be argued that compelling the state to pay lost future profits renders the compensation standards efficient. This is because the investor is left in exactly the same position he would have been in had the termination not occurred. Furthermore, the state would make a profit from its natural resource. The limitation of the efficient breach theory in an international investment law context, however, is that it assumes that the parties to a contract are invariably seeking to maximize profits. This is not actually the case with the state, whose primary function is to pursue legitimate public purposes. Typically, when a state terminates a contract, it is because it is making changes to its socio-economic policies. Whilst compelling the state to indemnify the investor encourages efficiency, it does not give the state sufficient flexibility to do so. This would suggest that some form of contractual flexibility is needed in the concession.

The difficulty with such a rigid approach lies primarily in the fact that the prices of natural resources such as oil and copper are mercurial. This means that they are subject to appreciations and depreciations over time. Stabilization clauses are not a very effective tool for adapting to such circumstances and the inflexibility of these clauses renders them a less effective tool in the face of the resource nationalism cycle. This was illustrated in Chapter 5, which was a case study on the Zambian windfall tax. This chapter is a good demonstration of the resource nationalism cycle. Zambia is a mono-economy that has relied on copper from her very inception. At independence her copper reserves were in private hands and dominated by two major corporations: the Roan Selection Trust and Anglo American.

These companies paid royalties and corporate tax to the British South Africa Company (BSAC), which held all mining rights in Northern Rhodesia. This prerogative shifted to the Government of Zambia, once she attained independence. However, the taxes and royalties received by the Government of Zambia paled in comparison to the profits the mining companies were making and externalizing. In fact, one of the concerns raised was that none of the revenue being generated was being reinvested in the mines. Moreover, there were concerns that with this domination by two foreign corporations, there was a danger that the interests of the people of Zambia were to become subservient to foreign ones.

Given this background, President Kaunda proceeded to nationalize the mines through the Mines and Minerals Act 1969. This was in order to advance the philosophy of 'humanism', under which it was seen as the Government of Zambia's responsibility to look after all citizens. The mines were thus placed under Zambia Consolidated Copper Mines Limited (ZCCM) in 1982. Contemporaneously, Zambia became a one-party state. Nationalization not only fostered job creation, but the revenues generated from the government controlled mines enabled the construction of roads, hospitals, schools and other social services. The sustainability of these social amenities, however, was contingent upon the copper prices remaining high. The oil crisis of 1974, coupled with the simultaneous depreciation in copper prices, forced the government to borrow money in order to maintain these services.

Subsequent to the reintroduction of multiparty democracy, and popular discontent with Zambia's worsening economic situation, Chiluba's MMD party won the elections held in 1991. As part of the MMD's promise to liberalize the Zambian economy, the government proceeded to privatize the Zambian mining industry.

Several advantages emanated from the privatization of the mines. The most notable advantage is that it has resuscitated an industry that had stagnated. There were, however, several disadvantages. These included mass redundancies, environmental degradation, lack of access to healthcare and a general deterioration of the standard of living. This was further compounded by the fact that profits generated were taxed at a preferential rate and were largely externalized. These profits increased further by a dramatic rise in the price of copper.

This windfall in copper prices led to calls for the government to rethink the tax incentives that mining companies were enjoying. This was owing to the fact that they were gaining immense profits to the detriment of the people of Zambia. In 2005/2006, Zambia had only made US$10 million in tax revenues. This is comparatively low when contrasted with other copper producers such as Chile, which made US$8 billion in revenues during the same period. The potential for increased revenue led the Government of Zambia to introduce the windfall tax in 2008. In order to foster this, the government passed the Mines and Minerals Development Act No. 7 of 2008. Article 160 of the Act terminated all existing concessions between the government and the mining companies. The government then increased the corporate tax and the royalty rate.

However, many of the terminated concessions contained tax stability clauses. They stipulated that, for a period of 15 years, the tax rates would not be increased in a manner that would have a 'material adverse effect' on the distributable profits of the foreign owned mining companies. From this chapter, it can be seen that the insertion of tax stability clauses rendered the development agreements too rigid. Without them, however, it is unlikely that investors would have entered into the concession at all. It is clear, however, from this and preceding chapters that a host state is unlikely to abide by contracts that are too rigid. It is in the interests of both the investor and the state to allow some form of flexibility in the contracts.

It is for this reason that this book advocates the insertion of renegotiation clauses into the concession agreement. This book has shown that renegotiation is also possible in instances where there is no clause in the contract. The principle of *rebus sic stantibus* is well recognized under international law, civil law and the common law. Universally, however, it has been seen that the changed circumstances must be unforeseen, and must have an adverse effect on the economic viability of the contract. Moreover, it has been seen that the principle only applies in very limited case because the courts, both international and domestic, respect the sanctity of contracts and are only prepared to depart from it in the extraordinary and limited circumstances highlighted above.

The principle of *rebus sic stantibus* is thus not a reliable starting point because it would seem to apply only to circumstances which adversely affect the parties, which is not the case when one is referring to windfall profits. Windfall profits, after all, deal with a situation where one party, the investor, is in a better off position owing to higher mineral prices. Moreover, it would only apply in limited circumstances and, because of the variations in legal systems, the powers of the courts or tribunal depend on the jurisdiction or choice of law. This would suggest that renegotiation should be facilitated through a contractual mechanism. This could be accomplished through the insertion of a renegotiation clause. This would identify renegotiation clauses as contractual mechanisms that could be inserted into concession agreements to foster the process of renegotiation. Such a clause should identify the triggering event, the effect of the trigger event, the objectives of the renegotiation and, finally, the course of action if the renegotiation fails.

In the event where the renegotiation fails, it should be specified that the matter should go before an arbitral tribunal. The state and the investor will have to specify in the contract that they have granted the arbitral tribunal the authority or jurisdiction to amend concession agreements. Arbitrators will not be willing to do so in the absence of jurisdiction and if they did it may be a ground upon which the award they render could be refused recognition and enforcement under Article V(1)(c) of the New York Convention of 1958. Therefore, in order to ensure that they have jurisdiction, arbitrators would need the consent of the parties, which is derived from the arbitration agreement itself. In this regard, the parties would have to stipulate this in the agreement.

It could thus be concluded that when the state breaches a contract containing stabilization clauses, then the state is liable to compensate the investor. This will include lost future profits. Whilst the compensation standards under international investment law ensure efficiency, it is asserted in this book that the assumption when looking at efficient breach is that the aim of both parties is to maximize wealth. This is not often the case with the state. Invariably, the goal of the state is to pursue legitimate public functions and the current compensation regime does not permit that. This in itself necessitates flexibility in contractual agreements between the state and foreign investors. This can be facilitated through the insertion of renegotiation clauses in the concession agreement. The renegotiation clauses advocated in the literature studied are only triggered when the change of circumstances adversely affects the investor. This book proposed renegotiation clauses that are triggered when a change of circumstances occurs that benefits the investor, usually in the form of windfall profits.

Bibliography

Books

Aharoni, Y., *The Foreign Investment Decision Process* (Library of Congress 1966)

Atiyah, P., *An Introduction to the Law of Contract* (6th edn, OUP 2005)

Atiyah, P.S., and Smith, S.A., *Atiyah's Introduction to the Law of Contract* (6th edn, Clarendon Press 2006)

Baker, J.C., *Foreign Direct Investment in Less Developed Countries: The Role of ICSID and MIGA* (Quorum Books 1999)

Bayulgen, O., *Foreign Investment and Political Regimes: The Oil Sector in Azerbaijan, Russia and Norway* (Cambridge University Press 2010)

Beveridge, A.A., *African Businessmen and Development in Zambia* (Princeton 1979)

Boyle, A. and Chinkin, C., *The Making of International Law* (OUP 2007)

Bremmer, I., *The End of the Free Market* (Portfolio 2010)

Brooker, P., *Non-Democratic Regimes: Theory, Government and Politics* (Macmillan 2000)

Brownlie, I., *Principles of International Law* (6th edn, OUP 2003)

Brownlie, I., *Principles of Public International Law* (7th edn, OUP 2008)

Burawoy, M., *The Colour of Class on the Copper Mines: From African Advancement to Zambianization* (Manchester University Press 1971)

Burns, J.H., and Hart, H.L.A., (eds), *The Collected Works of Jeremy Bentham* (London 1977)

Butler, L., *Copper Empire: Mining and the Colonial State in Northern Rhodesia, c. 1930–64* (Palgrave 2007)

Calabresi, G. and Bobbit, P., *Tragic Choices* (WW Norton & Company 1978)

Campbell, O. and Bhatia, A., *Privatization in Africa* (World Bank 1998)

Coleman, F.L., *The Northern Rhodesia Copperbelt 1899–1962* (Manchester University Press 1971)

Corrales, J. and Penfold, M., *Dragon in the Tropics: Hugo Chávez and the Political Economy of Revolution in Venezuela* (Brookings Institute 2011)

Crawford, J., *The Creation of States in International Law* (2nd edn, OUP 2006)

Crawford, J., *The International Law Commission's Articles on State Responsibility, Introduction, Text and Commentaries* (Cambridge University Press 2002)

Diamond, L., *Developing Democracy: Toward Consolidation* (Johns Hopkins University Press 1999)

Dolzer, R. and Schreuer, C., *Principles of International Investment Law* (2nd edn, OUP 2012)

Dolzer, R., and Schreuer, C., *Principles of International Investment Law* (OUP 2008)

Fatouros, A.A., *Government Guarantees to Foreign Investors* (Columbia University Press 1962) 16

Bibliography 167

Ferguson, J., *Expectations of Modernity: Myths and Meanings of Urban Life on the Zambian Copperbelt* (University of California Press 1999)

Fox, W., *International Commercial Agreements: A Primer on Drafting, Negotiating and Resolving Disputes* (Kluwer Law International 1998)

Fraser, A. and Lungu, J., *For Whom the Windfalls: Winners and Losers in the Privatisation of Zambia's Copper Mines* (Civil Society Trade Network of Zambia 2006)

Garner, B.A. (ed), *Black's Law Dictionary* (Thomson West 2009)

Graham, C., *Safety Nets, Politics and the Poor* (The Brookings Institute 1994)

Hackworth, G., *Digest of International Law: Volume 3* (US Government Printing Office 1942)

Hofstede, G., *Culture's Consequences: International Differences in Work-related Values* (SAGE Publications 1984)

Holmes, O.W., *The Common Law* (Macmillan 1882)

Horn, N., *Legal Problems of Codes of Conduct for Multinational Enterprises* (Kluwer 1980)

Hughes Parry, Sir D.A., *Sanctity of Contracts in English Law* (Stevens 1959)

Jensen, N.M., *Nation-States and the Multinational Corporation* (Princeton 2006)

Karl, T.L., *The Paradox of Plenty: Oil Booms and Petro-States* (University of California 1997)

Kaunda, K.D. and Moss, C.M., *A Humanist in Africa* (Longman 1966)

Lowenfeld, A.F., *International Economic Law* (2nd edn, OUP 2008)

Lungu, J., *The Politics of Reforming Zambia's Mining Tax Regime* (Southern Africa Resource Watch 2009)

Mann, F.A., *Studies in International Law* (OUP 1972)

Marboe, I., *Calculation of Compensation and Damages in International Investment Law* (OUP 2009)

Markesinis, B.S., Unberath, H. and Johnston, A., *The German Law of Contract: A Comparative Treatise* (2nd edn, Hart Publishing 2006)

Martin, A., *Mining Their Own Business: Zambia's Struggle Against Western Control* (Hutchinson 1972)

McLachlan, C., Shore, L. and Weiniger, M., *International Investment Arbitration: Substantive Principles* (OUP 2010)

Muchlinski, P., *Multinational Enterprises and the Law* (OUP 2007)

Mvunga, M.P., *Land Law and Policy in Zambia* (Institute for African Studies 1982)

Mwambwa, S., Griffiths, A. and Kahler, A., *A Fool's Paradise? Zambia's Mining Tax Regime* (Centre for Trade Policy and Development 2010)

Mwenda, K.K., *Contemporary Issues in Corporate Finance and Investment Law* (Penn Press 2000)

Ndulo, M., *Mining Rights in Zambia* (Kenneth Kaunda Foundation 1988)

Nicholas, B., *The French Law of Contract* (2nd edn, OUP 1992)

Nkrumah, K., *Consciencism: Philosophy and Ideology for Decolonisation and Development With Particular Reference to the African Revolution* (Heinemann 1964)

Noreng, Ø., *Oil and Islam: Social and Economic Issues* (Wiley 1997)

Nwogugu, E.I., *The Legal Problems of Foreign Investment in Developing Countries* (Manchester University Press 1965)

Nyerere, J.K., *Ujamaa: Essays on Socialism* (OUP 1968)

Parra, F., *Oil Politics: A Modern History of Petroleum* (IB Tauris 2004)

Peel, E., *Treitel: The Law of Contract* (13th edn, Sweet & Maxwell 2011)

Peet, R., *Global Capitalism: Theories of Societal Development* (Routledge 1991)

Peter, W., *Arbitration and Renegotiation of International Investment Agreements* (Kluwer Law International 1995)

Petrov, N., Lipman, M. and Hale, H.H., *Overmanaged Democracy in Russia: Governance Implications of Hybrid Regimes* (Carnegie Endowment for International Peace 2010)

Posner, E.A. and Sykes, A.O., *Economic Foundations of International Law* (Harvard University Press 2013)

Posner, R.A., *Economic Analysis of Law* (8th edn, Wolters Kluwer 2011)

Posner, R.A., *The Economics of Justice* (Harvard University Press 1981)

Salacuse, J.W., *The Law of Investment Treaties* (OUP 2010)

Salacuse, J.W., *The Three Laws of International Investment: National, Contractual, and International Frameworks for Foreign Capital* (OUP 2013)

Salter, M. and Mason, J., *Writing Law Dissertations: An Introduction and Guide to the Conduct of Legal Research* (Pearson 2007)

Sands, P. and Klein, P., *Bowett's Law of International Institutions* (6th edn, Sweet & Maxwell 2009)

Sardanis, A., *A Venture in Africa: The Challenges of African Business* (IB Tauris 2007)

Sardanis, A., *Africa: Another Side of the Coin: Northern Rhodesia's Final Years and Zambia's Nationhood* (IB Tauris 2011)

Schachter, O., *International Law in Theory and Practice* (Brill 1991)

Schill, S.W., *The Multilateralization of International Investment Law* (Cambridge University Press 2014)

Schreuer, C., *The ICSID Convention: A Commentary* (Cambridge University Press 2001)

Schrijver, N., *Sovereignty Over Natural Resources: Balancing Rights and Duties* (Cambridge University Press 1997)

Smith, S.A., *Contract Theory* (Clarendon Press 2004)

Sornarajah, M., *The International Law on Foreign Investment* (3rd edn, Cambridge University Press 2010)

Sornarajah, M., *The Settlement of Foreign Investment Disputes* (Kluwer 2000)

Steingruber, A.M., *Consent in International Arbitration* (OUP 2012)

Subedi, S., *International Investment Law: Reconciling Policy and Principle* (2nd edn, Hart Publishing 2012)

Taverne, B., *Petroleum, Industry and Governments: A Global Study of the Involvement of Industry and Government in the Production and Use of Petroleum* (2nd edn, Kluwer 2008)

Treitel, G.H., *Frustration and Force Majeure* (Sweet & Maxwell 1994)

Upex, R. and Bennett, G., *Davies on Contract* (10th edn, Sweet & Maxwell 2008)

Várady, T., Barceló III, J.J. and von Mehren, A.T., *International Commercial Arbitration: A Transnational Perspective* (3rd edn, Thomson West 2006)

Vernon, R., *Sovereignty at Bay: The Multinational Spread of US Enterprises* (Longman 1971)

Whiteman, M.M., *Damages in International Law: Volume 3* (United States Government Printing Office 1943)

Yates, D.A., *The Rentier State in Africa: Oil Rent Dependency and Neo-colonialism in the Republic of Gabon* (Africa World Press 1996)

Book chapters

Asante, S.K.B., 'The Concept of Stability of Contractual Relations in the Transnational Investment Process' in Hossain, K. (ed), *Legal Aspects of the New International Economic Order* (Frances Pinter 1980)

Chowdhury, S.R., 'Permanent Sovereignty Over Natural Resources: Substratum of the Seoul Declaration' in de Wart, P., Peters, P. and Denters, E. (eds), *International Law and Development* (Martinus Nijhoff 1988)

Bibliography 169

Chowdhury, S.R., 'Permanent Sovereignty Over Natural Resources' in Hossain, K. and Chowdhury, S.R. (eds), *Permanent Sovereignty Over Natural Resources in International Law* (Frances Pinter 1984)

Cunningham, S.M., 'Multinationals and Restructuring in Latin America' in Dixon, C.J., Drakakis-Smith, D. and Watts, H. (eds), *Multinational Corporations and the Third World* (Routledge 1986)

Faber, M.L.O., 'The Recovery of the Mineral Rights' in Faber, M.L.O. and Potter, J.G. (eds), *Towards Economic Independence: Papers on the Nationalization of the Copper Industry in Zambia* (Cambridge 1971)

Fraser, A., 'Introduction: Boom and Bust on the Zambian Copperbelt' in Fraser, A. and Larmer, M. (eds), *Zambia, Mining, and Neoliberalism Boom and Bust on the Globalized Copperbelt* (Palgrave Macmillan 2010)

Garrett, G. and Lange, P., 'Internationalization, Institutions and Political Change' in Keohane, R.O. and Milner, H.V. (eds), *Internationalization and Domestic Politics* (Cambridge University Press 1996)

Gewald, J. and Soeters, S., 'African Miners and Shape-shifting Capital Flight: The Case of Luanshya/Baluba' in Fraser, A. and Larmer, M. (eds), *Zambia, Mining, and Neoliberalism: Boom and Bust on the Globalized Copperbelt* (Palgrave Macmillan 2010)

Horn, N., 'Changes in Circumstances and the Revision of Contracts in Some European Laws and International Law' in Horn, N. (ed), *Adaptation and Renegotiation of Contracts in International Trade and Finance* (Kluwer 1995)

Hossain, K., 'Introduction' in Hossain, K. and Chowdhury, S.R. (eds), *Permanent Sovereignty Over Natural Resources* (Frances Printer 1984)

Jaenicke, G., 'Consequences of a Breach of an Investment Agreement Governed by International Law, by General Principles of Law or by Domestic Law of the Host State' in Dicke, D. (ed), *Foreign Investment in the Present and New International Economic Order*, Vol 2 (Warburg 1987)

Jimenez de Aréchaga, E., 'Application of the Rules of States' Responsibility to the Nationalization of Foreign-owned Property' in Hossain, K. (ed), *Legal Aspects of the New International Economic Order* (Frances Pinter 1980)

Kröll, S.M., 'The Renegotiation and Adaptation of Investment Contracts' in Horn, N. and Kröll, S.M. (eds), *Arbitrating Foreign Investment Disputes* (Kluwer Law International 2004)

Larmer, M., 'Enemies Within? Opposition to the Zambian One-party State 1972–1980' in Gewald, J., Hinfelaar, M. and Macola, G. (eds), *One Zambia, Many Histories* (Library of Congress 2008)

Lowenfeld, A.F., 'Lex Mercatoria: An Arbitrator's View' in Carbonneau, T.E. (ed), *Lex Mercatoria and Arbitration* (Kluwer 1998)

Potter, J.G., 'The 51 Per Cent Nationalization of the Zambian Copper Mines' in Faber, M.L.O. and Potter, J.G. (eds), *Towards Economic Independence: Papers on the Nationalization of the Copper Industry in Zambia* (Cambridge University Press 1971)

Rakner, L., van de Walle, N. and Mulaisho, D., 'Zambia' in Devarajan, S., Dollar, D.R. and Holmgren, T. (eds), *Aid and reform in Africa: Volume 1* (World Bank 2001)

Schlemmer, E.C., 'Investment, Investor, Nationality and Shareholders' in Muchlinski, P., Ortino, F. and Schreuer, C. (eds), *The Oxford Handbook of International Investment Law* (OUP 2008)

Shan, W., and Gallagher, N., 'China' in Brown, C. (ed), *Commentaries on Selected Model Investment Treaties* (OUP 2013)

170 Resource nationalism in international investment law

Schrijver, N., 'Natural Resource Management and Sustainable Development' in Weiss, T.G. and Daws, S. (eds), *The Oxford Handbook on the United Nations* (OUP 2007)

Simutanyi, N., 'The Politics of Constitutional Reform in Zambia: From Executive Dominance to Public Participation?' in Chirwa, D.M. and Nijzink, L. (eds), *Accountable Government in Africa: Perspectives from Public Law and Political Studies* (United Nations 2012)

Vargiu, P., 'Environmental Expropriation in International Investment Law' in Treves, T., Seatzu, F. and Trevisanut, S. (eds), *Foreign Investment and Common Concerns: An International Law Perspective* (Routledge 2013)

Weil, P., 'Les clauses de stabilization ou d'intangibilité insérées dans les accords de développement économique' in *Mélangues offerts à Charles Rousseau* (A Pedone 1974)

Zakariya, H.S., 'Changed Circumstances and the Continued Validity of Mineral Development Contracts' in Hossain, K. (ed), *Legal Aspects of the New International Economic Order* (Frances Pinter 1980)

Zakariya, H.S., 'Sovereignty Over Natural Resources and the Search for a New International Order' in Hossain, K. (ed), *Legal Aspects of the New International Economic Order* (Frances Pinter 1980)

Ziegler, A.R. and Gratton, L., 'Investment Insurance' in Muchlinski, P., Ortino, F. and Schreuer, C. (eds), *The Oxford Handbook of International Investment Law* (OUP 2008)

Articles

Adler, B.E., 'Efficient Breach Theory Through the Looking Glass' (2008) 83 *New York University Law Review* 1679

Afrin, Z., 'Foreign Direct Investments and Sustainable Development in the Least Developed Countries' (2004) 10 *Annual Survey of International & Comparative Law* 215

Akinsanya, A., 'Permanent Sovereignty Over Natural Resources and the Future of Foreign Investment' (1978) 7 *Journal of International Studies* 124

Al Qurashi, Z.A., 'Renegotiation of International Petroleum Agreements' (2005) 22 *Journal of International Arbitration* 261

Alavi, M., Kayworth, T.R. and Leidner, D.E., 'An Empirical Examination of the Influence of Organisational Culture on Knowledge Management Practices' (2005) 22 *Journal of Management Information Systems* 191

Al-Emadi, T.A. and Al-Asmakh, M.A., 'Cultural Differences and Their Impact: Some Brief Comments' (2006) 5 *Chinese Journal of International Law* 807

Amerasinghe, C.F., 'State Breaches of Contracts with Aliens and International Law' (1964) 58 *American Journal of International Law* 881

Arbtali, E., 'Political Regimes, Investment Risk and Resource Nationalism: An Empirical Analysis' http://regconf.hse.ru/uploads/7da62134fab330f54f067e5cd2e603c40298cd7e.pdf

Asante, S., 'Stability of Contractual Relations in Transnational Investment Process' (1979) 28 *International and Comparative Law Quarterly* 401

Asante, S.K.B., 'Restructuring Transnational Mineral Agreements' (1979) 73 *American Journal of International Law* 335

Barrera-Hernándes, L., 'Sovereignty Over Natural Resources Under Examination: The Inter-American System for Human Rights and Natural Resource Allocation' (2006) 12 *Annual Survey of International and Comparative Law* 43

Baxter, R.R., 'International Law in "Her Infinite Variety"' (1980) 29 *International and Comparative Law Quarterly* 549

Baylies, C. and Szeftel, M., 'The Fall and Rise of Multiparty Politics in Zambia' (1992) 54 *Review of African Political Economy* 75

Berger, K.P., 'Renegotiation and Adaptation of International Investment Contracts: The Role of Contract Drafters and Arbitrators' (2003) 36 *Vanderbilt Journal of Transnational Law* 1347

Bernardini, P., 'Investment Protection under Bilateral Investment Treaties and Investment Contracts' (2001) 2 *Journal of World Investment* 235

Bernardini, P., 'Stabilization and Adaptation in Oil and Gas Investments' (2008) 1 *Journal of World Energy Law and Business* 98

Bernardini, P., 'The Renegotiation of the Investment Contract' (1998) 13 *Foreign Investment Law Journal* 411

Bernardini, P., 'Stabilization and Adaptation in Oil and Gas Investments' (2008) 1 *Journal of World Energy Law and Business* 98

Birmingham, R., 'Breach of Contract, Damage Measures, and Economic Efficiency' (1970) 24 *Rutgers Law Review* 273

Bleicher, S.A., 'The Legal Significance of Re-citation of General Assembly Resolutions' (1969) 63 *American Journal of International Law* 444

Borehand, E.M., 'Contractual Claims in International Law' (1913) 13 *Columbia Law Review* 457

Boubakri, N., Cosset, J. and Guedhami, O., 'Liberalization, Corporate Governance and the Performance of Privatized Firms in Developing Countries' (2005) 11 *Journal of Corporate Finance* 767

Bowett, D.W., 'State Contracts With Aliens: Contemporary Developments on Compensation for Termination or Breach' (1988) 49 *British Yearbook of International Law* 49

Bratton, M., 'Zambia Starts Over' (1992) 3 *Journal of Democracy* 81

Brooks, R.R.W., 'The Efficient Performance Hypothesis' (2006) 116 *Yale Law Journal* 571

Burdette, M., 'Nationalization in Zambia: A Critique of Bargaining Theory' (1977) 11 *Canadian Journal of African Studies* 471

Büthe, T. and Milner, H., 'The Politics of Foreign Direct Investment into Developing Countries: Increasing FDI Through International Trade Agreements?' (2008) 52 *American Journal of Political Science* 741

Butler, A., 'Resource Nationalism and the African National Congress' (2013) 113 *Journal of the Southern African Institute of Mining and Metallury* 11

Cantegreil, J., 'The Audacity of the Texaco/Calasiatic Award: Rene-Jean Dupuy and the Internationalization of Foreign Investment Law' (2011) 22 *European Journal of International Law* 441

Chamisa, E.E., 'The Relevance and Observance of IASC Standards in Developing Countries and the Particular Case of Zimbabwe' (2000) 35 *International Journal of Accounting* 267

Chatterjee, S.K., 'The Stabilization Clause Myth in Investment Agreements' (1988) 5 *Journal of International Arbitration* 97

Chua, A., 'The Paradox of Free Market Democracy: Rethinking Development Policy' (2000) 41 *Harvard International Law Journal* 287

Chua, A., 'The Privatization–Nationalization Cycle: The Link Between Markets and Ethnicity in Developing Countries' (1995) 95 *Columbia Law Review* 262

Chua, C., 'Markets, Democracy and Ethnicity: Toward a New Paradigm for Law and Development' (1998) 108 *Yale Law Journal* 1

Coale, M.T.B., 'Stabilization Clauses in International Petroleum Transactions' (2002) 30 *Denver Journal of International Law and Policy* 217

Coleman, J.L., 'Efficiency, Utility, and Wealth Maximization' (1980) 8 *Hofstra Law Review* 509

Cotula, L. 'Reconciling Regulatory Stability and Evolution of Environmental Standards in Investment Contracts: Towards a Rethink of Stabilization Clauses' (2008) 1 *Journal of World Energy Law & Business* 158

Cotula, L., 'Regulatory Takings, Stabilization Clauses and Sustainable Development' (2008) *OECD Global Forum on International Investment* 13 http://www.oecd.org/investment/globalforum/40311122.pdf

Craig, J., 'Evaluating Privatization in Zambia: A Tale of Two Processes' 27 *Review of African Political Economy* 357

Craig, J., 'Putting Privatisation Into Practice: The Case of Zambia Consolidated Copper Mines Ltd' (2001) 3 *Journal of Modern African Studies* 389

Crawford, J.F. and Johnson, W.R., 'Arbitrating with Foreign States and Their Instrumentalities' (1986) 5 *International Financial Law Review* 11

Culda, S., 'The Theory of Imprevision' (2010) 52 *Fiat Iustitia* 4

Curtis, C.T., 'The Legal Security of Economic Development Agreements' (1988) 29 *Harvard International Law Journal* 317

Dawson, F.G. and Weston, B.H., 'Prompt, Adequate and Effective: A Universal Standard of Compensation?' (1962) 32 *Fordham Law Review* 727

De Vries, H., 'The Enforcement of Economic Development Agreements with Foreign States' (1984) 62 *University of Detroit Law Review* 1

Delaume, G.R., 'ICSID Arbitration: Practical Considerations' (1984) *Journal of International Arbitration* 101

Dolzer, R., 'New Foundations of the Law of Expropriation of Alien Property' (1981) 75 *American Journal of International Law* 553

Dolzer, R., 'Expropriation for Nationalization' (1985) 8 *Encyclopedia of Public International Law* 214

Dufresne, R., 'The Opacity of Oil: Oil Corporations, Internal Violence, and International Law' (2004) 36 *New York University Journal of International Law and Politics* 331

Duncan, R., 'Price or Politics? An Investigation of the Causes of Expropriation' (2006) 50 *Australian Journal of Agricultural and Resource Economics* 85

Duriugbo, E., 'Permanent Sovereignty and Peoples' Ownership of Natural Resources in International Law' (2006) 38 *George Washington International Law Review* 33

Eisenberg, A., 'Different Constitutional Formulations of Compensation Clauses' (1993) 9 *South African Journal of Human Rights* 412

Eisenberg, M.A., 'Actual and Virtual Specific Performance, the Theory of Efficient Breach, and the Indifference Principle in Contract Law' (2005) 94 *California Law Review* 975

Eljuri, E. and Treviño, C., 'Venezuela: On the Path to Complete "Oil Sovereignty", or the Beginning of a New Era of Investment?' (2009) 2 *Journal of World Energy Law & Business* 259

Emeka, J.N., 'Anchoring Stabilization Clauses in International Petroleum Contracts' (2008) 42 *International Lawyer* 1317

Fales, H., 'A Comparison of Compensation for Nationalization of Alien Property With Standards of Compensation under United States Domestic Law' (1983) 5 *Northwestern Journal of International Law & Business* 871

Faruque, A., 'Renegotiation and Adaptation of Petroleum Contracts: The Quest for Equilibrium and Stability' (2008) 9 *Journal of World Investment and Trade* 113

Faruque, A., 'Validity and Efficacy of Stabilization Clauses: Legal Protection vs Functional Value' (2006) 23 *Journal of International Arbitration* 317

Bibliography 173

Fatouros, A.A., 'International Law and the Internationalized Contract' (1980) 74 *American Journal of International Law* 134

Foster, G.K., 'Managing Expropriation Risks in the Energy Sector: Steps for Foreign Investors to Minimise their Exposure and Maximise Prospects for Recovery When Takings Occur' (2005) 23 *Journal of Energy & Natural Resources Law* 36

Fried, C., 'Contract As Promise Thirty Years On' (2012) 45 *Suffolk University Law Review* 961

Fried, C., 'The Convergence of Contract and Promise' (2007) 120 *Harvard Law Review Forum* 1

Friedland, P.D. and Wong, E., 'Measuring Damages for the Deprivation of Income-producing Assets: ICSID Case Studies' (1991) 6 *ICSID Review Foreign Investment Law Journal* 400

Friedman, D., 'The Efficient Breach Fallacy' (1989) 18 *Journal of Legal Studies* 1

Gann, P.B., 'Compensation Standard for Expropriation' (1984) 23 *Columbia Journal of Transnational Law* 615

Geiger, R., 'The Unilateral Change of Economic Development Agreements' (1974) 23 *International and Comparative Law Quarterly* 78

Gess, K.N., 'Permanent Sovereignty over Natural Resources: An Analytical Review of the United Nations Declaration and Its Genesis' (1964) 13 *International and Comparative Law Quarterly* 398

Gotanda, J.Y., 'Recovering Lost Profits in International Disputes' (2005) 36 *Georgetown Journal of International Law* 61

Gotanda, J.Y., 'Renegotiation and Adaptation Clauses in International Contracts Revisited' (2003) 36 *Vanderbilt Journal of Transnational Law* 1461

Gould, J., 'Zambia's 2006 Elections: the Ethnicization of Politics?' (2007) The Nordic Africa Institute http://www.nai.uu.se/publications/news/archives/071gould/index.xml

Guriev, S., Kolotilin, A. and Sonin, K., 'Determinants of Nationalization in the Oil Sector: A Theory and Evidence from Panel Data' (2009) 27 *Journal of Law, Economics & Organization* 301

Guzman, A., 'Why LDCs Sign Treaties That Hurt Them: Explaining the Popularity of Bilateral Investment Treaties' (1998) 38 *Virginia Journal of International Law* 639

Haglund, D., 'Regulating FDI in Weak African States: A Case Study of Chinese Copper Mining in Zambia' (2008) 46 *Journal of Modern African Studies* 547

Handley, A., 'Business, Government and the Privatisation of the Ashanti Goldfields Company in Ghana' (2007) 41 *Canadian Journal of African Studies* 1

Holmes, O.W., 'The Path of the Law' (1897) 10 *Harvard Law Review* 457

Hyde, J.N., 'Permanent Sovereignty Over Natural Wealth and Resources' (1956) 50 *American Society of International Law* 854

Ibhawo, B. and Dibua, J.I., 'Deconstructing Ujamaa: The Legacy of Julius Nyerere in the Quest for Social and Economic Development in Africa' (2003) 8 *African Journal of Political Science* 59

Inniss, A.B., 'Rethinking Political Risk Insurance: Incentives for Investor Risk Mitigation' (2010) 16 *Southwestern Journal of International Law* 477

Jennings, R.Y., 'State Contracts in International Law' (1961) 37 *British Yearbook of International Law* 156

Jensen, N., 'Political Risk, Democratic Institutions and Foreign Direct Investment' (2008) 70 *The Journal of Politics* 1040

Jensen, N.M., 'Democratic Governance and Multinational Corporations: Political Regimes and Inflows of Foreign Direct Investment' (2003) 57 *International Organization* 587

Jiménez de Aréchaga, E., 'State Responsibility for the Nationalization of Foreign Owned Property' (1978) 11 *New York University Journal of International Law and Politics* 179

Joffé, G., Stevens, P., George, T., Lux, J. and Searle, C., 'Expropriation of Oil and Gas Investments: Historical, Legal and Economic Perspectives in a New Age of Resource Nationalism' (2009) 2 *Journal of World Energy and Business* 3

Kaplow, L. and Shavell, S., 'Fairness Versus Welfare' (2001) 114 *Harvard Law Review* 961

Katz, A., 'Virtue Ethics and Efficient Breach' (2012) 45 *Suffolk University Law Review* 777

Kerwin, G.J., 'The Role of United Nations General Assembly Resolutions in Determining Principles of International Law in United States Courts' (1983) 4 *Duke Law Journal* 876

Kolo, A. and Wälde, T.W., 'Renegotiation and Contract Adaptation in International Investment Projects: Applicable Legal Principles and Industry Practices' (2000) 1 *Journal of World Investment and Trade* 5

Konarski, H., 'Force Majeure and Hardship Clauses in International Contractual Practice' (2003) 4 *International Business Law Journal* 405

Koskemeni, M., 'What Use for Sovereignty Today' (2011) 1 *Asian Journal of International Law* 61

Kraus, J.S., 'A Critique of the Efficient Performance Hypothesis' (2007) 116 *Yale Law Journal Pocket Part* 423

Li, Q., 'Democracy, Autocracy and Expropriation of Foreign Direct Investment' (2009) 42 *Comparative Political Studies* 1098

Lieblich, W.C., 'Determinations by International Tribunals of the Economic Value of Expropriated Enterprises' (1990) 7 *Journal of International Arbitration* 37

Limpitlaw, D., 'Nationalization and Mining: Lessons from Zambia' (2011) 111 *Journal of the Southern African Institute of Mining and Metallurgy* 737

Lowenfeld, A., 'Investment Agreements and International Law' (2003) 42 *Columbia Journal of Transnational Law* 123

Luchembe, C.C., 'Legacy of Late Nineteenth Century Capitalism: The Cases of W.R. Grace and C.J. Rhodes' (1996) 10 *Botswana Journal of African Studies* 40

Lungu, J., 'Copper Mining Agreements in Zambia: Renegotiation or Law Reform?' (2008) 117 *Review of African Political Economy* 403

Maniruzzaman, A.F.M., 'International Development Law as Applicable Law to Economic Development Agreements: A Prognostic View' (2001) 20 *Wisconsin International Law Journal* 1, 23

Maniruzzaman, A.F.M., 'Some Reflections on Stabilisation Techniques in International Petroleum, Gas and Mineral Agreements' (2005) *International Energy Law and Taxation Review* 96

Maniruzzaman, A.F.M., 'The Issue of Resource Nationalism: Risk Engineering and Dispute Management in the Oil and Gas Industry' (2009) 5 *Texas Journal of Oil Gas and Energy Law* 79

Maniruzzaman, A.F.M., 'The Pursuit of Stability in International Energy Investment Contracts: A Critical Appraisal of the Emerging Trends' (2008) 1 *Journal of World Energy Law and Business* 121

Mann, F.A., 'The Aminoil Arbitration' (1984) 14 *British Yearbook of International Law* 213

Marboe, I., 'Compensation and Damages in International Law: The Limits of "Fair Market Value"' (2006) 7 *Journal of World Investment and Trade* 723

Markovits, D. and Schwartz, A., 'The Myth of Efficient Breach: New Defenses of the Expectation Interest' (2011) *Virginia Law Review* 1939

Bibliography 175

Markowitz, R.S., 'Constructive Critique of the Traditional Definition and Use of the Concept of the Effect of a Choice on Allocative (Economic) Efficiency: Why the Kaldor-Hicks Test, the Coase Theorem, and Virtually all Law-and-Economics Welfare Arguments are Wrong' (1993) *University of Illinois Law Review* 485

Marsh, B., 'Preventing the Inevitable: The Benefits of Contractual Risk Engineering in the Light of Venezuela's Recent Oil Field Nationalization' (2008) 13 *Stanford Journal of Law Business & Finance* 453

Mato, H.T., 'The Role of Stability and Renegotiation in Transnational Petroleum Agreements' (2012) 5 *Journal of Politics and Law* 33

Mendelson, M.H., 'Compensation for Expropriation: The Case Law' (1985) 79 *American Journal of International Law* 414

Metz, S., 'The Socialist Theories of Nkrumah and Nyerere' (1982) 20 *Journal of Modern African Studies* 377

Mezzacano, P.J., 'Force Majeure, Impossibility, Frustration and the Like: Excuses for Non-performance; the Historical Origins and Development of an Autonomous Commercial Norm in the CISG' (2011) *Nordic Journal of Commercial Law* 1

Miranda, L.A., 'The Role of International Law in Intrastate Natural Resource Allocation: Sovereignty, Human Rights, and People-Based Development' (2012) 45 *Vanderbilt Journal of Transnational Law* 785

Montembault, B., 'The Stabilisation of State Contracts Using the Example of Oil Contracts: A Return of the Gods of Olympia' (2003) 6 *International Business Law Journal* 593

Morrison, R., 'Efficient Breach of International Agreements' (1994) 23 *Denver Journal of International Law & Policy* 183

Mortenson, J.D., 'The Meaning of "Investment": ICSID's *Travaux* and the Domain of International Investment Law' (2010) 51 *Harvard International Law Journal* 257

Muller, M.H., 'Compensation for Nationalization: A North–South Dialogue' (1981) 19 *Columbia Journal of Transnational Law* 35

Muweme, M., 'Foreign Direct Investment: What Difference for Zambia?' (2001) *Jesuit Centre for Theological Research Bulletin, Number 50* http://www.jctr.zm/for-di-invest.htm

Mwenda, K.K., 'Legal Aspects of Foreign Direct Investment in Zambia' (1999) 6(4) *Murdoch University Electronic Journal of Law* http://www.murdoch.edu.au/elaw/issues/v6n4/mwenda64nf.html

Ndulo, M., 'Foreign Investment and Economic Development' (1984) 11 *Cornell Law Forum* 6

Ndulo, M., 'Mineral Taxation in Zambia' (1975–1977) 7–9 *Zambia Law Journal* 33

Ndulo, M., 'Mining Legislation and Mineral Development in Zambia' (1986) 19 *Cornell International Law Journal* 1

Ndulo, M., 'The Democratization Process and Structural Adjustment in Africa' (2003) 10 *Indiana Journal of Global and Legal Studies* 315

Ndulo, M., 'The Nationalization of the Zambian Copper Industry' (1974) 6 *Zambia Law Journal* 55

Ndulo, M., 'The Requirement of Domestic Participation in New Mining Ventures in Zambia' (1977) 7 *Georgia Journal of International and Comparative Law* 579

Negi, R., 'The Micropolitics of Mining and Development in Zambia: Insights from the Northwestern Province' (2011) 12 *African Studies Quarterly* 27

Ng'ambi, S., 'Stabilization Clauses and the Zambian Windfall Tax' (2010) 1 *Zambia Social Science Journal* 107

Ng'ambi, S.P., 'The Effect of Stabilization Clauses in Concession Agreements' (2012) 43 *Zambia Law Journal* 57

Nussbaum, A., 'The Arbitration between the Lena Goldfields Ltd and the Soviet Government' (1950–51) *Cornell Law Quarterly* 31, 42

Nwaokoro, J., 'Enforcing Stabilization of International Energy Contracts' (2013) 3 *Journal of World Energy Law & Business* 103, 105

O'Neal, J.R. and O'Neal, F.H., 'Hegemony, Imperialism and the Profitability of Foreign Investment' (1988) 42 *International Organization* 347

Oshionebo, E., 'Stabilization Clauses in Natural Resource Extraction Contracts: Legal, Economic and Social Implications for Developing Countries' (2010) 10 *Asper Review of International Business & Trade Law* 1

Paasirvirta, E., 'Internationalization and Stabilization of Contracts versus State Sovereignty' (1989) 60 *British Yearbook of International Law* 315

Pate, T.J., 'Evaluating Stabilization Clauses in Venezuela's Strategic Association Agreements for Heavy-Crude Extraction in the Orinoco Belt: The Return of a Forgotten Contractual Risk Reduction Mechanism for the Petroleum Industry' (2009) 40 *University of Miami Inter-American Law Review* 347

Penrose, E., Joffé, G. and Stevens, P., 'Nationalization of Foreign-owned Property for a Public Purpose: An Economic Perspective on Appropriate Compensation' (1992) 55 *Modern Law Review* 351

Phiri, B., 'Colonial Legacy and the Role of Society in the Creation and Demise of Autocracy in Zambia, 1964–1991' (2001) 10(2) *Nordic Journal of African Studies* 224

Pierce, J., 'A South American Energy Treaty: How the Region Might Attract Foreign Investment in the Wake of Resource Nationalism' (2011) 44 *Cornell International Law Journal* 417

Posner, R.A., 'Utilitarianism, Economics, and Legal Theory' (1979) 8 *Journal of Legal Studies* 103

Rand, W., Hornick, N.N. and Friedland, P., 'ICSID's Emerging Jurisprudence: The Scope of ICSID's Jurisdiction' (1986) 19 *New York University Journal of International Law and Politics* 33

Rosado de Sá Ribeiro, M., 'Sovereignty Over Natural Resources Investment Law and Expropriation: The Case of Bolivia and Brazil' (2009) 2 *Journal of World Energy Law & Business* 129

Rosen, J.A., 'Arbitration Under Private International Law: The Doctrines of Separability and Compétence de la Compétence' (1993) 17 *Fordham International Law Journal* 599

Rossi-Guerrero, F.P., 'The Transition from Private to Public Control in the Venezuelan Petroleum Industry' (1976) 9 *Vanderbilt Journal of Transnational Law* 475

Russi, L., 'Chronicles of a Failure: From a Renegotiation Clause to Arbitration of Transnational Contracts' (2008) 24 *Connecticut Journal of International Law* 77

Salacuse, J.W., 'Renegotiating International Project Agreements' (2000) 24 *Fordham International Law Journal* 1319

Salas, M.T., 'Staying the Course: United States Oil Companies in Venezuela, 1945–1958' (2005) 32 *Latin American Perspectives* 147

Salomon, M.E., 'From NIEO to Now and the Unfinishable Story of Economic Justice' (2013) 62 *International & Comparative Law Quarterly* 31

Schachter, O., 'Compensation for Expropriation' (1984) 78 *American Journal of International Law* 121

Schmitter, P.C. and Karl, T.L., 'What Democracy Is . . . and Is Not' (1991) 2 *Journal of Democracy* 75

Schrijver, N., 'Natural Resources, Permanent Sovereignty Over' (2010) *Max Planck Encyclopedia of Public International Law* 8 http://ilmc.univie.ac.at/uploads/media/PSNR_empil.pdf

Schwebel, S.M., 'The Story of the U.N.'s Declaration on Permanent Sovereignty over Natural Resources' (1963) 49 *American Bar Association Journal* 463

Sereni, A.P., 'International Economic Institutions and the Municipal Law of States' (1959) 96 *Recueil des cours* 129

Shan, W., 'Is Calvo Dead?' (2007) 55 *American Journal of Comparative Law* 123

Shan, W., Gallagher, N. and Zhang, S., 'National Treatment for Foreign Investment in China: A Changing Landscape' (2012) 27 *ICSID Review* 120

Shiffrin, S.V., 'The Divergence of Contract and Promise' (2007) 120 *Harvard Law Review* 708

Shihata, I.F.I., 'The Multilateral Investment Guarantee Agency' (1986) 20 *International Lawyer* 485

Sieck, D.R., 'Confronting the Obsolescing Bargain: Transacting Around Political Risk in Developing and Transitioning Economies Through Renewable Energy Foreign Direct Investment' (2010) 33 *Suffolk Transnational Law Review* 319

Smith, R.J., 'The United States Government Perspective on Expropriation and Investment in Developing Countries' (1976) 9 *Vanderbilt Journal of Transnational Law* 517

Sornarajah, M., 'Compensation for Expropriation: The Emergence of New Standards' (1979) 13 *Journal of World Trade Law* 108

Stevens, P., 'National Oil Companies and International Oil Companies in the Middle East: Under the Shadow of Government and the Resource Nationalism Cycle' (2008) 1 *Journal of World Energy Law & Business* 5

Suratgar, D., 'Considerations Affecting Choice of Law Clauses in Contracts Between Governments and Foreign Nationals' (1962) 2 *Indian Journal of International Law* 273

Te'llez, F.M., 'Conditions and Criteria for the Protection of Legitimate Expectations Under International Investment Law' (2012) 27 *ICSID Review* 432

Ushewokunze, C., 'The Legal Framework of Copper Production in Zambia' (1974) 6 *Zambia Law Journal* 75

Van Aaken, A., 'International Investment Law Between Commitment and Flexibility: A Contract Theory Analysis' (2009) 12 *Journal of International Economic Law* 507

Vargiu, P., 'Beyond Hallmarks and Formal Requirements: a *"Jurisprudence Constante"* on the Notion of Investment in the ICSID Convention' (2009) 10 *Journal of World Investment and Trade* 753

Vedeer, V.V., 'The Lena Goldfields Arbitration: the Historical Roots of the Three Ideas' (1998) 47 *International and Comparative Law Quarterly* 747

Veneziano, A., 'UNIDROIT Principles and CISG: Change of Circumstances and Duty to Renegotiate according to the Belgian Supreme Court' (2010) 15 *Uniform Law Review* 137

Vivoda, V., 'Resource Nationalism, Bargaining and International Oil Companies: Challenges and Change in the New Millennium' (2009) 14 *New Political Economy* 517

Von Mehren, R.B. and Kourides, N.P., 'International Arbitration Between States and Foreign Private Parties: The Libyan Nationalization Cases' (1981) 75 *American Journal of International Law* 476

Von Soest, C., 'How Does Neopatrimonialism Affect the African State's Revenues? The Case of Tax Collection in Zambia' (2007) 45 *Journal of Modern African Studies* 621

Wälde, T.W. and Ndi, G., 'Stabilizing International Investment Commitments: International Law Versus Contract Interpretation' (1996) 31 *Texas International Law Journal* 215

178 Resource nationalism in international investment law

Wälde, T.W., 'Renegotiating Acquired Rights in the Oil and Gas Industries: Industry and Political Cycles Meet the Rule of Law' (2008) 1 *Journal of World Energy Law and Business* 55

Warden-Fernandez, J., 'The Permanent Sovereignty Over Natural Resources: How it Has Been Accommodated Within the Evolving Economy' (2000) *CEPMLP Annual Review Article 4*, 3 http://www.dundee.ac.uk/cepmlp/car/html/car4_art4.htm

Wehberg, H., '*Pacta Sunt Servanda*' (1959) 53 *American Journal of International Law* 775

Wells, L.T., 'Double Dipping in the Arbitration Awards? An Economist Questions Damages Awarded to Karaha Bodas Company in Indonesia' (2003) 19 *Arbitration International* 471

Williams, S.L., 'Political and Other Risk Insurance: OPIC, MIGA, EXIMBANK and Other Providers' (1993) 5 *Pace International Law Review* 59

Wolff, M., 'Some Observations on the Autonomy of Contracting Parties in the Conflict of Laws' (1950) 35 *Transactions of the Grotius Society* 143

Woodhouse, E.J., 'The Obsolescing Bargain Redux? Foreign Investment in the Electric Power Sector in Developing Countries' (2006) 38 *New York University Journal of International Law and Politics* 121

Yackee, J., '*Pacta Sunt Servanda* and State Promises to Foreign Investors Before Bilateral Investment Treaties: Myth and Reality' (2009) 32 *Fordham International Law Journal* 1550

Zongwe, D., 'The Contribution of *Campbell v Zimbabwe* to the Foreign Investment Law on Expropriations' (2010) 2 *Namibia Law Journal* 31

Reports and government statements

2010 Census of Population and Housing (Zambia Central Statistical Office 2011) 2 http://unstats. un.org/unsd/demographic/sources/census/2010_phc/Zambia/PreliminaryReport.pdf

Budget Address by The Hon. Ng'andu P. Magande, MP Minister of Finance and National Planning: Delivered to the National Assembly on 25 January 2008 http://www. parliament.gov.zm/index.php?option=com_docman&task=doc_view&gid=242

Christopher Adam and Anthony M. Simpasa, 'Harnessing Resource Revenues for Prosperity in Zambia' (OxCarre Research Paper 36, Revised Draft) 25–27 http://www. oxcarre.ox.ac.uk/images/stories/papers/RevenueWatch/oxcarrerp201036.pdf

First National Development Plan 1966–1970 (Office of National Development and Planning, Lusaka, July 1966)

First Quantum Minerals Ltd, *Annual Report* 2005 http://www.first-quantum.com/files/ doc_financials/2005AR.pdf

F.V. Garcia Amador, 'Fourth Report on State Responsibility' (1959) 2 *Yearbook of the International Law Commission* 32

International Monetary Fund, Balance of Payments Manual (International Monetary Fund 1993)

Investment Law Reform: A Handbook for Development Practitioners (World Bank 2010)

Libya: Law on Nationalization of Oil Companies Legislation and Regulations (1974) 13 ILM 60

Libya: Law on Nationalization of British Petroleum Exploration Company (1972) 11 ILM 380

Ministerial Statement on the Status of Mining Taxation http://www.parliament.gov.zm/ index.php?option=com_docman&task=doc_view&gid=770

Overseas Private Investment Corporation, OPIC Handbook (2006) 4 http://www.opic. gov/sites/default/files/docs/OPIC_Handbook.pdf

Report of the Executive Directors, on the Convention on the Settlement of Investment Disputes Between States and Nationals of Other States, International Bank for Reconstruction and Development (18 March 1965) https://icsid.worldbank.org/ICSID/StaticFiles/basicdoc/partB.htm

Seymour J. Rubin, 'World Bank: Report to the Development Committee and Guidelines on the Treatment of Foreign Direct Investment' (1992) 31 ILM 1363

UNCTAD World Investment Report 2006

United Nations Conference on Trade and Development Investment Policy Review Zambia (UN 2006)

United Nations Conference on Trade and Development: Investment Policy Review Zambia (UN 2006), UNCTAD/ITE/IPC/2006/14

Vedanta Resources Plc, Annual Report 2006 http://www.vedantaresources.com/uploads/vedanta2006annualreportv1.pdf

'World Bank Guidelines, on the Treatment of Foreign Direct Investment' (1992) 31 ILM 1379

World Bank, Legal Framework for the Treatment of Foreign Investment (World Bank 1992)

World Intellectual Property Organization Guide to WIPO Mediation, quoted in Tibor Várady, John J. Barceló and Arthur T. von Mehren, *International Commercial Arbitration: A Transnational Perspective* (3rd edn, Thomson 2006)

Zambia: Sectoral Study of the Effective Tax Burden (December 2004) Foreign Investment and Advisory Service (FIAS), a joint service of the World Bank and IFC, 39 http://siteresources.worldbank.org/EXTEXPCOMNET/Resources/2463593-1213973103977/10_Zambia.pdf

Zambia's Mining Industry the First 50 Years (Roan Consolidated Mining Ltd 1978)

Newspaper and magazine articles

'Anglo America Quits Zambia' BBC News (Tuesday 20 August 2002) http://news.bbc.co.uk/1/hi/business/2205509.stm

'First Quantum Dealings' Editorial in *The Post* (Monday 28 October 2013) http://www.postzambia.com/post-read_article.php?articleId=39866

'Mining: Nationalisation in Zambia' *Time Magazine* (Friday 22 August 1969) http://www.time.com/time/magazine/article/0,9171,898567,00.html

Joan Chirwa, 'Be Open on Mine Taxes, Sichinga Advises Govt' (2008) *Business Post* (1 April 2008)

Working papers and theses

Al-Emadi, T.A., 'The Renegotiating Clause in Petroleum International Joint Venture Agreements' (Oxford Student Legal Studies Paper No. 04/2012 2012) http://papers.ssrn.com/sol3/papers.cfm?abstract_id=2073340

Chang, R., Hevia, C. and Loayza, N., 'Privatization and Nationalization Cycles' (2010) National Bureau of Economic Research Working Paper Series, Working Paper 16126 http://www.nber.org/papers/w16126 6

Kapwadi, L., 'Renegotiating a Long Term Investment Contract: The Case of Mining Contracts in DRC' (LLM Thesis, University of Pretoria 2012)

Li, P., 'The Myth and Reality of Chinese Investors: A Case Study of Chinese Investment in Zambia's Copper Industry' (2010) *Southern African Institute of International Affairs*, Occasional Paper Number 62 http://www.eisourcebook.org/cms/June%202013/Myth

%20&%20Reality%20of%20Chinese%20Investors,%20Zambian%20Copper%20Case%20Study.pdf

Websites

Electoral Commission of Zambia: http://www.elections.org.zm/elections_faq.php
London Metal Exchange: http://www.lme.com/copper_graphs.asp
United States Energy Information Administration (2012): http://www.eia.gov/countries/analysisbriefs/Venezuela/venezuela.pdf

Index

abuse of rights 88–91
acid rain 119
Action for Southern Africa (ACTSA) 122
Adam, C. 115
Adler, B.E. 77
Afrin, Z. 2
agriculture 27
Aharoni, Y. 13, 26
Akinsanya, A. 46
Al-Emadi, T.A. 127, 134, 135
Al Faruque, A. 52, 53, 54, 131, 133, 135, 145, 146, 147, 151
Al Qurashi, Z. 140, 146
Alavi, M. 135
Amerasinghe, C.F. 56
American Insurance Group (AIG) 39
Anglo American Corporation (AAC) 10, 96, 99, 101, 103, 105–6, 110–11, 112, 113, 125, 163
Anglo Iranian Oil Company 53–4
arbitration clause 5, 14, 39, 40, 43, 55, 63, 64, 72–3, 161; renegotiation clause and 151–2, 156, 157, 165; separability principle 41; *see also* International Centre for Settlement of Investment Disputes (ICSID)
arbitration on failure to agree during renegotiation 151–4
Arbtali, E. 34, 35
army 5
Asante, S.K.B. 7, 46, 130, 132, 144, 158
Atiyah, P.S. 56, 140
authoritarian regimes 4, 34, 35, 37

Bahrain 150
Baker, J.C. 3, 26
bargaining power: obsolescing bargain model 5, 9, 25, 28–9, 94, 95, 157, 161

Barrera-Hernándes, L. 46
Baxter, R.R. 51
Baylies, C. 108, 109
Bayulgen, O. 27, 29, 35
benefits of foreign capital 26–8
Berger, K.P. 136, 145, 147, 148, 157
Bernardini, P. 5, 8, 45, 57, 144, 145, 146, 147, 148, 151, 154, 155, 156
Betancourt, Rómulo 30–1
Beveridge, A.A. 101
Birmingham, R. 93
Bleicher, S.A. 50
book value approach 80
Borehand, E.M. 59
Boubakri, , N. 33
Bowett, D.W. 57, 83
Boyle, A. 49
Bratton, M. 108
Bremmer, I. 33
British South Africa Company (BSAC) 10, 102, 103, 105, 163
Brooker, P. 35
Brooks, R.R.W. 94
Brownlie, I. 76, 79, 83
Burawoy, M. 106
Burdette, M. 37, 38
Burns, J.H. 91
Büthe, T. 2
Butler, A. 34, 37
Butler, L. 103
Bwana Mukubwa Mines Ltd 114

Calabresi, G. 92
Caldera, Rafael 31
Campbell, O. 110
Cantegreil, J. 55
Central African Federation 103–4
Chambishi disaster of 2005 120–1

182 Index

Chambishi Mines Plc 114
Chamisa, E.E. 134
Chang, R. 33
changed circumstances (*rebus sic stantibus*)
11, 135–42, 143–4, 158, 164; applicable
law 136; civil law systems 137, 141–2;
common law systems 137, 140–1;
contractual term 136; under
international law 137–9
Charter of Economic Rights and Duties of
States (CERDS) 46, 47, 48–9, 51, 67,
72; appropriate compensation 81
Chatterjee, S.K. 56, 57, 135
Chávez, Hugo 31, 32, 33
Chibuluma Mines Plc 114
Chile 122
Chiluba, Frederick 11, 108, 109, 110,
163
China 28, 119–21
Chirwa, J. 122
choice of law clause 41, 63, 64–5, 66, 137,
164
Chowdhury, S.R. 46, 48, 49, 52
Christian Aid 122
Chua, A. 37, 38
Chubb 39
civil law systems 137, 141–2
Clifford Chance 113
Coale, M.T.B. 55, 60
Coleman, F.L. 102
Coleman, J.L. 91, 92, 96
colonialism 45–6, 97, 99, 101, 102–4
commercial impracticability 140–1
common law systems 137, 140–1
compensation 6, 8, 9–10, 57, 72, 73,
76–8, 162, 165; abuse of rights 88–91;
appropriate 49, 76, 78, 80–2, 83, 90,
162; Charter of Economic Rights and
Duties of States (CERDS) 49; duty 49,
51, 77, 90, 95, 97; efficient breach
theory 10, 77, 91–7, 98, 162–3, 165;
experts 85, 87; full 49, 82; Hull principle
67, 76, 78–80, 82–3, 162; interest 87;
lawful and unlawful takings 74, 83, 85,
90, 98; lost future profits (*lucrum cessans*)
10, 59, 67, 74, 76, 78, 79, 83–91,
93–4, 95, 96, 97, 98, 106, 125, 126,
162; no track record of profitability
87–8; veto on pursuing legitimate
purpose 96; Zambia 2, 106, 113, 125,
126
Congo 69, 86–7, 105
consciencism 104

contractual clauses: dispute settlement
clauses 40–1; stabilization clauses *see
separate entry*
Convention on the International Sale of
Goods 139
Convention on the Recognition and
Enforcement of Foreign Arbitral
Awards 40, 152–4, 159, 165
Corrales, J. 32, 38
corruption 110
Cotula, L. 57, 127
Craig, J. 109, 110, 111
Crawford, J.F. 57
Crawford, J.R. 49, 79, 83
Culda, S. 142
culture 134–5
Cunningham, S.M. 27
currency: exchange controls 112;
exchange rates 27, 109
Curtis, C.T. 53, 54
customary international law 50–1, 67
customs duties 2

Dawson, F.G. 82
De Vries, , H. 55
de-industrialization 27
debt relief 112, 117
definition of foreign direct investment
14–25; foreign 23–4; investment 15–22
Delaume, G.R. 15, 155
democratic regimes 4, 34–6, 37
dependency theorists 26–8
devaluation 109
Diamond, L. 35
diplomatic protection 59
discounted cash flow method 76
discrimination 106
dispute settlement clauses 40–1
diversification of economy 27
Dolzer, R. 1, 14, 41, 42, 54, 68, 74, 81, 82,
94, 146
Dufresne, R. 52
Duncan, R. 33
Duruigbo, E. 46, 47
'Dutch Disease' 27

economic stabilization clauses 54–5
efficient breach theory 10, 77, 91–7, 98,
162–3, 165
Egypt 142
Eisenberg, A. 81
Eisenberg, M.A. 94
Eljuri, E. 30

Al-Emadi, T.A. 127, 134, 135
Emeka, J.N. 45
employment 27; laws 28, 100, 121;
Venezuela 31; Zambia 118, 119–20,
121, 125
enforcement 40, 90, 95, 152–4, 165
environment: pollution 119, 121, 127–8
Enya Holdings BV 114
ethnicity 38
European Court of Human Rights 81–2
ex aequo et bono 87, 157
exchange controls 112
exchange rates 27, 109
extra-contract renegotiation 131

Faber, M.L.O. 102
Fales, H. 94
Faruque, A. 52, 53, 54, 131, 133, 135, 145,
146, 147, 151
Fatouros, A.A. 25, 26, 29, 53
Ferguson, J. 108
financial crisis 125
First Quantum Minerals Ltd 112, 114,
122, 125
fixed-term contracts 118, 119–20
food subsidies 109
force majeure 139, 144
foreign, meaning of 23–4
Foster, G.K. 135
Fox, W. 146
France: *imprévison* 141, 142, 144
Fraser, A. 100, 101, 103, 104, 105, 107,
109, 110, 114, 117, 118, 119, 120, 123
Fried, C. 91, 93
Friedland, P.D. 80
Friedman, D. 93, 94
frustration of contract 140, 144

Gabon 27, 54
Gaddafi, Muammar 65
Gann, P.B. 78, 83, 85, 87
Garcia Amador, F.V. 55
Garner, B.A. 91
Garrett, G. 35
Geiger, R. 141, 142
general principles of law 59, 64–5, 66
Germany: *Störung der Geschäftsgrundlage*
141–2, 144
Gess, K.N. 51
Gewald, J.-B. 7
Ghana 104, 111, 112; Ghana/Shell clause
145, 147
going concern approach 79

good faith 8, 66–7, 89, 132, 137, 144, 148,
149, 150–1, 156; Germany 141
Gotanda, J.Y. 88, 131, 133
Gould, J. 123
Graham, C. 105, 108
Greece 142
Guriev, S. 34
Guzman, A. 67

Hackworth, G. 78
Haglund, D. 121
Handley, A. 111
hardship clauses 142–4
health: respiratory diseases 119
healthcare 107, 119, 120
Hofstede, G. 134
Holmes, O.W. 92
Horn, N. 136, 138
Hossain, K. 52
Hughes Parry, D. 140
human rights 127
humanism 10, 99, 105, 108, 163
hybrid systems 4, 35, 36, 37
Hyde, J.N. 47

Ibhawo, B. 104
ICC (International Chamber of
Commerce) 142–3, 149
ICSID *see* International Centre for
Settlement of Investment Disputes
imports 27
impracticability, commercial 140–1
imprévison (France) 141, 142, 144
Indonesia 54, 88–90
inflation 76, 85
Inniss, A.B. 39
insurance 1–2, 13–14, 39–40, 95, 161;
renegotiation clauses 157–8
intangibility clauses 54
interest 87
International Centre for Settlement of
Investment Disputes (ICSID): failure of
renegotiation 149, 154–6, 159; foreign
23–4; investment 15–22; legal dispute
149, 154–5; loss of future profits 86–8;
shareholders 24
International Chamber of Commerce
(ICC) 149; Model Hardship Clause
142–3
International Monetary Fund (IMF) 1;
Zambia 100, 101, 109, 117, 118
investment, interpretation of 15–22;
jurisdictional approach 16–19, 20–1;

jurisprudence constante 20–2; typical characteristics approach 16, 19–20, 22
Iran 31, 65; 1933 Concession Agreement: Anglo Iranian Oil Company and 53–4
Iraq 31
Italy 142

J&W Group 114
Jaenicke, G. 75
Jennings, R.Y. 56
Jensen, N.M. 26, 35, 36
Jimenez de Aréchaga, E. 51, 52, 76, 78, 80
Joffé, G. 4, 7, 8, 34, 157
judiciary 36
juridiction: arbitration 15–25, 152, 154–6, 157, 165

Kaldor-Hicks efficiency 91–2
Kantor, M. 89
Kaplow, L. 91
Kapwadi, L. 139, 142
Kapwepwe, Simon Mwansa 106
Karl, T.L. 30, 31
Katz, A. 93
Kaunda, Kenneth D. 10–11, 37–8, 99, 101, 104, 105–6, 107, 109, 163
Kerwin, G.J. 49
Kienbaum Development Services GmbH 111
Kolo, A. 140, 141
kompetenz-kompetenz rule 152
Konarski, H. 142
Konkola Copper Mines (KCM) 110–11, 113–14; earnings 122; stabilization clause 116
Koskenniemi, M. 62
Kraus, J.S. 94
Kröll, S.M. 143
Kuwait 31, 70–2, 85–6

labour laws 28, 100, 121
Larmer, M. 105
Lasmo clause 145, 147
Latin America 33
legitimate expectations 8, 45, 62, 85, 126, 128, 129, 158, 159
Lewanika, Chief 10, 102
Li, P. 119, 120
Li, Q. 35, 36
Libya: nationalization cases 62–8, 74, 85
Lieblich, W.C. 83, 90
Limpitlaw, D. 96

Lloyd's of London 39
lost future profits *(lucrum cessans)* 10, 59, 67, 74, 76, 78, 79, 83–91, 162; efficient breach theory 93–4, 95, 96, 97, 98; Zambia 106, 125, 126
Lowenfeld, A. 51, 55, 70, 77, 83
Luanshya Mines Plc 114
Luchembe, C.C. 102
Lungu, J. 6, 7, 100, 101, 104, 108, 109, 110, 113, 114, 116, 121, 122, 123, 124, 127

McLachlan, C. 79, 80, 83, 88
Magande, Ng'andu P. 117
Malaysia 38
Maniruzzaman, A.F.M. 14, 25, 30, 39, 42, 44, 52, 53, 57, 72, 155
Mann, F.A. 45, 56, 151
manufacturing industry 27
Marboe, I. 76, 83
Markesinis, B.S. 141
market value: US valuation methods 78–80
Markovits, D. 93
Markowitz, R.S. 91
Marsh, B. 25, 28, 30, 95
Martin, A. 99, 101
Mato, H.T. 136
mediation 40
Mendelson, M.H. 83
Metorex 114
Metz, S. 104
Mezzacano, P.J. 141, 142
Mineworkers' Union of Zambia 107, 109, 110, 117–18
Miranda, L.A. 46, 47
Montembault, B. 53
Morrison, R. 96
Mortenson, J.D. 15
Movement for Multiparty Democracy (MMD) 11, 100, 108, 109, 110, 113, 115, 123, 163
Muchimba, C. 118
Muchlinski, P. 58, 130
Muller, M.H. 96
Multilateral Investment Guarantee Agency (MIGA) 1–2, 14, 39–40, 95, 161
Musokotwane, Situmbeko 117, 123, 124
Muweme, M. 6
Mvunga, M.P. 102
Mwambwa, S. 99, 125

Mwanawasa, Levy 113–14
Mwenda, K.K. 13, 112

Namibia 2
national systems and institutions, role of 34–7
nationalization 4, 5, 8, 13, 25, 30, 51, 74–5; efficient breach theory 94, 95–6; ethnicity 38; expression of nationalism 37–8; Kuwait 70–2, 85; Libyan cases 62–8, 74, 85; prices and 33–4; renegotiation clauses and 132, 133; right 57, 81, 82, 94; specific performance 94; Venezuela 30, 31, 32, 33, 96, 97; Zambia 10, 37–8, 96, 99, 101, 103, 104–8, 163
Nawakwi, Edith 117
Ndulo, M. 26, 27, 29, 77, 99, 102, 103, 104, 105, 106, 107, 122, 125
need for foreign capital 26–8
Negi, R. 33
Netherlands 27, 157
New York Convention 40, 152–4, 159, 165
Ng'ambi, S. 7, 44, 57, 64, 67, 130
Nkhata, L. 117
Nkrumah, Kwame 104
Non-Ferrous Metals Co 114, 119–20
Noreng, Ø. 34
Nussbaum, A. 59, 84
Nwaokoro, J. 29, 52, 57
Nwogugu, E.I. 25, 26
Nyerere, J.K. 104

obsolescing bargain model 5, 9, 25, 28–9, 94, 95, 157, 161
oil/petroleum 6, 11, 33, 34; exploration 52–3; Gabon 27; Ghana/Shell clause 145, 147; Libya 62–8; OPEC 30–1; Qatar 149–51; Venezuela 30–2, 97; Zambia 38, 101, 108, 163
Ok Tedi clause 145
O'Neal, J.R. 27
OPEC (Organization of Petroleum Exporting Countries) 30–1, 70
organizational culture 135
Oshionebo, E. 7, 100, 116, 125
Overseas Private Investment Corporation (OPIC) 13–14, 39, 68, 161

Paasivirta, E. 49, 54, 55
pacta sunt servanda 8, 9, 55–6, 58, 61, 63, 66, 67, 72, 73, 75, 162; civil law systems 141; *rebus sic stantibus* (changed

circumstances) 136, 138, 158; UNIDROIT Principles of International Commercial Contracts 138
Pakistan 105
Pareto efficiency 91, 92, 93, 95, 162
Parra, F. 31
Pate, T.J. 31
Patriotic Front 11, 115, 123
Peel, E. 56, 92
Peet, R. 26
Penrose, E. 94
pensions 118
permanent sovereignty over natural resources 9, 45–52, 61, 67, 71, 74, 75, 162; evolution of doctrine 47–9; legal status 49–52
Peter, W. 149
Petrov, N. 36
Phiri, B. 99
Pierce, J. 31
Poland 142
pollution 119, 121, 127–8
portfolio investment 14
Posner, E.A. 29, 77, 91, 94, 95, 97
Posner, R.A. 91, 93, 96
post-contract renegotiation 131–2
Potter, J.G. 106
poverty 26, 96, 120
price controls 109
prices of natural resources 6, 25, 29, 32, 33, 53, 126–7, 163; appreciation in 6–8, 11, 13, 25, 30, 33–4, 104, 107, 113–14, 115, 121, 122, 133, 164; OPEC 31; renegotiation clauses 144, 156–8; Zambia 6–7, 11, 99–100, 101, 104, 107–8, 111, 113–14, 115, 117, 121, 122, 125, 126, 163, 164
privatization 2, 32–3, 95; Venezuela 30, 31, 32; Zambia 6, 11, 100, 101, 103, 108, 109–14, 117–21, 126, 163–4
profit transfers 2, 101, 121, 133, 164

Qatar 149–51; Model Exploration and Production Sharing Agreement of 1994 144
Al Qurashi, Z. 140, 146

racial discrimination 106
Rakner, L. 109
Rand, W. 15
rebus sic stantibus (changed circumstances) 11, 135–42, 143–4, 158, 164; applicable law 136; civil law systems 137, 141–2;

common law systems 137, 140–1; contractual term 136; under international law 137–9
recession 31
renegotiation clauses 3, 8, 11–12, 14, 42, 75, 97, 98, 127, 128, 130–59, 160, 164–5; contracts with 144–58; contracts without 135–44; culture 134–5; definition 131–2; effect of change on contract 146–7; failure of renegotiation 149–56; legal validity 131; objectives of renegotiation 147; procedure 148–9; reasons for desire to renegotiate 132–5; stabilization clauses and 132, 135, 157–8; triggering event 145–6, 156, 165; windfall profits: proposed 156–7
rentier states 27
replacement cost approach 79
resource nationalism cycle 3–4, 13, 42–3, 98, 160–1, 163; foreign direct investment (FDI) and 25–38; renegotiation clauses and 132; Zambia 99–129
respiratory diseases 119
Rhodes, Cecil 102
Roan Antelope Mining Corporation of Zambia (RAMCOZ) 114
Roan Selection Trust (RST) 10, 96, 99, 101, 103, 105–6, 125, 163
Rosado de Sá Ribeiro, M. 48
Rosen, J.A. 41
Rossi-Guerrero, F.P. 97
Rothschild 113
Royal Dutch Oil Company 30
royalties 3, 4, 29, 33; loss of future profits and 84, 85, 86; Zambia 6–7, 100, 102, 103, 105–6, 113, 116, 121, 126, 163, 164
Rubin, S.J. 26
Russi, L. 152, 153
Russia 4, 33

safety in mines 119
Salacuse, J.W. 8, 13, 94, 130, 131, 134, 149
Salas, M.T. 30
Salomon, M.E. 96
Sands, P. 49
Sardanis, A. 37, 99, 105, 106, 108
Sata, Michael 115
Saudi Arabia 30
Schachter, O. 56, 82
Schill, S.W. 73

Schlemmer, E.C. 14, 24
Schmitter, P.C. 35
Schreuer, C. 15, 154
Schrijver, N. 48, 49, 51, 52
Schwebel, S.M. 51, 81
Scottish Catholic International Aid Fund (SCAIF) 122
self-determination 47–8
separability principle 41
Sereni, A.P. 57
Shakafuswa, Jonas 123
Shan, W. 28, 83
shareholders: ICSID 24
Shell 145, 147
Shiffrin, S.V. 93
Shihata, I.F.I. 2
Sieck, D.R. 33
Simutanyi, N. 101
Smith, R.J. 78, 79, 80, 87
Smith, S.A. 91, 92
Sornarajah, M. 1, 5, 13, 14, 23, 40, 42, 50, 53, 56, 81, 132, 134
South Africa 38, 110
Sovereign Risk Insurance Limited 39
sovereignty over natural resources, permanent 9, 45–52, 61, 67, 71, 74, 75, 162; evolution of doctrine 47–9; legal status 49–52
specific performance 6, 73, 92, 94, 97
stabilization clauses 3, 5–8, 9, 14, 41–2, 44–5, 52–3, 74–5, 130, 161–2, 163; case law on 58–74; 'compliance with international law' 127; earlier decisions 58–62; economic 54–5; effect of 55–8; environmental degradation 127; evolutionary approach 127–8; intangibility clause 54; Libyan nationalization cases 62–8, 74; renegotiation clauses and 132, 135, 157–8; subsequent decisions 68–74; *stricto sensu* 53–4; types of 53–5; Zambia 7, 11, 100, 116–17, 125, 126, 127–8
Standard Oil Company 30
Steingruber, A.M. 2, 15
Stevens, P. 13, 30, 96, 133
Störung der Geschäftsgrundlage 141–2, 144
sub-contractors 118–19, 120
Subedi, S. 39, 76
subsidiaries 26–7; meaning of foreign 23–4

Sudan 105
Suratgar, D. 55
Sweden 157

Tanzania 104
Taverne, B. 65
taxation 2, 3–4, 5, 8, 13, 25, 29, 30, 33, 34;
    loss of future profits and 84, 85, 86;
    renegotiation clauses 144; tax stability
    clauses 42, 54, 68, 100, 116–17, 125,
    126, 164; valuation methods and 79;
    Venezuela 30, 31; Zambia 6–7, 10, 11,
    97, 100, 103, 112, 113, 114–28, 126,
    163, 164
Te'llez, F.M. 57
transaction costs 93
Transparency International 110
treaties and contracts 56–7, 73
Treitel, G.H. 140

Ujamaa 104
UNCITRAL proceedings 21
unemployment 118, 119, 120
UNIDROIT Principles of International
    Commercial Contracts 138–9
Uniform Commercial Code (US) 140–1
United Kingdom 65, 81–2, 101, 102, 103;
    frustration of contract 140
United National Independence Party
    (UNIP) 10–11, 99, 104, 106, 108, 109
United Nations: Conference on Trade and
    Development (UNCTAD) 14; Draft
    Code of Conduct for Transnational
    Corporations 138; General Assembly
    46, 47–8, 49–51, 66, 81
United States 39, 65, 154; commercial
    impracticability 140–1; compensation
    78–80, 81, 82, 87, 90
unjust enrichment 59, 84
Upex, R. 92
Ushewokunze, C. 103
utilitarianism 91

Van Aaken, A. 3
Várady, T. 40, 64, 152
Vargiu, P. 17, 18, 20, 21, 22, 77
Vedanta 113–14, 121
Vedeer, V.V. 59
Veneziano, A. 139
Venezuela 30–2, 33, 96, 97
Vernon, R. 5, 25, 28
Vienna Convention on the Law of Treaties
    56–7, 137

Vietnam: Lasmo clause 145, 147
Vivoda, V. 29, 44
Von Mehren, R.B. 63, 65
Von Soest, C. 100

Wälde, T.W. 3, 4, 7, 14, 32, 45, 53, 132
Warden-Fernandez, J. 48
water rates 119
wealth maximization 8, 10, 77, 91, 96, 97,
    98, 165
Wehberg, H. 56
Weil, P. 62
Wells, L.T. 90, 95
Whiteman, M.M. 87, 88
Williams, S.L. 95
Wolff, M. 57
Woodhouse, E.J. 44
World Bank 1–2, 26, 39; compensation 82;
    Zambia 100, 101, 109, 110, 112, 117,
    118, 121, 123

Yackee, J.W. 6, 47, 58, 59, 67, 68, 72, 84
Yates, D.A. 27

Zakariya, H.S. 25, 136, 142
Zambia 6, 10–11, 37–8, 96–7, 99–129,
    163; commercial mining in northern
    Rhodesia 101–4; Constitution 106,
    108, 113, 115, 123; Development
    Agency Act 2006 2; evolution of mining
    in 101–14; from privatization to the
    windfall tax 114–28; humanism 10, 99,
    105, 108, 163; low taxation and high
    copper prices 121–2; Mines and
    Minerals Development Act 2008 7, 11,
    124, 164; mono-economy 10, 99, 104,
    128, 163; nationalization 10, 37–8,
    96, 99, 101, 103, 104–8, 163;
    privatization 6, 11, 100, 101, 103,
    108, 109–14, 117–21, 126, 163–4;
    proposed renegotiation clause 156;
    social services and amenities 107, 119,
    120, 163–4; stabilization clauses 7, 11,
    100, 116–17, 125, 126, 127–8;
    Zambianization 107
Zambia Consolidated Copper Mines
    Limited (ZCCM) 6, 10, 99–100, 101,
    106, 107, 110–12, 113, 117, 119, 120,
    122, 163
Ziegler, A.R. 46
Zimbabwe 97
Zongwe, D. 97
Zurich Emerging Markets Solutions 39